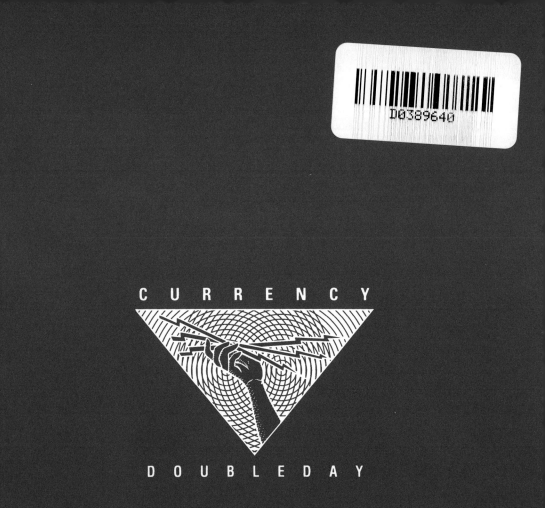

C U R R E N C Y

D O U B L E D A Y

THE LAST WORD ON POWER

CURRENCY

DOUBLEDAY

NEW YORK

LONDON

TORONTO

SYDNEY

AUCKLAND

THE
LAST
WORD
ON
POWER

TRACY GOSS

RE-INVENTION

FOR LEADERS

AND ANYONE

WHO MUST

MAKE THE

IMPOSSIBLE HAPPEN

A CURRENCY BOOK
PUBLISHED BY DOUBLEDAY
a division of Bantam Doubleday Dell Publishing Group, Inc.
1540 Broadway, New York, New York 10036

CURRENCY and DOUBLEDAY are trademarks of Doubleday,
a division of Bantam Doubleday Dell Publishing Group, Inc.

Library of Congress Cataloging-in-Publication Data

Goss, Tracy.
The last word on power / by Tracy Goss.
p.   cm.
1. Leadership.   I. Title.
HD57.7.G67   1996
658.4'092—dc20   95-21269
CIP

ISBN 0-385-47492-X
Copyright © 1996 by Tracy Goss

Printed in the United States of America

January 1996

1   3   5   7   9   10   8   6   4   2

First Edition

To
Julie and George Goss
Sam and Doris Reid
for a lifetime
of
Making the Impossible Happen

AUTHOR'S NOTE

GREAT IDEAS very frequently come from great partnerships. The entire body of work I've called Re-Invention—both Executive Re-Invention and Organizational Re-Invention—is a direct by-product of my partnership with Sheila Reid.

Sheila operates her life and our organization making the impossible happen. This book was created, in great part, through her extraordinary skills and leadership as the Managing Partner of Goss-Reid Associates and the President of the Leadership Center for Re-Invention. She is a major contributor to the design of this work, and her expertise in delivering and coaching the Re-Invention methodology to all levels of leadership was a source of invaluable knowledge. The work that she and I designed and conducted together for a variety of organizations worldwide provided the client experience that is the foundation for this book.

Most important, from the very beginning Sheila took the stand that I would express our work on Re-invention in a way that would make it universally available. Her unrelenting stand was the source of power during the two years it took to complete the book. Without her resourcefulness, tireless selflessness, total commitment, dedication, and loyalty, neither the Executive Re-Invention program nor this book would have been possible.

I salute her as a woman, a business leader, and a friend; and I thank her for the fifteen years of collaboration we have shared.

Tracy Goss

Lake Travis, Austin, Texas
July 1995

ACKNOWLEDGMENTS

WHILE I HAVE BEEN a lecturer and consultant in the field of transformation and transformational leadership for twenty years, until three years ago I had not expressed any of my work in writing. The fact that this book now exists, and has the possibility of being a catalyst for transformation for many more people than I might ever reach in person, is due to the extraordinary human beings with whom it has been my privilege to be associated. Specifically, I wish to express my appreciation to:

The wonderful thinkers, writers, and editors who played an essential role in turning the possibility of a book on Executive Re-Invention into a reality:

Gail Raben intentionally created the possibility of *The Last Word on Power* by introducing me to Betty Sue Flowers. "When you two meet, there will be a book," she said.

Betty Sue Flowers continuously generated the opportunity for *The Last Word on Power.* Her commitment to the success of the book was and is never-ending, starting with bringing me to Harriet Rubin and then nurturing the process all the way through by making significant contributions as a scholar, editor, and coach. Having Betty Sue on your team is like having a fairy godmother—somehow whatever is needed magically appears at exactly the right moment.

Richard Christian is the only person I know who is truly an expert on all aspects of creativity, artistry, and politics. Richard's work with me as a writer crystallized the focus and style of my "voice," and with his assistance and coaching the manuscript moved to an entirely new level.

Art Kleiner, with great supportiveness and professionalism, helped me to cross the threshold that allowed the book's draft to come into its final form. His expertise has been a creative signature for this and the many other books he has edited and coached. His artistic eye and unique creativity were sources of continued inspiration and contributed directly to bringing the manuscript to life. His patience, artistry, and sense of humor are gratefully appreciated. Finally, he is a brilliant, talented, and delightful human being with whom it was a pleasure to work.

During the initial stages of my work with Art, when we tore up and reassembled the manuscript in a very short time, we relied on Virginia O'Brien for key editorial work. I appreciated her ear for language and diligence under pressure. She made an essential contribution to the final draft. Jennifer Breheny made time stand still.

Finally, and most important, there is Harriet Rubin, my editor at Doubleday Currency. Harriet is the future of the publishing industry. Just as when a first-time violinist plays a Stradivarius and recognizes that nothing else will do, as a first-time author I recognized immediately that Harriet was, without doubt, the only person with whom to create this book. Her instincts are always right. I am deeply grateful for her expertise as an editor and writer, her stand on me as an author, and her unshakable commitment to the possibility of this book being a catalyst for a revolution in leadership. Harriet is a rare combination of a true operatic diva and Glenda the Good Witch of the North; she can hold her own with anyone in the arena of making the impossible happen.

All those whose life work has powerfully impacted my thinking, my professional work, and my life, especially Philip Amato, Hubert Dreyfus, Charles Wesley Emerson, Werner Erhard, Fernando Flores, Buckminster Fuller, Michael Goldstein, Martin Heidegger, Joan Holmes, Randy MacNamara, Jim Selman, William Shakespeare, and Constantine Stanislavsky.

Distinguished colleagues all over the world who are engaged in one or another aspect of organizational transformation, many of whom have enthusiastically shared my work and the Executive Re-Invention Program with their associates, clients, and colleagues, particularly Nancy Dorrier and Judith Underwood; Mike Cook and Terry Miller; Allan Scherr; Maurice Cohen, Jerry

Strauss, and David Spiwak; Bill Broussard, Bob Chapman, and Mike King; Vince DiBianca and Bob Berkman; Nathan Rosenberg; Marty Leaf; Rik Super; Harry Rosenberg, Barbara Holmes, and Brian Regniee; Joan Rosenberg, Tirzah Cohen, Michael Reid, and Arlene Reid; Mike McMaster; Jim Selman; and David Norris.

All of the executives and client organizations that we have had the privilege of engaging in Executive or Organizational Re-Invention, especially Jean-Luc Schwitzgubel, Head of Textile Dyes Division, Ciba-Geigy Limited, Peter Schutz, Head of Ciba Pigments Division, and Jean Schaefle, President of Ciba Pigments Division USA, and their executive teams; Bob Meers, Executive VP and President of Reebok Specialty Business Group; Charles Butt, Chairman and CEO of H. E. Butt Grocery Company in Texas, COO Fully Clingman, and the H. E. Butt and Pantry Division executive teams; Greg Thomson, SVP at Owens-Corning and his leadership team; Jerry Carr, Chairman and CEO of Rochester Tel, and his associates, Richard Smith, Controller, and Catherine Deagman, Corporate Materials Management; and the Honorable John Snobelen, Minister of Education and Training, Province of Ontario. I offer special thanks to Earl Lestz, President of the Studio Group at Paramount Pictures and his executive team, especially Larry Owens, VP Administration, Christine Essel, VP Planning and Development and Public Affairs, and Tom Bruehl, SVP Video Operations, for pioneering the Re-Invention work in its early stages.

All the members of the Leadership Center for Re-Invention's Executive Association for their willingness to create and demonstrate the reality of leaders operating in the mode of transformation and continuously pioneer the next level of making the impossible happen in their companies. As a group they are an important laboratory for transformation. I very much appreciate everyone's input over the past year, and especially the valuable comments and critiques of Walter Kiechel and MaryBeth Rogers on the final draft.

Richard Pascale and Tony Athos, my coauthors for the Harvard Business Review *article "The Re-Invention Roller Coaster: Risking the Present for a Powerful Future,"* the first publication of the principles of Re-Invention. Readers probably know them from their best-selling book *The Art of Japanese Management* and from Richard's groundbreaking book *Managing on the Edge.* From the first moment I introduced the Executive Re-Invention program to Richard Pascale in 1990, he insisted that it was a missing dimension for successful corporate transformation, and immediately became a strong stand for my work and a driving force in support of getting my work in writing. I very much appreciate his contribution to me.

A chairman/CEO I worked with called Tony Athos a "national treasure." I couldn't agree more. I am grateful to him, not only for his powerful influence on the *HBR* article and its publication but for his unique distinction as a teacher and mentor to CEOs. Working with Tony has profoundly impacted me, my work, and this book.

The staff of Goss-Reid Associates and the Leadership Center for Re-Invention for their joyful willingness to do whatever was needed, whenever it was needed, both in service of this book and in our stand for a revolution in leadership. I especially acknowledge Deborah Reid for re-inventing our organizational structures and ongoingly generating opportunities for a new future, Bill Sutherland for his caring and loyalty no matter what, and Debbie Byrns for her trust and partnership.

The entire Goss-Reid Family for their never-ending love and support of me and my commitments: Michael Goss, my brother, who led me into the world of transformation, Julie Goss, Doris Reid, Sam Reid, Matt, Caitlin, and Melinda Goss, Deborah Reid, Grant, Christie, Joshua Reid, Lynda Williams, and Sam L. Reid and his family, Bill Sutherland, Aunty Alice, Bill Sr., and Norma, Alex Courtney, Lynell Bangs, Marty Merrill, our "godfather," and our dear friend Mel Welles.

Acknowledgment is gratefully given to Werner Erhard, who developed the body of work on which this book is built. Although his work is the source of much of the material presented, the interpretation and presentation are mine alone. If there is any divergence from the original work, the responsibility is mine.

This book is not for people who want to become successful, but for those who have already won at the game of success and want much more.

CONTENTS

THE LAST WORD ON POWER

CHAPTER 1

THE POWER TO "MAKE THE IMPOSSIBLE HAPPEN"

THE POWER that brought you to your current position of prominence and responsibility as a leader—the power that is the source of your success in the past—is now preventing you from making the impossible happen in your life and in your work.

If you are an executive or manager who is charged with leading a re-invention effort, before you can successfully re-invent your organization, institution, community, or country, you must first acquire a new kind of power: the power to consistently make the impossible happen. The absence of this power is what has made an ever-growing number of organizational re-invention efforts fail.

The pathway to this new power is to completely and intentionally "re-invent" yourself: to

put at risk the success you've become for the power of making the impossible happen.

There are millions of people who genuinely want to make something happen that they, and frequently everyone else, consider impossible. But they feel powerless to do so. It's not that they're incapable. Most of them have already won at the traditional games of life, or feel they're on their way to winning. They have leadership positions in large organizations or responsible professional posts. They have comfortable, rewarding, and fulfilling lives. They are influential members of business, government, or nonprofit communities. If they were ever psychologically troubled, they have learned to transcend those troubles or to apply them as a springboard for success. They have developed fruitful strategies all through their lives for achieving what they want and what they think is right.

But now they want much more. They want to achieve something meaningful, beyond merely holding an influential position—to start a new sort of organization, redefine the nature of their industry, make government work effectively, right a deeply inbred and prevalent abuse, reshape their workplace, bring a new technology into the world, or simply to be great at what they do. In some cases, their goals led them to seek their positions and challenges in the first place, as if they were compelled by a calling to make a better world. In other cases, external events have led them to doing battle with the impossible.

Once upon a time, there was an executive who realized his life's ambition. At age fifty-five, he had reached the top position, the post of chairman and CEO of a high-technology company so prominent that it was known throughout the world simply by its initials. During the course of his fast-track career, this man, known for his unique and innovative solutions, encountered many difficult challenges. In each case he triumphed. As CEO, his actions, his strategies, his ideas, and his power would finally have a chance to influence the whole world, at a scale beyond any he had known. In fact, the board had made him CEO expecting he would do just that. But within a few years, all his old skills and powers, which had brought him to the opportunity of a lifetime, seemed to get in the way of his ability to deliver. His understanding of the business turned sour. Allies turned on him. Amid several embarrassing legal battles and market losses, the company's stock price plunged. After demonstrations by shareholders, the board told him to step down.

There was once a young woman who inherited a small manufacturing business from her father and built it up into a leader in its market. While in college, she had worked in the plant or the offices every summer, learning the operation from the ground up. After graduating first in her MBA class at one of the highest ranked business schools, she joined the firm and took over the presidency ten years later, becoming one of the first women entrepreneurs to lead a manufacturing company. By the time she was forty-five, she had moved the company from $5 million to $50 million in annual revenues—a goal that, back in college, had seemed like it might take a lifetime. But by this time she had decided to make it a $1-billion company before she retired. Five years into this project, however, having tried every growth strategy she could think of, she was ready to throw in the towel. "It's impossible to build a billion-dollar company in this market," she concluded, and prepared to spend the rest of her professional life merely improving what she had already achieved, instead of trying to accomplish anything else spectacular with her life.

At the same time there lived a young man who wanted more than anything else to be president of his country. He knew that if he could be elected, he would be able to finally solve the problems that nobody else had been able to tackle: growing the country out of its economic doldrums, investing in its future, and cleaning up the environment. With his unusual ability to appeal to the ideals of a wide range of people, galvanize and inspire them to action, and lead them to embrace a common ground, he would redefine not only the nature of the presidency but also the purpose of his country's government: to make it a government of service. From his college days, he devoted himself almost obsessively to becoming the sort of man who could become president, learning how to navigate through the political barriers and competitions effectively. And it worked—he was chosen for his country's highest political office, amid a melee of celebration and high hopes. But he had hardly moved into the president's house before he became mired in the sort of partisan politics he had hoped to transcend. For reasons he couldn't fathom, he found it impossible to rise above a contemptuous, cynical climate, which he knew he was contributing to, though he couldn't see how. Unknown to him, everything he had learned along the road to becoming president was preventing him from doing the things that had made him want to become his country's leader in the first place. The very power that got him elected prevented him from being the great public servant he wanted to be.

You may have guessed who some of these people are. And you're right—whomever you've guessed. All three of them are legion. The CEO could be almost any chief executive of a large mainstream corporation—and certainly any chief executive of a company engaged in a wholesale overhaul of the organization, such as a reengineering or restructuring. The entrepreneur could stand in for most professionals of either gender—not just entrepreneurs, but health care officials, educators, and managers of enterprises large and small. And the president's story could be told about nearly every elected official, of any party, in any country.

For many executives, from the vantage point of their hard-won position, their most desired goals seem more unrealizable than ever. The resistance that blocks them is intangible yet impenetrable; obvious and yet almost impossible to describe. The more successful they have been in the past, the more they understand how impossible the impossible can be. Often the only sensible option is to settle instead for short-term success, produced by continuous improvement, leading in surprisingly many cases to long, slow decline.

This book is written for those people—people who want much more. Don't even read it unless you can authentically say something like the following: "There's something I desire to accomplish, in my life, or in my work, or in the world, that is currently not possible. The more experience I've gained in the world, the more I've learned exactly how impossible it is to achieve what I really want to accomplish. I know that it can't be done, or can't be done by me at this time, but if it could, I would invest myself in attaining it, with all my heart."

You are right that you can't do it—at least not from the power available to you as a leader today. But if you are serious about acquiring the power to accomplish the impossible, then I invite you to embark on Executive Re-Invention and transform yourself as a leader, right down to the core of your identity.

Executive Re-Invention is an invitation to successful people who want to play the most challenging game of all—the game of making the impossible happen. These are usually people who are pursuing something beyond success—who are engaged in making an impact on the world—whether that's the world of their specific organization or industry, or the world of business, education, government, health care, the military, the arts, or anything else. They want to leave a legacy that continues after them. I think no one has expressed this commitment more passionately than George Bernard Shaw:

> This is the true joy in life, the being recognized by yourself as a mighty one; the being thoroughly worn out before you are thrown on the scrap heap; the being a force of nature instead of a feverish selfish little clod of ailments and grievances complaining that the world will not devote itself to making you happy.
>
> I am of the opinion that my life belongs to the whole community and as long as I live it is my privilege to do for it whatever I can. I want to be thoroughly used up when I die, for the harder I work the more I live. I rejoice in life for its own sake. Life is no brief candle to me. It is a sort of splendid torch which I have got hold of for the moment, and I want to make it burn as brightly as possible before handing it on to future generations.

The outcome of Executive Re-Invention, for those who take it on, is an entirely different relationship with reality, not only with the future but also with the past and the present. Lawrence of Arabia described that relationship this way:

Those who dream by night in the dusty recesses of their minds wake in the day to find that all was vanity;

but the dreamers of the day are dangerous people,
for they may act their dream with open eyes,
and make it possible.

MOVING BEYOND ''POWER 101''

Power to make something impossible happen is a very sophisticated form of power. It is completely different from the forms
of power that most people, even successful people, have learned
during the course of their lives. It bears no relation to authority
(the ability to compel things to happen by virtue of your position). It has nothing to do with competence (the ability to fix
problems and perform effectively). And it does not require influence (the ability to get people to do what you want through
such "soft" power methods as nurturing, decentralizing, and
mentoring).

I think of those types of power as the kind that someone
might teach in an introductory course—valid and worthwhile to
learn, but representing only the beginning stages of mastery. At
an advanced level, you discover a form of power as different, in
its methods and forms, as calculus is from arithmetic. Just like
calculus, it feels a bit alien and counterintuitive to learn, and yet
no one who seeks to be an effective leader can do without it.
Like most advanced subjects, it takes you beyond the precepts
that seemed so valuable during the introductory stages. It brings
you face-to-face with a whole new set of precepts and practices.

**I define this advanced level of power as the ability to take
something that you believe could never come to pass, declare
it possible, and then move that possibility into a tangible reality.** Mastering this power gives you the capacity to act without
being constrained by the habitual ways of thinking from the
past—your own past, the history of your organization, and even
the heritage of your culture. It allows you to act without feeling
dependent on circumstances—without having to wait, in other
words, for events to align in your favor.

Power to make the impossible happen is the only lasting type of power. Authority is bestowed upon you by others. It can be taken away or lost. Competence is earned by producing results, and it is lost when you stop producing. In a turbulent world, no one's competence continues indefinitely. Even influence is limited by your relationships to individuals. When your relationships change, your ability to persuade and inspire people dwindles.

Once you acquire the capacity to generate the power to make the impossible happen, it cannot be taken away from you. In fact, it increases over time. That is why executives and leaders must re-invent themselves *before* they can re-invent an organization, institution, or country effectively. Without the capacity to generate the power to make the impossible happen, how can they possibly succeed?

Fortunately, this power can be acquired by anyone—anyone who is committed to something in his or her life that is currently not possible and who is willing to "re-invent" himself or herself to accomplish it. When you acquire this power, you can operate with a quality and integrity that frees you to take the risks and actions necessary to change the world.

A TASTE OF POWER

Everyone has had a taste of this freedom sometime in his or her life. Think, for a moment, of an area where you have a great deal of skill and mastery—something you can do better than almost anyone you know. This area might be hunting, cooking, making speeches, handling finance, teaching, writing, decorating, traveling, guiding, being a parent. Whatever it is, it is a unique arena for you: The kind of power you have in that arena is different from your power in other parts of your life.

In that arena, you look forward to tough challenges. "Send me your worst," you tell the Fates, because you want to find out what will happen when you are tested. You know, even if the challenge leads to a devastating failure, it will be interesting. You'll learn from it. And on some level, where it's most significant, you'll be able to handle it. You don't need a rule book when you leave on a hunt, or stand up to make a speech, or whatever your arena might be. You know that you have the skills, ability, and confidence to handle the consequences of any event that comes along.

Most important, you are not threatened by the consequences of wrong decisions. Power, in this arena, does not control the outcomes of your decisions. In your mind there is no way that things "should" turn out—whatever happens, you know it was worthwhile showing up. In fact, *your power stems from the absence of control.* You know that the more you try for a specific outcome, the smaller the results will be. Instead of needing to anticipate and direct the outcome of events ahead of time, you accept events as they occur.

> As a man's real power grows and his knowledge widens, ever the way he can follow grows narrower: until at last he chooses nothing, but does only and wholly what he must do.
>
> —Ursula le Guin, *A Wizard of Earthsea*

Now imagine if you could bring the confidence and power you feel in this particular arena to all the spheres of activity in your life. I invite you to envision the unlimited possibility available to you as a leader if your relationship to the most critical and challenging opportunities is one of complete freedom.

The most capable, legendary, inspiring leaders we know of have one thing in common. They have made the impossible happen. This aspect of their lives, not any position they may have held as a head of state or corporate executive, has been the source of their significance. Wilbur and Orville Wright developed the power to fulfill a dream as old as the human species. Mahatma Gandhi called forth the power to compel the British to walk out of India. Rosa Parks, in refusing to give her seat to a white man, did not merely spark a revolutionary alteration in racial attitudes; she embodied a powerful stand that forced an entire country to take notice. Betty Friedan reframed the mainstream American culture's attitude toward women; Betty Ford reframed its attitude about addiction.

In business, a list of powerful leaders, so well known to everyone they are almost a cliché in management literature, would include Sam Walton, Steven Jobs, and Fred Smith. It even makes us uncomfortable to hear them mentioned sometimes, because it reminds us of how few business and organizational leaders live up to their example. Leaders may try to learn what Walton or Jobs or Smith did, and duplicate those practices; but the real source of power these leaders wielded was the ability to declare something impossible a possibility and bring it into reality. *Nobody can achieve that sort of power by copying what someone else did.*

But imagine that there was a set of theories and techniques—a methodology, if you will—for learning to make the impossible happen. It would take you on a ride with roller-coaster speed. As with all the most memorable rides, when you were done, you would not be the same person you were before you began. In fact, you would no longer be the person you have been for most of your professional life. You would still have all your existing capabilities, competencies, and controls available to you. But in addition, you would know how to become expert, over time, at making the impossible happen consistently and skillfully.

There *is* such a methodology, accessible to anyone who is serious about learning it. It's based on in-depth philosophical theory, dramatic tradition, and fifteen years of working with top management executives, entrepreneurs, professionals, and public servants. I have put it in a form designed so that anyone who is committed can master it, without leaving the existing concerns of his or her life and work behind. I call this methodology *Executive Re-Invention.*

WHAT IS EXECUTIVE RE-INVENTION?

Executive Re-Invention is a series of radical transformations in which you put at stake the success you've become for the power of making the impossible happen. Through seven

distinct transformations, you completely re-invent yourself as a leader by redefining your reality of the past, present, and future and your relationship to taking risks, winning, action, and being extraordinary. Executive Re-Invention provides you, and allows you to provide others, with the capacity for making the impossible happen regardless of past experience or current circumstances.

Executive Re-Invention in my view and others' is the key ingredient that determines success or failure for most of the organizational strategies that have emerged over the past few years: building "learning" organizations, reengineering business processes and management practices, and re-creating industrial "core competencies." The demands of these strategies call for the power to make the impossible happen.

Some people are concerned that the imperative to "re-invent themselves before they re-invent the organization" implies that there is something wrong with them. Nothing could be further from the truth. Executive Re-Invention is not remedial work. It does not even "improve" the leader's skills. It takes leaders someplace new, to unknown and unfamiliar territory.

Executive Re-Invention is not a psychological journey. It is not designed to "fix problems" in the personality, character, or style of leaders. It's not about "getting in touch with" your feelings or delving into the subconscious mind.

It's not a theological journey. It has nothing to do with your relationship to a higher power, and it will not threaten anyone's religious practice.

It's not even a philosophical journey—at least not in the sense of being theoretical. It is intimately tied to action—not just actions in the abstract, but the actions you are able, and not able, to take as a leader.

Executive Re-Invention is primarily an ontological journey. Ontology is that branch of philosophy that deals with the nature of reality and different ways of *being.* Executive Re-Invention is concerned with the different ways that you as a leader are *being* and how that determines your reality of what's possible and not possible.

If you committedly take yourself through this methodology, you will gain an awareness of the fundamental links between your view of the world at any moment and the ultimate scope of your achievements and failures.

I invite you to read this book in a way that allows something powerful to happen for you as a leader, beyond the learning of new ideas and concepts.

The purpose of this book is fivefold:

- To introduce the path of Executive Re-Invention for leaders and engage them in making the impossible happen
- To incite people to see the value of following this path, to re-invent themselves and the leaders of their organizations
- To dispel the myths and habits that hold people back from their own destiny
- To end the despair about resistance to change in organizations, and, as a result of the first four purposes:
- To catalyze the emergence of extraordinary leadership in all aspects of everyday life.

LEADERS MUST RE-INVENT THEMSELVES FIRST

If you are going to re-invent your organization, then in order to succeed, you must *first* re-invent *yourself.* Organizational re-invention efforts are failing because without re-inventing themselves, executives do not have the kind of power necessary to succeed.

Consider the implications of that statement. It means that re-inventing yourself is a prerequisite for re-inventing your organization.

Powerful re-inventions require powerful leaders, from the shop floor to the executive tower. Unless re-inventing the leaders becomes a top priority, successful organizational re-invention will continue to be rare. The leaders who must be re-invented include anyone at the top of any company undergoing a serious reengineering, strategic re-invention, or learning-organization effort, as well as their management cadre who must implement these initiatives. It also includes people with responsibility at all levels of the organization where some aspect of implementation will require making the impossible happen.

The way these leaders think and act has been a key force in giving the organization its current identity and practices. Therefore, if you are one of these people, and you do not re-invent yourself before you begin, then your re-invention effort will not accomplish what you want.

This fact is borne out by many experiences in real organizations. Robert Heller, in his history of the turbulence at IBM in the mid-1990s, notes that the re-invention effort failed because the leaders didn't re-invent themselves:

> Where [CEO John] Akers failed, in the eyes of the board, investors, and his successor, was in the wrong execution of the right strategy. . . . Akers had plainly failed to achieve the true object of reinvention: to change, not the organization, but the behavior of those within. . . . None of the remedies had worked, because the reinventors couldn't reinvent the most crucial element of all: themselves.[1]

To understand what happens to corporate leaders who don't re-invent themselves, imagine that you are a member of an elite military squad—a Navy SEAL, Army Green Beret, or Navy Top Gun pilot—being sent into your first covert, difficult mission. Everyone knows the mission is "impossible" by conventional military standards. That's why your special unit got the assignment.

Where would you get the power to undertake this mission? Not from your innate capabilities and track record. That was merely your entry card into the squad. Only the top 1 percent, "the best of the best," of the young officers are accepted for these elite military units in the first place.

After joining, you are put through a rigorous training program, designed to prepare you to operate beyond the capabilities of "ordinary" leaders. The training is so tough that after completing it, you are not the same "already successful" person who began the course. You have extraordinary skills and extraordinary prowess. You routinely take risks that someone else would shrink from. Because of your training, while you are not unaware of the risks, the consequences are not threatening to you. The shift that has taken place in yourself has provided you with confidence and the willingness to be "extraordinary" at need. Most of all, it has provided you with a source of power you did not have before.

Now imagine taking on a similar mission as a "green" recruit—without the benefits of the highly specialized training designed for such missions. You become lost, uncertain, and probably destined to fail, but you would never let anyone see your terror. After all, you are still the best of the best. You're not supposed to feel afraid. When you fail, you go down in flames, not knowing why.

And that is precisely the situation of corporate leaders in business today. They take on the "top gun" missions of complete corporate re-invention but without any training. Only the top 1 percent of managers ever reach the senior position at the helm of an organization. Since they're the "best of the best," it's assumed they already know what they need to know. Nobody even acknowledges that these re-inventions may require the senior leaders to learn new skills. Even if it were acknowledged in the abstract, in practice everyone knows that the senior leaders can't spare the time to leave their offices to learn something new. And with their authority and salary at stake, they can't risk looking like they don't know all the answers.

In the absence of knowledge and special training, they do what anyone would do in their position—everything they can to minimize their risks. Instead of taking on what is not possible, they immerse themselves in what is obviously possible. They try to stay on top of the latest thinking by reading books or working with consultants. They become preoccupied with the currently popular process of benchmarking: What has worked in other organizations? What hasn't worked? Thus they lose sight of their original "mission impossible" goals. They forget about what they really want to create. They settle, instead, for improving what is already possible by implementing new processes—changing what they are *doing.* They hope for an occasional breakthrough, and pray that, at worst, the organization will sail along on continuous improvement, without incident, long enough for them to move on or retire.

If you have been reading all this thinking that it doesn't apply to you—that you, personally, have little or no resistance to change, and other people in the organization are the only ones holding back your re-invention efforts—please think again. *If you are a breathing human being, you are resistant to change. Like all your fellow human beings, you are designed to be incapable of starting with a clean sheet of paper.* That is why it is necessary to re-invent yourself first. If you are accountable for the success of the organization, re-inventing yourself is the only way to create an environment in which resistance to change can dissolve. Without such an environment, at best you will achieve an atmosphere of continuous improvement of the past.

Until you have re-invented yourself to be personally free from the constraints and limitations of your own past (including your own past success), you will not have the power to deal effectively with what is at the source of resistance to change—either your own or that of others. You will not be able to get to "the clean sheet of paper" that Michael Hammer and James Champy insist is essential to successful reengineering. You will not be able to lead your company to "jettison its past," which C. K. Prahalad and Gary Hamel insist is essential to re-invent your industry. You will not be able to produce the "shift of mind from seeing parts to seeing wholes" that Peter Senge insists is essential to the "fifth discipline" of systems thinking, the cornerstone of building a learning organization. For example, when the consulting firm Deloitte & Touche interviewed managers from companies whose efforts had failed, 62 percent of the interviewees listed resistance to change as the main reason. While resistance to change is the label given to the problem, the actual problem is much more fundamental than resistance.

It's not that human beings are resisting. It's that they do not have the capacity to start from a clean sheet of paper. *By design,* human beings are incapable of this. Before anyone else makes a mark on that blank page, it's *already* filled—with your past, the company's past, the things you think are appropriate for the business, and the qualities you think a company should and shouldn't have. To really start over with a clean sheet of paper, you'd have to redesign not only the organization but the identities of every key person, from the CEO on down. This is not a matter of changing what you are *doing,* but of transforming your way of *being.*

TRANSFORMING YOUR WAY OF *BEING* VERSUS CHANGING WHAT YOU ARE *DOING*

Executive Re-Invention requires a series of transformations in yourself as a leader. Thus, to re-invent yourself (and your organization), you must become an expert in the territory that is at the heart of transformation: the territory of *being.* The way you are *being* at any given time determines your reality of what's possible and not possible.

Unfortunately, the term "transformation" is frequently misused in business literature today to refer to a "big change" or a "significant change." Managers look at the outcome of a change effort, and if the results are grand enough, they say that "a transformation has happened in that person, or organization, or industry."

In reality, the concept of "transformational change" is an oxymoron. Transformation and change are different phenomena. **CHANGE is a function of altering what you are *doing*—to improve something that is already possible in your reality (better, different, or more). TRANSFORMATION is a function of altering the way you are *being*—to create something that is currently not possible in your reality.** This may seem at first glance like just a matter of semantics, but in practice, the confusion between change and transformation has kept many managers stuck in a cycle of continual improvement, when what they really want is to shake up their foundations and re-invent their entire organization.

Unlike change, improvement, or reform, a transformation is a fundamental and significant alteration in the way that you are *being* or your organization is *being*. In the case of the organization, its way of *being* reverberates at many spheres and levels and affects the entire organization down to its core.

When you alter the way you are *being*, with effectiveness and competence, you gain the capacity to make the impossible into a reality. This can include a minor impossibility, like getting through an impossible deadline, or a major impossibility, like taking the lead in your industry when that lead has been held for decades by a larger or older competitor, or eliminating the resistance to change necessary to the success of today's leading business strategies.

Some people assume that *being* is a matter of "feeling," "meditation," or "passive reflection." Nothing could be further from the truth. **The way you are *being* is the source of your reality, which in turn is the source of your actions.** For example, all human beings grow up believing that life should turn out one way or another. This drives you, as an individual, to constantly compare your current reality with the ideal in your mind of how life "should" turn out—which in turn affects a startling amount of what you do. (I'll return to this point in more detail in Chapter 3.)

The domain of *being* is hidden, in part, because it is not referred to in everyday, action-oriented language. (*Being,* wrote the philosopher Martin Heidegger, "denies its own coming to presence.")[2] Most common phrasings refer to "doing" or "having" instead. For example, if a key player is refusing to participate in an important project, you might say, "What are you *doing* about Jane's refusal to participate?" You would not typically say, "How are you *being* with regard to Jane's refusal to participate?" **It is difficult to realize, in the environment of typical business language, that your actions are always the expression of some overall way of being unknown to you, of which your will and decisions are just a part.**

THE CONTEXT IS DECISIVE

To alter the way you are *being*, you must engage with the phenomenon of context. *Context is the human environment that determines the limitations of your actions and the scope of the results your actions can produce.*

This explains why copying someone else's strategy—while it may improve your reputation—never seems to lead to effective action. You might hear of an extraordinary manager named Peter, at one of your competitors' companies, and you might catch up with Peter at a conference and ask him what he is "doing" to achieve his spectacular results. Or you might read books about Peter or attend seminars in which Peter's "deeds" are described, down to the most detailed particular. But when you return to your organization and implement Peter's practices, they won't have the same effects, even if you copy his practices perfectly.

Peter's results were not just created by what he "did" but by the context within which he did it: the habitual ways of thinking, talking, and acting in his part of his organization, including all the forces that had produced that context over time. Your context is completely different. Transplanting what Peter "did" is like planting an Arizona cactus in the Greenland snow. Peter's context and the context of the organization, like the climate of Greenland, is the decisive factor.

If you want Peter's results, you must "unconceal" (as ontologists say) your own context—the way you are *being.* Then you can begin to alter the way you are *being.* This does not mean adopting Peter's context or the context of Peter's organization. That's just a more sophisticated way of trying to copy what Peter is *doing.* (Some American managers tried this when they thought they could instill the Japanese context by introducing group calisthenics and songs in their factories.) To alter the context of your organization, you must re-invent your own way of *being* by creating a new context from which to relate to the world.

The context also explains why managers who excel in one position so often become stymied in another. William Weiss,

CEO of Ameritech, noticed this problem recurring among the corporate executives he promoted:

> Well, we're on our fourth or fifth generation of presidents of our Bell operating companies. The people I picked had seemed to be aggressive enough to drive forward. But when they got into more serious positions, all of a sudden they became traditionalists. They wouldn't make the hard decisions. They became risk averse, reluctant to get into conflict. So, we had to turn over the leadership groups several times before we found people capable of making a bold transformational change.[3]

Reengineer James Champy talks vaguely of changing "who [managers] are," and goes on to describe specific techniques for mobilizing, enabling, defining, measuring, and communicating— all forms of change that start by *doing* things differently. I argue that what Champy is really calling for is an alteration in the way managers are *being*.

Changing processes will not get to the heart of transformation because you cannot get to being *from* doing. *Processes and* doing *do not provide people with the power to alter their context.*

Good actors understand innately what it means to alter one's context. When an actor studies a new role, there is more to the job than merely learning to speak a new way, or practicing a new form of body movement, or changing the outward styles of behavior. The actor has to learn to see the world, to listen to dialogue, and to think things through in the same way that the character would. When an actor asks the question "What's my motivation?" he is really asking, "Who is this character supposed to 'be' in relation to the events taking place around him?" That context is very different from the way the actor would be when out of character in the same situation. The actor knows that everything else will follow once that way of *being* has been set. **Creating context is a cornerstone in the foundation of Executive Re-Invention. You shift the way you are being by creating a new context from which to relate to reality.** In this way it is possible to transform your way of *being* in a very short time. This is accomplished through language—by altering the way you speak and listen.

LANGUAGE IS THE HOUSE OF *BEING*

Language is the only leverage for changing the context of the world around you. This is because people apprehend and construct reality through the way they speak and listen. Or, as Martin Heidegger put it, "Language is the house of being." On a day-to-day basis, you can alter the way you are *being* by altering the conversations in which you are engaged.

The idea of changing your actions (and the events in the world around you) through conversation feels alien for many people, partly because it is so abstract, and partly because it contradicts the conventional psychological view of a person's personality. From a psychological perspective, actions stem from deeply seated motives in a person's subconscious. You have to probe deeply into a person's past to see what's really going on behind his or her actions. Psychologically, no one can really alter those deep motives except, perhaps, through years of arduous analysis.

From an ontological perspective, by contrast, everything is apparent in the conversation being held at that moment. This gives everyone a starting place for making dramatic alterations and the tools for doing so. **By learning to uncover the concealed aspects of your current conversations and learning to engage in different types of new conversation, you can alter the way you are being, which, in turn, alters what's possible.**

When you create a new context, you create a new realm of possibility, one that did not previously exist. Consider the power of the context created during the American Revolution. Before 1776, human beings did not have sovereign rights simply by virtue of being human. Kings and heads of churches had had rights since antiquity; nobles had had rights since their declaration of the Magna Carta. But ordinary human beings lived at the sufferance of their rulers.

The leaders of the American Revolution created a new realm of possibility for humanity. They did this by declaring, "Human beings have rights." This brought about a new political environment. Human beings would have rights to "life, liberty, and the pursuit of happiness," granted "self-evidentially," and rulers would rule at the sufferance of their citizens.

This was not an improved evolution of the previous British form of government or even of the colonial governors' practices. There were some philosophical precedents for the new country, but no sovereign state had existed, in modern times, based on the same premises.

The American leaders could only bring this new realm of possibility into existence by making a declaration—a form of conversation. Once human rights were declared, actions that would never have been conceived before came naturally to mind. Assertions about taxation without representation, the control of commerce, and the ownership of property were now natural to make. The power generated by the new collective stand, like adrenaline in times of danger, allowed the citizenry to transcend their normal fears. The realm of possibility they created was so significant that it became a worldwide line of demarcation. No country, anywhere in the world, was ever the same. Such is the power of context.

One man who discovered this form of power was Jack Younger (not his real name), a manager of the information systems group at a large western retail company. A business school graduate in his midforties, he had a reputation of being extremely competent and "one of the nicest guys" in the company. He had always been able to get disparate people to work together on teams, and he always seemed to gravitate to positions where that skill was needed. The CEO had considered him for vice-presidential positions and turned him down on the grounds that he had never really been tested.

But shortly thereafter, the head of a prominent division—one of the company's three major chains—left to take another job. The CEO chose to give Younger the opportunity. He did so with trepidation. The division's second-in-command, an older man with twenty years' experience in this form of retailing, had expected the job himself. But the CEO had little confidence in the second-in-command, who had remained there, everyone knew, by making himself seem indispensable. Thus, even before Younger got there, the division had grouped itself into antagonistic camps, for and against him. Members of the second-in-command's camp were perceived by both the CEO and the COO as not carrying their weight.

Every one of the senior executives worried that Younger was in over his head. It wasn't clear he had the financial and marketing skills, but he especially seemed to lack political savvy. The job would require someone to take charge and reshape the division, and Younger wasn't an aggressive type of person. Nor did he want to become aggressive. If reshaping the division meant becoming a latter-day Attila the Hun, he wasn't sure he wanted to play.

After a year in his new position, Younger was treading water—not failing, but certainly not succeeding at reshaping the division. When he asked for a performance review, the CEO told him point-blank: "You don't want one this year. Don't ask me for it."

But he forced himself to look closely at the limitations on his leadership in running the company so far. On this job, he wouldn't have the luxury of dealing with people in his customary fashion. He would have to dramatically alter himself and his way of looking at the world, or he would fail.

After engaging in the Executive Re-Invention process, he created a new context both for himself as a leader and for his life. He created the context "take the lead boldly," which allowed him to continuously put himself on the line. Three months after the CEO told him not to ask for a performance review, he walked into the CEO's office and said, "Here's my promise. Within a year you will have absolutely no concern about this division. We will be producing unprecedented results. If we're not, I'll step down and leave the company. I'll place my job at stake."

He became the leader he needed to be in order to deliver on that promise. He confronted the second-in-command directly and challenged him to either support the new regime or transfer to another division. In the past, he would have spent months trying to get this guy to come around. (The second-in-command transferred.) He galvanized other managers throughout the division and gave them the training they needed to transform their own operations. He took three months out to go to Harvard Business School himself—not to get a degree or credential, or to improve or "fix" himself as a leader (as he would have in the past), but to rapaciously learn anything that would be consistent with taking the lead in re-inventing the division. In school and back at the company, he continually challenged those he talked to, trying to draw their best out from them, communicating his sincere need to hear their best in the very way he spoke to them and listened to them. He reshaped the communications, marketing, and human resource practices. And in the end, his division's performance was strong enough that he not only kept his job but was honored.

The details of Younger's actions were not the critical factor in his triumph. It's important, however, to note that his actions were now all shaped by the new context he created. He worked hard, but his hard work was more of an effect than a cause of the transformation he created. The critical factor was the context. Context is always decisive, and everything he did was altered naturally to be consistent with the context *take the lead boldly.*

Re-Invention does not stop there. Having learned the principles and power of Re-Invention, Jack Younger will never stop transforming himself. He has moved from being a closed system, reacting to outside events and limited to incremental improvement, to being an open system: creating, generating, taking risks, and driven by any future he wishes to create. Instead of shutting himself off to possibilities, he will now attract them; instead of standing still, he will move with velocity to take powerful action.

It is possible for you, too, to make a similar transformation. As Jack Younger did, you must start by looking at yourself carefully and learning as much as possible about the context that determines the limits of your action.

THE STAGES OF RE-INVENTION

"Some are born great, some achieve greatness, and some have greatness thrust upon them." Those words were spoken in *Twelfth Night* by Malvolio, one of Shakespeare's most celebrated fools. But fools are frequently the source of wisdom. If you are over thirty, it's probably too late for you to be born great. You might hope that before you die, greatness will be thrust upon you. That leaves a lot to chance. Or you can actively take on achieving greatness by re-inventing yourself.

> *If I don't manage to fly, someone else will.*
> *The spirit wants only that there be flying.*
>   *As for who happens to do it,*
>   *In that he has only a passing interest.*
>   —RAINER MARIA RILKE

Rilke's poem suggests that somewhere in the world today great leaders are becoming ready to emerge, because the "spirit" of the time is calling for them. I happen to believe that is true. The question for any individual leader is: Will you be among them, sprouting wings and becoming an eagle yourself? Or will you be left behind?

Conventional wisdom holds that great leaders are born, not bred; or, if bred, they are a rare breed who cannot be replicated.

I reject that notion. All organizations can have a cadre of extraordinary leaders who have acquired the power normally associated with rare, legendary individuals.

In the following chapters, I will show not only that people can re-invent themselves but exactly how to go about it. In that context, I strongly urge senior executives of organizations to make re-inventing themselves as high a priority as re-inventing their strategic plan, reengineering their business processes, or revitalizing their information systems.

Before undertaking Re-Invention, people need a map of where they're going. Otherwise, when they run up against their own limits and discomfort, they—like all healthy human beings—will react with irritation and turn away. "This is irresponsible," they may say. "We should do something less disruptive. We need to go back to the basics." At that point, the Re-Invention initiative will be aborted.

Hence the structure of this book: As a methodology, it takes readers through seven separate transformations. They're presented here as stages, each with its own chapter, each as a prerequisite for the next, but they are not really as programmatic as this presentation would make them seem. Each one involves new skills and new ways of thinking. Each requires some practice, and some willingness to experiment. Each offers an opportunity for broadening your own capabilities, for making the impossible happen in your own life and in the lives of those around you.

The first four stages have to do with freeing yourself from the constraints of the past:

1. **Uncovering your Winning Strategy:** learning to recognize the existing sources of power underlying your own individual success in the past. Continuing to operate with this kind of power will prevent you from creating and implementing any desired future outside the realm of what you currently consider possible.

2. **Experiencing the limits of the Universal Human Paradigm at work in your actions:** undoing the context, and the way of *being,* that lead you to seek continuous improvement instead of Re-Invention

3. **Learning to put everything at risk:** becoming willing to operate with no guarantee you will succeed, and with your eyes wide open to the high odds of failure and the accompanying consequences. Samurai warriors used to call this stage "dying before you go into battle."

4. **Inventing a new master paradigm that provides you with a new source of power:** making a series of declarations that constitute a new master paradigm that allows you to engage the forces around you in an unprecedented manner

The last three stages build your capacity for making the impossible happen:

5. **Inventing an impossible game to play:** creating the future that re-invents *you* as a leader, and making bold promises in the game you have chosen to play, so that you do not spend your life carrying a spear in someone else's opera

6. **Breaking the addiction to interpretation:** operating in a reality where there are no "shoulds," and where every problem and dilemma is seen from the standpoint of an invented future rather than through the filters of history

7. **Operating beyond the limits of your Winning Strategy:** learning to operate beyond compensating for what's not possible. Like building a new set of muscles, this stage develops the capacity to have your everyday acting express the "impossible future" you have invented.

How long will these stages take? That depends. If you're like most readers of this book, you have built up your current ways of thinking during the past thirty to fifty years. But it will not require another thirty to fifty years to undo them. A caterpillar becomes a butterfly, after all, in a matter of weeks. When people ask me how long it takes, I like to tell the story of the Japanese apprentice Matajura.

Matajura wanted to become a great swordsman, but his father said he could never learn, because he wasn't quick enough. So Matajura went to the famous dueler Banzo and asked to become his pupil. "How long will it take me to become a master?" he asked. "Suppose I become your servant, to be with you every minute, how long?"

"Ten years," said Banzo.

"My father is getting old," pleaded Matajura. "Before ten years have passed I will have to return home to take care of him. Suppose I work twice as hard. How long will it take me?"

"Thirty years," said Banzo.

"How is that?" asked Matajura. "When I offer to work twice as hard, you say it will take three times as long. Let me make myself clear. I will work unceasingly. No hardship will be too much. How long will it take?"

"Seventy years," said Banzo. "A pupil in such a hurry learns slowly."

Matajura understood. Without asking for any promises in terms of time, he became Banzo's servant. Three years passed. Matajura cleaned, cooked, washed, and gardened. He was ordered never to speak of fencing or to touch a sword. He was very sad at this, but he had given his promise to the master and resolved to keep his word.

One day while Matajura was gardening, Banzo came up quietly behind him and gave him a terrible whack with a wooden sword. The next day in the kitchen, the same blow fell again. Thereafter, day in and day out, from every corner and at any moment, Matajura was attacked by Banzo's wooden sword. He learned to live on the balls of his feet, ready to dodge at any moment. He became a body with no desires, no thought, only external readiness and quickness. Banzo smiled and started lessons. Soon, Matajura was the greatest swordsman in Japan.

THE ROOTS OF RE-INVENTION

During the early 1980s, my business partner, Sheila Reid, and I developed a series of workshops on career transformation for people in the entertainment industry. We focused on coaching people to produce impossible results—from getting acting roles, to acquiring the money to finance a film, to finishing an artistic project. The methods were so effective that close to three hundred people would show up at 6:00 A.M., five days a week, for an entire year. Within four years we had worked with over four thousand professionals: actors, directors, agents, executives, writers, designers, one end of the industry to the other. As word spread, executives in the entertainment industry and throughout the corporate world who similarly wanted to achieve such seemingly impossible results were soon occupying our full commitment.

Around 1986, our work was in great demand. However, I began to feel that in some important ways, we were not making enough of a difference. The more I worked with people, particularly the most senior people in an organization, the more I saw that they needed to move beyond personal effectiveness and completely and fundamentally re-invent themselves as leaders before taking on large-scale re-invention efforts in their companies. Moreover, they needed to transform their entire leadership body.

What was needed was to produce a series of transformations in the executives I was working with, so that they would re-invent themselves into extraordinary leaders. This was the era when management books talked about "extraordinary leadership"; I wanted to move beyond talk, and see that leadership in action.

After hearing me complain about this, Sheila said, "Well, it seems very simple to me. Why don't we just stop what we're doing and go design a way of working with top executives that produces the transformation we want?" Her suggestion seemed so simple and so obvious, and yet I hadn't thought of it.

We spent the next year in research and design, conducting pilot experiments and developing a methodology that we called "Executive Re-Invention."

We first developed a ten-day workshop designed for people who were successful but who were not making the difference they really wanted to make.

That was eight years ago. Since then, Sheila and I have continued to develop the Re-Invention Methodology and work with top executives who are using it. We have applied it in business, education, leadership, parenting, and government; we have custom-designed it for entire organizations and for specific divisions or business units. While the implementation of the methodology is different in each of those circumstances (and should be), the principles are the same. In each case, it starts with the Re-Invention of the people who charge themselves with this task.

These last eight years have been extremely satisfying. I am now doing exactly what I want to do, and I'm as passionate about it now as I was eight years ago. The people I've worked with consistently report that as a result of our work together, they have undergone remarkable, beneficial transformations.

However, when I measure what I'm accomplishing now against my commitment to bring into existence a whole new breed of leaders—ordinary people who are willing to promise and deliver extraordinary outcomes previously considered impossible—I come up short. I now see it is essential to move beyond the limitations of face-to-face consulting: delivering programs to executives and executive teams, lecturing to associations of top executives, speaking at conferences, and spreading the methodology through organizational consulting and advising. I believe there is a crisis of leadership right now in the West, and it is necessary to re-invent leadership itself. It is necessary for making the impossible happen to be an idea whose time has come and to provide the means for people to re-invent themselves so that they are equipped to lead the transformations necessary to accomplish this.

This book is the start of that public conversation.

"Making the impossible happen" is not an accomplishment, but a career choice, like medicine or business or art. Like any career choice, there are certain commitments, abilities, and areas of expertise required to work in the field. The skills and expertise necessary to be extraordinary are not taught in MBA programs, nor can they be acquired through ordinary business experience. They are the result of a direct and intentional intervention in the way you are *being*.

WHO ARE THE CANDIDATES FOR RE-INVENTING THEMSELVES?

While this book can be of benefit to all who are seriously interested in re-inventing themselves, the people with whom I work are usually in one of three situations. I draw them as concentric circles, because each group is contained in the next. All "impassioned CEOs," for instance, are also "executive transformational catalysts" and are also engaged with a "designated impossibility."

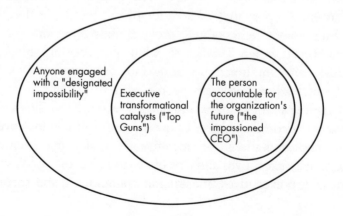

The "impassioned CEO," or anyone accountable for an organization's future

You are responsible for leading your organization into a future that at the moment is considered impossible.

You may be about to take on a major reengineering effort or an attempt to transform your company into a learning organization. Or you have already begun the organizational re-invention and are facing the breakdown of implementation. Now you find yourself in a territory for which there are no maps. You know that whatever you've learned from the past will not be sufficient in dealing with the tasks in front of you.

Anyone in the position of being an "executive transformational catalyst"

You are in an organization in transition, or you are about to make a transition. Somehow you have become part of the cadre of people leading this transition—possibly by choice, possibly because you were drafted or already in the appropriate position. You know that this transformation, if it is to succeed, will require a different kind of leadership, and it is your part to be one of the new type of leaders.

Anyone engaged with a "designated impossibility"

For whatever reason, there is some specific impossibility that you must make happen. Perhaps you want to change the world of business, or government, or education, or health care, or the media, or women or religion or the military, or, or, or . . . or perhaps you're simply dissatisfied.

You may well have accomplished what you once set out to. You might have a good life and are probably doing well; by other people's standards, you may be making a great contribution. But your mood is like the Peggy Lee song "Is That All There Is?" You think of doing more of the same for the next five, ten, or fifteen years with revulsion. You recognize that you have not made the contribution that you came to your current position to make. So you ask yourself, "Now what?"

THE "TICKET" INTO RE-INVENTION

Before beginning the stages of transformation, there is one more consideration: You should take some time to reflect on why you are here. Ask yourself, "What, specifically, am I interested in accomplishing that requires me to re-invent myself to accomplish it?" Or, to be more precise: "What 'designated impossibility' *would* I be committed to accomplishing—if only it were possible?"

This question, if you take it seriously, elicits what you ultimately have at stake. It reveals the motivation you have to re-invent yourself. It's not a difficult question, but it often brings up intense discomfort, and many people tend to discount it the instant it comes up. "You're asking me to talk about what's impossible," people say.

"Precisely correct," I respond. Indeed, I often phrase the question this way: What are you *not* committed to, only because you don't believe it can be done? What are you *not* beating down doors to do? What are you not actively taking on but *would if you could*?

The most important part of the question is the implicit phrase "You would if you could." There are millions of impossible things you're *not* committed to taking on, because they do not interest you. For instance, most people are not committed to learning to fly, without machine help, from one skyscraper roof to another.

But if you're like most people, there *are* impossible goals that you would take on *if you could.* You have a passion for these "impossibilities" designated in your mind. They call to you, capture your imagination, and make you feel alive. It may have hurt you terribly the day you finally accepted the idea that it was irresponsible to pursue these goals—irresponsible to invest time, energy, and resources in something impossible. Now the "ticket question" asks you to exhume those phantoms and bring them to the surface again. This time, accomplishing these goals is the most *responsible* thing imaginable.

The Re-Invention of yourself is enjoyable at times, but it is also a provocative, challenging, and disruptive process. There needs to be an extremely compelling motive—something in it for you that says, "This interests me. I want this a lot. I'm committed to playing in this game. And I even look forward to the disruption it will bring." That's why I call it the *designated* impossibility, meaning that you must designate it as significant to yourself, and you must recognize that you cannot accomplish it with the power you currently have. You know that you must re-invent yourself or it will remain impossible.

It may be of interest to learn what early answers some people have given to this question:

A vice-president: "To reorient the telecommunications company, where I work, around a commitment to apply our technology to transform education for the better. That would require justifying this commitment in business terms, which in turn would mean altering the business mission of this company."

CEO of a family-owned business: "To step back from trying to do everything for everyone in my company, and go sailing."

First-time television producer: "To get a new television show on the air within six months, with no experience or track record as a producer—an impossibility in standard entertainment industry practice."

Senior executive at a retail chain: "To break through the industry-wide assumptions about what is possible in quality, service, and profitability."

Former board member: "To return to a post on a non-profit arts agency board, but this time to do it without sacrificing the rest of my life or my abilities as an artist."

Inevitably, some answers are vague. Some are specific. Few of them are honed down to the point where we will take them as we move through the stages of Re-Invention. Beginning to think about this driving motivation is crucial, however, for without it you have no reason to continue.

Before moving on, then, ask yourself these questions.

(They're all different ways of phrasing the same question; answer the one that's most evocative for you.)

What are you interested in accomplishing that requires you to re-invent yourself to accomplish it?

What *would* you be committed to accomplishing—if only it were possible?

What's worth accomplishing—so much so that it would be worth re-inventing your whole self?

Having gained some idea of the designated impossibility that brings you to re-invent yourself as a leader, it's now possible to move forward and begin to work with the most vital concept of the Re-Invention process: discovering your Winning Strategy.

CHAPTER 2

UNCOVERING YOUR WINNING STRATEGY

Discovering the source of your success, which is also the source of your limitation

Little Miss Muffet sat on a tuffet
Eating her curds and whey.
Along came a spider and sat down beside her.
She picked up her spoon, beat the hell out of it
and escaped danger to great applause.

IT'S BEEN WORKING EVER SINCE.

IN THE EARLY 1980s, a manager whom I'll call Geoffrey was hired to head the management information services department of a leading financial services corporation. At age forty-one, Geoff was one of the most promising young MIS people in the country. (His name and some of his circumstances have been changed in this story.) Having built his career in banks, he was known for his ability to anticipate technical needs. A manager could talk vaguely about finding a way to link together a widespread group of people on the same database, and Geoff would begin describing the implementation in detail, mentioning problems and solutions that no one else would have noticed until months in the future. Since computer use in those days required the creation of a well-crafted, coordinated system, Geoff's ability to do this had been increasingly important throughout his career.

Now, after twenty years in the field, he had an opportunity to show what he could do with his own department. In his first meetings, he talked of designing a massive networked computer system from the ground up, which would serve and coordinate the information processing needs of the whole company. And he continued to describe problems that other people didn't see coming.

Everyone with whom Geoff worked, from the CEO down to the fifth-level managers, initially reacted with enthusiasm. After two or three months, however, everything seemed to change. He would go to meetings, talk about how his system would help people, and see their eyes glaze over. When it came time for budget allocations, his department was cut back; the money went instead to buying new personal computers with spreadsheet programs, on which people could run their own projections and store their own data.

Geoff, of course, had foreseen the popularity of personal computers. In fact, he had worked out in advance a methodology with which the company could train people in using them and integrate the new machines with the old system. In this way, once again, he was immersed in the future, years ahead of his time. Indeed, his foresight had helped him land the MIS job. But now that he was in the job, no one seemed interested in thinking ahead. They seemed more interested in having him answer their immediate questions and purchase computers at lower costs.

As the 1980s rolled by, Geoff heard more and more accusations that he was slipping in the routine tasks of his department. He felt less and less valued. A few years later, he left the company. He now considers the episode a major failure in his career. He knows that he contributed to this failure somehow, but if he had to do it all over again, he can't imagine what he might do differently.

Geoff's problem is the kind of problem that faces everyone at some point in their career. Unknown to him, he has been guided all his life by a "Winning Strategy."

A Winning Strategy is a lifelong, unconscious formula for achieving success. You did not design this Winning Strategy, it designed you. As a human being and as a leader, it is the source of your success and at the same time the source of your limitations. It defines your reality, your way of being, and your way of thinking. This, in turn, focuses your attention and shapes your actions, thereby determining what's possible and not possible for you as a leader.

From childhood onward, Geoff had been rewarded in both tangible and intangible ways for asking the question "Are things on or off track?" In school, he might have been the sort of kid who "kept his eye on the ball," who always looked ahead to make sure there would be a bat on the baseball field or gas in the car for Friday night. He had always sought, on some deep level, the goal of being valued; everyone should see him as important. Together, these elements had constituted a strategy of always looking for what was next; then organizing, convincing, and inspiring others to prevent problems before they arose. This was Geoff's individual Winning Strategy, and he had followed it, without really thinking about it, all his life. It had given him a way of *being* likable, thoughtful, and energetic—and ultimately it had brought him to the professional position he coveted, head of the MIS department for a major company, where he thought he might really make a difference.

But once Geoff took that new position, his Winning Strategy stopped boosting him forward. Instead, it held him back. In the new environment of personal computers, people didn't care so much about what's in the future and solving uncommon problems. They wanted flexibility and fluidity in getting their work done. What had always been heroic about Geoff's behavior in the past was now preventing people from working effectively.

Since he didn't know his own Winning Strategy, he couldn't understand this. His strategy kept him in mystery. Given his Winning Strategy, he could never hear the message; he never grasped why people were not satisfied with him. He never saw that his new role called for him to take on the impossible—to find a way of being patient, cognizant of the people's individual needs, and self-effacing. That's what the company needed from its MIS chief at this moment. While this might be relatively easy for someone else, for Geoff it fell into the category of impossible. Geoff short-circuited. When the other managers of the company didn't listen to him with respect, he concluded, "They've stopped apreciating my contribution here." Or "They won't let me do the job they hired me to do." Or "They're not interested in a well-managed future." Or "I failed to organize, convince, and inspire them." These conclusions were simply ways that his Winning Strategy, which he still did not explicitly recognize, occurred for him.

Geoff spend the next year looking for a job, trying to find another organization where his Winning Strategy would be welcome, although he didn't see that this was his main criterion. He thought he was merely looking for an environment where "people knew what they wanted."

Geoff's story is one of many that could be told about people who rose, and rose, and rose—producing results by getting better and better at their Winning Strategy—until they were forced to produce a result that was outside of their reality, and their Winning Strategy prevented them from accomplishing this.

SUCCESS IS NEVER FREE

Every human being has his or her own Winning Strategy—a Strategy for winning the games of life, for "making it" in life—or even for surviving in life. This is not a Strategy that you sat down and designed, and then decided to use. It is a Strategy that designed and uses you. This Strategy is so much a part of you that you are almost completely unaware of its existence. It operates as a hidden underlying force in every aspect of your life.

One person's Winning Strategy might center around the implicit injunction "Be able to fix whatever is broken." Whatever comes up in life, this person responds by looking for something broken to fix. Another person's Winning Strategy might involve doing "the difficult thing that nobody else will do." A third Strategy might be "Take control of the situation." Winning Strategies might be centered around challenging and provoking others; relating and communicating well; avoiding being ordinary; preventing problems; facilitating and empowering; creating chaos; being admired and respected; being convincing and motivating; seeking pleasure; providing security; or any of a number of other avenues for producing results.

The particulars of each person's own Winning Strategy are unique, but they always represent the ways that you, as an individual, have learned to "win" in life and get what you want. You first developed your Strategy beginning with your earliest childhood and have been refining it ever since. The development of your Winning Strategy happened at a very early age—as soon as you began interpreting your experience, giving meaning to things, drawing conclusions, and having all the other thought processes that come with the acquisition of language. As your individual Winning Strategy developed and evolved, it directed all the twists and turns of your childhood, your gains and losses since then, and your relationships with friends, family members, and coworkers. Most important, your Winning Strategy continues to shape each aspect of your life today.

Your Winning Strategy is not what you do. It is the source of what you do. It is a manifestation of who you are being. That is why, to a surprising degree, your behavior (what you are *doing*) is governed by your Winning Strategy. The times when you speak and listen, the choices you make of what to pay attention to and what to ignore, the conclusions you draw, the deals you engage in, and the actions you take are all expressions of the Winning

Strategy that has brought you success in the past. *For as long as your Winning Strategy is your ground of being, it will never occur to you to take any actions beyond it.* In fact, when other people suggest actions that are contrary to, or beyond the limits of, your Winning Strategy, those suggestions will occur to you as being "preordained to lead to failure," and you may not even hear them.

For much of your life, your Winning Strategy was a benign ally, providing you with a formula for living effectively, helping you make your way into and through adulthood. Even now, the reason for focusing on your Winning Strategy is not that it's faulty. It still works as well as it ever has. If you never take on some "designated impossibility" of your own, your Winning Strategy will never get "used up." You will keep improving and succeeding, because the Winning Strategy is intimately woven, by design, with your ability to keep improving your own life— within the Strategy's own limits.

But as soon as you must take on the impossible, the Winning Strategy will not only cease to be useful, it will impede you from succeeding.

Sooner or later, you will probably leave the arena of improving what's possible and move into the territory of making the impossible happen. At that point, whatever its particulars may be, your Winning Strategy will keep you from being able to do the things you need to do.

Here are three examples that may help give a clear idea of how a Winning Strategy works:

■ John, the CEO of a well-established, family-run business in the South, was committed to growing his $80-million business into a $200-million venture as quickly as possible. He had been working very hard for a number of years to accomplish this, but was chronically dissatisfied with the slow, incremental improvement and the constant strain on the company's resources. Several times, John had engaged a team of experts to design and implement growth plans. The growth plans always called for bringing some new blood—people with new skills and expertise—into the organization at a senior level. This would inevitably bring up conflicts with existing executives and managers, many of whom were members of John's family.

Every time a plan moved into a crucial, "do or die" phase, John would intervene—either refusing to endorse it or stopping implementation. His Winning Strategy centered around creating powerful relationships and avoiding conflicts. He was an *expert* at making sure everyone was happy, particularly the members of his family, while maintaining control of any conflicts. His Winning Strategy thus stopped him from taking actions necessary to implement the growth plans.

John was totally unaware of his role in the failure of his company to move ahead. If you had asked him, at the end of any day, how he had spent that day, he would have said, "I spent it working on the growth of the company." But as long as John was trapped within the boundaries of a Winning Strategy that had always helped him succeed by making his family happy, he would not be able to bring into existence the family's own dream of moving the organization to the next level.

■ Fran's goal was to create a new model of innovative, independent leadership in the management teams of her retail company. If this model could succeed, Fran knew it would foster a climate of innovation and entrepreneurship throughout the entire business. And she knew, perhaps better than any other senior executive in the company, how valuable that would be.

But consistently in Fran's career, she had achieved success through a Winning Strategy of taking charge in order to prevent problems from emerging. She was an expert at nipping problems in the bud. She sincerely wanted to give up maintaining control, but "taking charge and preventing problems" represented her way of succeeding and surviving.

Thus, when teams were created to open new stores, Fran worked out the details for them, reasoning that she wanted to help them avoid any pitfalls that could lead to failure. Whenever there was a conflict, she set things up so the team would defer to her—the expert—rather than work the conflict out themselves. Within a short time, the enthusiasm for "teamwork" and the "new model" diminished as managers realized the organization was still operating in the same old way: The teams were carrying out Fran's ideas rather than creating and implementing ideas of their own. Her Winning Strategy stopped her from allowing team leaders to face the problems and take the risks that would lead them to creative breakthroughs of their own.

■ One of the tragic stereotypes of modern political life is public officials who spend enormous effort gathering people around them who reinforce their Winning Strategy, only to get caught in the trap of a world that no longer wants what they have to give. Unfortunately, when this happens, they then apply, ever more vigorously, the skills and talents that worked in the past.

Sam, one such politician I know, is a classic example. He is a charismatic, popular, nationally known figure with a reputation for being a visionary. Sam had gathered a staff of similar visionaries to help him campaign for the mayoralty of a large southern city. The city had been dominated by "good ole boys" for as long as anyone could remember, but Sam promised to create a city government and city climate that were not just ethnically diverse but genuinely participatory. He won, by creating a powerful and exciting vision of the future.

Once in office, however, rather than surround himself with peple who knew how to deal with the hard realities of implementation, Sam continued to rely on his team of visionaries. The visionaries kept right on creating and planning and motivating; every week there was a new inspirational message, a new vision, a new statement of possibilities. None of it was ever followed through. In effect, Sam's Winning Strategy stopped not just him but everyone in his office from following through on the vision they had put forth. And Sam lost his bid for reelection.

Your Winning Strategy also determines what, from your point of view, is wrong with other people. You may have acquaintances, for example, whom you consider to be good, strong, intelligent people—*except* for the aspects of their lives to which they seem blind. If they could only see those aspects, they would be much more effective. But what they are blind to, in your view, is usually part of your *own* Winning Strategy, your own formula for success. For example, if your Winning Strategy is centered around creating relationships with people, you will be sure that those who don't create relationships well can never be successful. If they do succeed, you won't really believe it's success. It will be a fluke. On the other hand, if your Winning Strategy is centered around taking charge and driving the action, you will find it difficult to tolerate people around you in whom those capabilities are missing.

Winning Strategies are the reason why many meetings go on endlessly. If your Winning Strategy is focused on avoiding danger, you will not let a plan go forward until you have voiced all of the dangers and satisfied yourself that they are being considered. All the others in the meeting will also have to satisfy the imperative of *their* Winning Strategy—and make sure it has been considered—before they can go forward as a group. In many cases, the meetings make progress only because people can settle on *some* substantial issue left over after all the others have satisfied their own Winning Strategy requirements.

Sometimes the environment in an organization, relationship, or group changes, so that your Winning Strategy can no longer flourish. When that happens, you suffocate; you can't breathe. You *must* get out. When you uncover your own Winning Strategy, you'll be able to see how every important relationship, group, or organization that you ever left is in some way connected to this type of change. Sometimes you may be a leader so completely tied to the organization that getting out is not an option. Then, when your Winning Strategy can no longer flourish, you will unconsciously do everything you can to return the organization to its old condition. You will sacrifice whatever major transformation effort you had begun so that you can return to the environment that requires your Winning Strategy. For example, someone whose Winning Strategy is focused on uniquely solving unusual problems will unconsciously make choices to ensure that there are always unusual crisis-type problems at the forefront, demanding unusual heroics.

The purpose of this first stage of transformation is not to find a better Winning Strategy, but (1) to recognize your own individual Winning Strategy and (2) to recognize the Compensating Power Principle at work in your own Winning Strategy, and how this affects your current source of power.

THE COMPENSATING POWER PRINCIPLE

The foundation on which the Compensating Power Principle is built is that all human beings inherently believe that some things are not possible. To compensate for whatever is *not* possible you design a Winning Strategy to succeed at what *is* possible. Until you step beyond it, your Winning Strategy is your only source of power as a leader—the power to compensate for *not* making the impossible happen. Over the years this strategy has determined your reality of what is and is not possible.

The Compensating Power Principle: Every time you exercise your Winning Strategy and produce a "possible" result to compensate for what's "not possible," to an equal degree you expand the scope of what's "not possible," thereby keeping the cycle going. The structure for achieving something grows only to the extent that the foundation on which it is built grows. The foundation on which your Winning Strategy is built is "what's not possible, what can't ever be," and "what's not possible" keeps growing as the power of your Winning Strategy grows. When you strengthen one end, you strengthen the other.

Every win, every result you produce with your Winning Strategy, is built on and reinforces the interpretation that the world is not the way it should be, you are flawed and broken, and only certain things are possible. The more powerful your Winning Strategy gets (every time you succeed and win), the more you reinforce that there is something wrong with you, everyone else, and the world.

Every individual Winning Strategy implicitly declares that only some things are possible. Anything outside its realm of possibilities is excluded. It gives us the illusion of providing us unlimited power, but it only lets us travel within its inherent limits. Because the formula exists at such a deep level within us, most of us never bother to examine it; and we remain unaware of its power and its nature. We think of it, if at all, as simply "the way things should be done." We don't see how it determines the focus of our attention, shapes our actions, and, most important, limits the realm of possibility in which we operate. If we can't accomplish something through our Winning Strategy, we label it "impossible."

That is why the most conventionally successful engineers in the late nineteenth century were the *most* certain that manned flight was impossible. Their capabilities were balanced by a "compensating" power that kept them from taking the risks that a pair of bicycle-building brothers in Dayton, Ohio, were willing to take. Similarly, the better an organizational leader becomes at wielding his or her successful Winning Strategy, the harder it is to make the organization move in an "impossible" direction.

Every time you exercise your Winning Strategy and produce a result and win, you reinforce your existing perception of what is possible and not possible a bit more, until you get to the point where you unwittingly crowd out alternative approaches. Alternatives to your Winning Strategy don't even occur to you.

As your Winning Strategy gets stronger, so does your implicit perception that certain things are impossible and you can't do them (or, in fact, they can't be done). Every time you succeed, you reinforce the way of looking at the world that brought you success—and you make it harder to look at the world in any other way. Your limits grow in "compensation" for the success of your Winning Strategy—or, if you prefer, your Winning Strategy yields successful results that "compensate" you for the increasingly strong limitations on your action.

Once you are attuned to it in business, you will see many examples of the Compensating Power Principle at work. You will see how someone's Winning Strategy can determine the scope of what is possible for him or her. I think of Elizabeth, one of the few executive women in a very large manufacturing organization. She had the support, encouragement, and even insistence of her boss that she move into top management. But her actions were inconsistent with those of a credible senior manager.

It turned out that unbeknownst to Elizabeth, her actions were driven by the tactics that had always brought her power in the past: empowering and facilitating others around her, in order to be valued and to avoid being excluded. Always in great demand for teams and projects, because she was very capable of implementing others' ideas, she had parlayed her Winning Strategy into a vice-presidency. But once there, because of who she was *being,* she could not allow her own original thinking to take the lead. Thus her own thinking went unnoticed. It never occurred to her to step forward and lead—a missed opportunity for both her and the organization.

In re-inventing herself, Elizabeth altered her way of *being* from being trapped in her Winning Strategy. No longer did she compensate for what wasn't possible by empowering and facilitating changes within the realm of what was possible. In a matter of weeks, she dramatically shifted how her colleagues and boss perceived her. She did not lose her ability to inspire others; but in re-inventing herself, she naturally became someone who, every day, was drawing people around projects and goals that had never been taken on before. While they were currently impossible, they were the goals the organization needed to take on to accomplish its future. A few months later, she was named a member of the chairman's executive committee.

In another example, a Hollywood studio executive I know discovered that his Winning Strategy was centered around being responsible and avoiding unnecessary danger. Everything, from the layout of his office to his style of talking on the phone, was unconsciously designed to accomplish this. Once he became aware of this, he also saw that his entire organization reflected this same approach. His key executives operated with even more caution, and more excessive concern for "doing the right thing," than he had. This was only natural, given their desire to show him that they understood his concerns. Projects kept coming in late, always a little bit less colorful than what had been expected, with a surprising amount of the budget devoted to either literal insurance or figurative insurance—measures taken only because they provided a contingency in case something went wrong.

Given his Winning Strategy, the studio executive could neither reprimand his staff for caution nor set a better example. Only when he set about re-inventing himself could his division change. They all shifted their way of *being.* They had compensated for what wasn't possible by being cautious and "doing the right thing." Now they were free to take actions that required risk, innovation, and creativity. Once that happened, they built a reputation for consistently completing difficult and complicated projects in record-breaking time and under budget.

If your Winning Strategy outlives its usefulness, you will probably continue to be oblivious to it. Sooner or later, however, you will run up against situations where, through no fault of your own, your Winning Strategy won't work. Instead, it will lead to failure. But it will be so ingrained in you, so much a part of who you are *being,* that you will inevitably find it difficult, if not impossible, to give it up. You might even sacrifice your fondest hopes and aspirations for the sake of your Winning Strategy, telling yourself all the while that you are being "realistic" or that this behavior is "who I am and I can't hide it."

Re-inventing yourself does *not* mean replacing one Winning Strategy with another. Any Winning Strategy is as limiting as any other and keeps you trapped in the past. Re-inventing yourself deals with releasing yourself from the grip of all Winning Strategies. It means releasing yourself from the relentless lifelong practice of applying *any* formula that is a compensation for what's not possible.

YOUR INDIVIDUAL WINNING STRATEGY

The way to reveal your Winning Strategy is to unveil its anatomy.

It would be convenient if I could provide a list of "Common Winning Strategies" and invite you to simply pick the one that seems closest to your own. But that would do you a disservice. Everyone's Winning Strategy is entirely different; it has been honed and crafted, after all, during your individual life. No list that I (or anyone else) could generate would include yours. You must articulate it yourself.

This is not like unveiling your personality, your Myers-Briggs type, your leadership style, or your astrological birth sign. The process of divining your Winning Strategy involves reflection and directed self-examination—uncovering what you don't know you don't know about your hidden source of action. Remember, the purpose of this inquiry is re-inventing your "way of *being*," and you must start by learning more about how you are *being* now, by uncovering your individual Winning Strategy.

I have found it useful to conduct this investigation through three interrelated inquiries. Together, they make up a formula that, taken as a whole, articulates your Winning Strategy.

Start by asking yourself: In my everyday work life:

- *What do I listen for?* To what is your attention drawn? (This is the "listening for" component of your Winning Strategy formula.)
- *From what actions do I expect power?* What represents an essential solution or action, in any given situation, to produce a successful result? (This is the "so as to act by" component.)
- *What is the desired outcome of my life?* What's most important to you in the long run? (This is the "in order to" component.)

There is no set pattern for making these inquiries. You do not have to start with "listening for"; you can begin with any of the three questions. Nor must you approach them one at a time. Each element will probably give you a sense of its relationships to the others and a feel for your Winning Strategy as a whole. Gradually, you will develop an articulation that rings true to you as the formula for the way you have sought success all your life.

What Do You Listen For?

You might prefer to believe that you are open-minded, but even the most liberal people have a tendency to "listen for" specific possibilities that rule out all other possibilities, and filter everything we see and hear. The way you listen is the structure through which you interpret the world. How you listen to what's being said shapes how you speak, which, in turn, shapes the actions you take.

Thus, there is great leverage in transforming yourself and

your organization simply by paying attention to what you "listen for."

What you "listen for" often contains a heaping amount of prejudgment and preconception, especially around the familiar elements of your life. In most cases, before you even begin a conversation with a particular person on a particular topic, you have already made a judgment about what he or she will say. You will "listen for" him or her to meet your expectations.

Imagine, for instance, that you were the parent of a typical teenager. You came home one day and moaned, "Why can't you be tidy around the house?"

Then imagine that your teenager replied, "You know, I was just thinking that myself. I'm going to start right now by cleaning my room."

You might not even hear it at first. You might wonder, "Is something wrong with my child?" You would almost certainly do a double take, because it would contradict the expectations you typically "listen for."

When I mentioned this example in one of my sessions, an executive said, "We have a saying in our family: Don't discuss Ronald Reagan with my mother-in-law. She is always 'listening for' the idea that absolutely no good came from his administration."

"And you, in turn," I said, "are always 'listening for' her to hold forth with that opinion. Suppose you were with her one day, and someone brought up the topic of Reagan. Suppose she said, 'You know, I used to think differently, but now I actually think Ronald Reagan made a much greater contribution than I ever noticed.' "

"I'd call that *Invasion of the Body Snatchers,*" said the executive. If she had actually said as much, he might never have heard it, because his antennae were only calibrated to pick up the signals he expected from her.

It's hard to see what you are "listening for" at first, because it takes place on such an automatic, instantaneous level of your thinking. You interpret ruthlessly and instantly, based on the past and your Winning Strategy. This lies at the root of many communication breakdowns. What is distinctly clear to one person is not necessarily clear to another. One person feels such a strong, piercingly acute awareness of a problem that he feels like the problem is screaming through him. The other person barely hears, because she is not "listening for" that problem. The screams come across as barely audible whispers.

Think of this "listening for" element as an antenna built into your attention, operating at every moment. An antenna only picks up particular types of sound waves or those within certain ranges. Similarly, your attention is tuned to pick up only certain concerns. Antennae can be tuned into particular frequencies or aimed in particular directions. Similarly, your "listening for" attention is generally tuned and aimed toward certain questions or concerns, and away from others. If a particular phenomenon out in the world doesn't offer anything to answer your Winning Strategy, and you perceive that no action can be taken, then that phenomenon will not attract your antenna.

If your "listening for" is focused around answers to the question "What's the point?" you will filter every comment and every conversation through that question. If you can't get the point of a particular meeting or event, your attention will wander. If you get impatient about the lack of a point, you may put your foot down and stop the meeting until your concern is addressed. You would probably not be aware of the reason you are doing this, of its link to the way you are listening. You would more likely perceive yourself as merely needing more information or needing to be clearer about the circumstances. You might see your action as a matter of integrity: "It's irresponsible to go forward or invest my time until I know why we're here."

But when the dust clears (often in a matter of seconds or microseconds), the result is always the same: Either you have stopped the action long enough for you to get clear about what the point is (so that now you are ready for action) or you have removed yourself from an active role in the conversation. In doing so, you have stymied the productive work going on—even if that work was something you wholeheartedly supported. *One way or another, this "listening for" element determines whether or not you will move into action and shapes the action you will take.*

What you "listen for" is always in the form of a question.

There are an infinite number of these possible questions. Here are some examples:

"What's the whole picture?"
"How does this fit?"
"What is the opportunity?"
"What interests me?"
"What are the rules here?"

If you are a person who must make sure you are headed for the right direction in life, you might listen for "Where is this going?" You sort information according to its potential for helping you make connections, and you do not move forward unless those connections are visibly promised (which means you might miss more subtle opportunities).

Others might listen for "What's the truth?" They want to make sure they get to the "heart of the matter," and do not trust anything they hear unless it is objectively confirmable.

Another "listening for" focus might be "How can I use this?" If they don't hear anything that they perceive as useful, they write the experience off as a waste of time.

You can discover your "listening for" element by paying attention to language, to your own words, and by watching yourself in action.

I once worked with a manager named Melanie, who started out by saying, "I listen for the escape hatch, to find an escape route." That seemed like a narrow way of describing what one "listens for." (Indeed, most people start out describing their Winning Strategy in too narrow terms.) So I asked her to think more broadly: Consider that "finding the escape route" is an expression of what you listen for rather than the "listening for" itself.

"Well, I got to that," Melanie said, "because I was thinking I listen for 'What's really going on?' " If she knew what was really going on in a situation, she would always be able to see the escape hatch (as well as the entry route). She mulled this over and then said, "It's really most like the question 'What's the whole story?' " And it wasn't until she heard her voice asking that question, and recognized how familiar it sounded, that she felt as if she'd hit on the proper phrasing.

Here are some specific techniques for drawing forth this element:

- Observe yourself taking notes at meetings, when you attend programs, or when you take courses. What information do you write down? What determines your choice? What questions are your notes trying to answer?
- Notice when you feel you're "in the right place" and things are going well. What are the characteristics of the scene? What gave you the clue that things were okay? Chances are, the comfort you feel suggests that something you are "listening for" has been assuaged, like an itch that has been scratched.
- At the moment you are told that so-and-so is on the phone, pause before you pick up the line. What do you expect so-and-so to say? What are you already "listening for" him or her to say to you?
- Ask yourself during conversations, "In what way is what I 'listen for' expressing itself in the conversation that I'm presently having?" These conversations you have don't have to be with others; they are often internal conversations you have with yourself. Listen to yourself until you hear your "listening for" element talking to your children, spouses, friends, colleagues. Listen to the words in your head, the words that come out of your mouth, and the words you "listen for." Listen for your own "listening" so that it gets so loud that you can hear it whenever it emerges.
- "Listen for" what it is that prompts others around you to go into action too fast. What have they not taken into account?
- Find another person whom you have known awhile, someone who has seen you in many conversations. Explain the concepts of the Winning Strategy and "listening for" to them. Then ask them, "What do you feel I am 'listening

for' when you see me at work?" Consider what that person has told you. Does any of it seem to ring true?

When you hear your listening habits articulated, the phrasing will have a familiar ring. Play with the wording until you get it right: "It's not that I'm listening for 'What use is this?' I'm really listening for 'What do I really care about?' " The closer your phrasing gets to the core, the more familiar it will feel.

FROM WHAT ACTIONS DO YOU EXPECT POWER?

The old expression "To someone with a hammer, everything looks like a nail" conveys the essence of this element of your Winning Strategy. What are the actions, solutions, and other steps that represent "producing a successful result" to you, no matter what the situation may be?

In workshops, I describe this as the "so as to act by" component. Once your "listening for" component has been satisfied, you are ready to move the action forward or to stop the action.

How do you do that?

What is the implicit, habitual action, the everyday way of acting, that for you is essential for anything to succeed? What type of action, when you experience yourself doing it, makes you think you are handling life correctly?

Your first answer may be that there are many possible actions you might take, and they cover a wide range of possibilities. But when you look closely at them, all of the ways that it occurs to *you* to act are examples of one category of action—a category that, for you, lies at the heart of action. The task in this part of the exercise is to articulate that category.

This element represents the best solution, from your point of view, to anything: how you act to produce your most successful results. Whatever it may be, your "so as to act by" element is something at which you are an expert. You are even known for it by other people: "Jane is great at conciliating," they say, or "Mark is terrific at raising questions."

The way you act is second nature. Your actions are shaped

by what has worked in the past, developed over the years to demonstrate your skill and expertise. *You don't consciously dwell on your actions; they are automatic responses to the context created through your listening.*

If the "listening for" element is always a question, this element is always a verb (a transitive verb, ending in *-ing,* representing an ongoing activity).

In order to succeed, you might find it essential to "act by" understanding people; you might be a paragon of empathy, skilled at quickly getting a sense of why others do what they do. Or you might act by organizing. You might know exactly how to bring people together around a purpose and make sure each one can do his or her part. You might habitually find it essential to "act by" fixing things, analyzing, explaining, teaching, planning, solving problems, or fighting for a cause.

You gravitate to the kinds of actions that have always gotten you where you want to go.

Consider the case of Caroline, a senior vice-president of marketing in a Fortune 500 company. Caroline, at age forty, has fought her way to the top. She listens, she has learned, for answers to the question "What's beneath the surface here?" And her response, her "so as to" habitual action, is so instinctive that it is almost second nature. As soon as she spots a below-the-surface need, she begins to act by providing what's wanted and needed. Sometimes "what's wanted and needed" is advice; sometimes it's a kick in the pants. Other times it's a particular expertise that she offers or rounds up someone else to offer. Sometimes it's a matter of shifting resources around.

Caroline provides "what's needed" without ever making it seem like *she* is the one providing the resources. Things are miraculously ready when they are needed. One of her colleagues once said to her, "It's like there's an invisible army of elves in your office. Where do you keep them?"

This is the way Caroline has learned to get successful results. Yet, until she began to reflect on it, she never saw that, for her, "providing what's wanted and needed" was the solution to every situation. By listening for "What's beneath the surface?" and acting by "providing what's wanted and needed," she has developed a formula for succeeding. This formula, the first two elements of Caroline's Winning Strategy, is her source of power. Whenever she needs power to produce a result, she applies this formula. She listens for "What's beneath the surface here?" and goes into action by "providing what's wanted and needed." Sometimes that means taking over; sometimes it might mean getting out of the way; and sometimes it might simply mean reassuring everybody that everything is fine.

Revealing your "so as to act by" patterns can be more difficult than identifying your listening patterns because actions appear to be different depending on the circumstances. It takes time and concentration to tease out a sense of your habitual actions.

For example, Melanie (the manager described in the "listening for" example) worked her way to an understanding of her essential actions from which to draw power. She began by saying that she sought to "act by" teaching and communicating. But as she thought about it more, she realized that she most often acted to take charge of complex situations—to be responsible for them as a whole. I asked her what that looked like in action, and she laughed ruefully. "It is doing the whole thing. It's not that I do every part of the work—I do delegate—but I prefer to feel that I am making it possible to accomplish the whole thing. I like to set the terms." Melanie listens for "What's the whole story?" so as to act by "taking responsibility for the whole situation."

Here are some techniques:

■ Describe four or five examples of what you look like in action. Are you designing, confronting, persisting, helping, persuading, or taking responsibility? You should begin to see a pattern in your descriptions that expresses how you move forward in order to achieve success. Although the actual words might be different, on close examination you will see that an underlying theme emerges. For example, if you describe yourself as giving instructions, resolving conflicts, and solving problems, the common underlying theme is that you compensate for what's wrong by taking charge. You will recognize a particular pattern of acting as yours when you realize that if you don't act that way, you don't get results. And you cannot imagine yourself operating without acting in this manner.

This will hold true not only in business but across the board—at home, in the community, and in any volunteer work you do. It is who you are, and it is part of you all the time.

■ Think about your negative opinions of others. People often condemn others for not acting "properly"—in other words, for not following the same "so as to act by" element. You may feel that others won't be "successful" unless they act a certain way. Your opinion of them is a clue to *your* "so as to act by" element.

■ Consider this scenario. You've worked late. It's eleven at night when you finally leave the office and walk to your car, which is parked on a side street. When you reach the car, you see a body across the hood. The person is bleeding but alive. You don't have a cellular or car phone.

What is the first thing you would do in response?

Think for a moment, and *write down the answer now.*

What did you see yourself doing? What did those actions suggest about your habitual actions?

Some people will immediately speak to the person who is lying there to see if he or she is all right. Others will immediately look around to see if a perpetrator is present. Still others might not even approach the car but turn immediately to look for a phone.

People who immediately come to the victim's side are acting to help, in order to be valued. They are so driven by the urge to act (and by the need to listen for "What's needed?") that they may not realize that they have put themselves at risk.

People who look around for the perpetrator may be asking, "What's going on that I don't immediately see?" The action of investigating is a habitual response, a regular effort to avoid danger and ensure safety first.

People who look for a phone are acting to bring more help and resources to the scene. That is probably a component of their habitual action. They, too, may be listening for "What's needed?" but with a different result than the people who rush to the victim's side.

■ Here is another scenario to consider. At the last minute,

you are selected to fill in for a speaker who has suddenly taken ill. You will represent your entire industry at a worldwide satellite event taking place the next day. Your presentation will be five minutes long. You must be impressive.

What's the first action you take?

Once again, reflect and *write down the answer now.*

Some people will immediately begin to write a speech. They are apt to be "listening for" clarity of purpose and acting "so as to" be understood.

Others will collect data and seek out experts on the subject. They are "listening for" expert guidance, "so as to" be certain.

■ Examine your speaking—in both its verbal form and its written form.

The act of writing, more deliberate than speech, forces you to choose words that are significant. Which phrases occur again and again? What actions do they suggest?

Your writing holds clues to subtle nuances that reveal your approach to action. For example, two people might at first think they are acting "so as to" be respected. But as they closely examine their own words, one of them may discover phrases that have to do with gaining respect: "This will prove . . ." or "We need to substantiate . . ." The other may discover phrases that convey something closer to a drive for appreciation: "I have worked hard putting this material together . . ." or "We want to thank our predecessors . . ."

Don't focus on the literal meaning of the words you write or speak, but on what drives the choice of words. If you are acting "so as to" take charge, you may nonetheless see words like "delegation" and "decentralization." But if they appear in short, clipped, military-style sentences in which someone is clearly deputized to be in control at all times, that may be a clue to the habitual action component of your Winning Strategy.

WHAT IS THE DESIRED OUTCOME OF YOUR LIFE?

This is the third component, the "in order to" component, of your Winning Strategy. (I sometimes think of this as the "grand" component of the "grand strategy of your life.")

Your desired outcome is the "way of *being*" that you believe, in your heart, would make you feel fulfilled. It may be your most cherished dream ("to be the best" or "to be carefree"), or it may represent the nightmare you want to avoid at all costs ("to avoid loss of respect" or "to avoid being trapped").

You direct your efforts toward the desired outcome because you think that if you can *be* this particular way—"If I can be the best, be right, be in charge, be of value, be at peace, be secure"—your life will then turn out the way it should. Desired ways of *being* also include our efforts to avoid that which would have life turn out the way it shouldn't—being humiliated, criticized, betrayed, alone, confused, or ordinary.

I use the phrase "in order to" to help people get a sense of this component of their Winning Strategy. You act, move, study, talk, and make decisions *in order to* what? In order to achieve what outcome?

The outcome will express your version of how life should work out, including what to avoid to control life and keep it from "not turning out."

The desired outcome of a Winning Strategy is extremely important in influencing your decisions. In those times when you discover that you cannot implement your Winning Strategy's desired outcome, you may be drawn to frustration and despair. Often, people do anything they can to rid themselves of a situation that is threatening the outcome they seek. You might even quit jobs, leave relationships, and undo commitments, because you feel you are no longer in an arena where you can succeed at getting the results you want. You probably don't consciously realize *why* you feel threatened, however; you more likely feel like you don't quite know what is making you so edgy. You only know that you have to stop whatever is happening, because it threatens your power and control so fundamentally.

Consider the case of Jacqueline, who was the first female officer in one of her industry's leading companies. Jacqueline had always been "first": first woman to graduate from her business school, first member of her class to get a job at that company. Her divisioin was the first in the company to win a national quality award, first to exceed its goals five years in a row, and first to have 100 percent participation in the United Way. Jacqueline, to no one's surprise, discovered that her Winning Strategy's desired outcome was to "be first." She had always been driven by that goal, and she thought she always would be.

But she had run out of firsts to shoot for—and being first was essential for her life working out! There was only one first left: to make her company the leading enterprise of its kind in the world. To get this outcome, she would need to lead a company-wide transformation, and she entered into it with her customary zeal. But, as it turned out, no one else in the organization wanted the kind of transformation she did. No one else really wanted to be first, either. Her repeated attempts to incorporate new company-wide executive recruitment policies and development programs failed.

Finally, she realized that if she wanted to keep getting the boosts she felt from being first, she would have to leave the organization. If she wanted to stay in the company, she would have to get rid of her dependence on this desired outcome. It was a close call, but during Executive Re-Invention she ultimately decided and was able to give it up. She reversed her decision to leave for another firm, and went on to a higher leadership position in the company.

If you perceive yourself to be thwarted from achieving your desired outcome, then watch out! One way or another, as it did with Jacqueline, your Winning Strategy will drive you to change the situation somehow.

What techniques, then, can you use to articulate this component of your Winning Strategy?

▪ One approach is to examine your past. Look for an involvement—an organization, place, group, relationship, or project—that was once significant to you but which you left. Why did you leave?

Include, in this examination, situations where you left against your will. Why were you thrown out? What message was the relationship giving you?

If you can identify why you left, it will provide an indication of your "in order to"—what your Winning Strategy is always driving for and what it is always driving to avoid.

If you look at the times when you left, your immediate answer to the question "why?" would probably be something like, "There was no future for me there." Or "The company had changed so much that it was no longer the company I came to work for." Or "Everything that drew me here was now different and I no longer wanted to be there." Or "I found I had nothing in common with the people in that association any longer."

Look underneath that first answer and see that, while you may have explained it that way, you left to seek some "in order to," such as "to be respected" or "to be in charge" or "to be happy." At the time you left, it was apparent that this "in order to" was no longer available there, if it had ever been. Probably, it had become clear that it was never going to be available unless you moved on.

In one way or another, you were getting signals that, if you stayed, things would go in a direction that you must avoid. You would be placed in conflict; or you would be left out; or you would be bored; or whatever danger would be most meaningful to the "in order to" component of your Winning Strategy.

This tends to be true even if you didn't initiate the leaving—if you were laid off, or left to take another job, or left for reasons that had to do with a personal relationship or marriage. If you look underneath whatever reasons were given at the time, you will find the elements of your "in order to."

■ Ask yourself what the worst thing is that could happen to you.

This element is easiest to spot when it is threatened or thwarted. So try to describe the worst kind of failure you can imagine. For some people these elements include loss of power, love, reputation; for others, "lack of options for movement"; and for still others, financial failure, disrespect, exclusion.

Melanie, the manager from two previous examples, used this technique to reach an understanding of her desired outcome. What was the worst thing that could happen to her? To be embarrassed by failure. But what, exactly, did that mean? To be stuck in a situation where she felt empty, and not whole. She continually took responsibility, more than her share, because she never felt empty if she had enough responsibility.

■ This component of your Winning Strategy has a great deal

to do with feeling in control of life. In many organizations, the most damning accusation is to call someone "out of control." But different people mean different things by it. Simply being able to breathe means being "in control," in some form. What do *you* mean when you say someone is out of control? What characteristics does that person have? In what ways does being out of control make a person vulnerable?

EXPRESSING YOUR WINNING STRATEGY AS A WHOLE

Rather than work on three components of your Winning Strategy separately, it's helpful to think about them together. In corporate programs and executive groups, I often suggest that people draw up a table for themselves that looks something like this. (I've included several examples of the ways in which different people have ultimately responded.)

This table is not intended as a linear formula: You don't start at the left or the right column. You don't assume that "listening for" creates "in order to," or vice versa. Instead, you try to fill in all three columns, getting the language closer and closer to the truth, until you can recognize yourself in all of the pieces.

The formula is a way to reveal the hidden conversation that you are always *being* and holding within yourself. Sometimes it is spoken out loud. More often, it's internal—held within your reveries, your daydreams, and your reactions.

Revealing is truly a discovery process: You must unearth your own Winning Strategy. There is no set recipe. Examples of other people's Winning Strategies are just that—examples. Don't look for one that simply seems to fit you. Your Winning Strategy is as unique to you as your fingerprints.

CAN THE HOLD OF A WINNING STRATEGY BE BROKEN?

When you identify your Winning Strategy, your first response will most likely be one of enthusiastic approval. You like your

	Listening for . . .	. . . so as to act by . . .	. . . in order to . . .
Caroline (described above)	"What's underneath? What's hidden?"	. . . providing what's wanted and needed . . .	. . . be valued, and avoid being left out.
Geoff (described above)	"What could be done to make a better future?"	. . . organizing, gathering, bringing people together . . .	. . . be taken seriously and be respected.
Melanie (described above)	"What's the whole story?"	. . . taking responsibility for the whole situation . . .	. . . be in charge, and avoid being trapped.
Al	"What do they want that they don't know they want?"	. . . figuring it out and making it happen . . .	. . . call the shots, and avoid being controlled.
Patricia	"Where's the fun?"	. . . provoking, moving, arranging, and taking things lightly . . .	. . . be alive, feel everything, and avoid being trapped.
Jennifer	"Is it on or off track?"	. . . fixing, empowering . . .	. . . be carefree and fulfilled, and avoid getting out of control.
Faith	"What's the truth? What's really going on here?"	. . . doing what's appropriate, and doing the right thing . . .	. . . be certain and safe, and avoid betrayal.

Winning Strategy! Of *course* you like it. It's been the source of your power.

A second common response is astonishment. Your Winning Strategy is so vital that you have always assumed everyone felt the same way. Now you recognize that everyone has a different formula for success.

Your third response may well be the recognition of how addictive your Winning Strategy can be. The Winning Strategy gets its great addictive power through the results it produces. As people become experts at using their Winning Strategy, they get more and more successful in life. Every time you use it, you get a little "fix" of gratification, as the successful fruits of your efforts "kick in." You receive validation that your Winning Strategy is working, and you believe, all the more strongly, that the more you improve and fine-tune your Strategy, the faster you'll get to your goal, which will be a momentary version of your "in order to," whatever it may be.

Moreover, the Strategy is so deeply ingrained in most people that you probably can't imagine yourself listening or acting differently, or desiring a different outcome. Every time you have a problem or face a situation, you automatically and unconsciously turn to the familiar success patterns of your Winning Strategy. Indeed, it works in the same way that the misuse of narcotics or alcohol does, as a survival mechanism, which helps to explain why it is so difficult to get beyond it.

But as you move through life, your Winning Strategy requires increasingly great amounts of effort and energy to maintain. You might assume that outside circumstances are draining you. You might assume that your exhaustion stems from the amount of sleep you've had, the amount of stress in your life, the difficulties you face at work, the threat of competition, the problems in your family, or any number of external forces. But the actual source of your exhaustion is the relentless drain of effort to maintain the Winning Strategy at all costs.

The more exhausted you get, the more you are reinforced in believing in your own powerlessness. There isn't anything you can do about the circumstances in life *except* keep on with the only way of *being* that seems to be effective. And if that way of *being* is less effective, you assume, it's because life is tougher and tougher. As the "fixes" of gratification become shorter and shorter, you need more and more of them to compensate for the greater stress and exhaustion you feel. The whole process becomes a self-reinforcing spiral, from which it doesn't occur to you to escape.

Occasionally, you might wake up in the middle of the night and think, "I've got to change my ways." Yet you don't ever consider changing your formula for success—first, because you are unaware that it exists, and second, because your instincts tell you that if you changed it radically, things would be much worse. In short, while you may be momentarily experiencing its limitations, you are aware that it is the only source of power that you have at the moment.

Like Boston Charlie, the man who couldn't find his way off the trolley lines in the Kingston Trio's popular song, you might "ride forever" on the track of your Winning Strategy, going around and around and never escaping.

And there may be no need to escape. Your Winning Strategy can indeed bring success. But once you decide you want to create an impossible future, the only way to get there is to make a radical shift in the way you are *being*. This shift requires going beyond the limits of your Winning Strategy. It requires breaking the addiction.

Let me give you an example. It demonstrates how Executive Re-Invention transforms a successful person's understanding of his or her own Winning Strategy.

Mike is the chief operating officer of a $5-billion retail business. Recently, he found himself in the middle of an ongoing disagreement with the chairman of the company, with whom he had shared an extremely good relationship. They could not agree on the future of the company. The chairman wanted high-quality products, low prices, a great environment, and no increased spending. Mike thought the company could commit to two or even three of those goals, but he didn't think all four were possible. And the chairman's large-scale change effort, as it unfolded, seemed to support his beliefs. Although the company wanted to lower costs, an improved environment meant a change in pay structures, which increased costs dramatically.

When it became clear that costs would rise in the short term, Mike threw a fit. Not only money but time and energy were being wasted. The value of the goal of no increased spending was compromised, he argued, and it should be dropped. He insisted that only goals that could be achieved should be set.

The chairman, meanwhile, was equally adamant that the company commit to accomplishing all four goals. Mike blew a fuse; he thought there was either something wrong with the chairman for wanting the impossible or something wrong with himself for not being able to commit to unrealistic goals. He argued back and forth with himself: It wasn't right to commit to four goals. The organization was already having difficulty meeting one goal. There was absolutely no sense in saying you could do something if you couldn't. But how could the chairman be that wrong? Why didn't the chairman listen to him? What was wrong with the chairman? What was wrong with him? Why were they locked in this battle? What was the point of putting his reputation as a leader in jeopardy?

"You brought me here because of my expertise," he finally told the chairman, "but now when I try to tell you what can and can't be done, you don't want to listen to me." By then, events had reached the point where it was clear Mike would have to re-invent himself to successfully lead the company into the future.

In the Executive Re-Invention program, he began to look closely at his own Winning Strategy. He revealed his Winning Strategy to be:

	Listening for . . .	. . . so as to act by . . .	. . . in order to . . .
Mike	"What's the point?"	. . . taking charge . . .	. . . be respected, and avoid being weak.

Mike listens for "What's the point?" He's always asking himself, restlessly, why he should bother taking a project on and what difference it will make. In most situations, he habitually takes charge: moving as quickly as possible to mobilize people and act. His desired outcome, he realized, is to be respected as a leader. Mike does not think much of leaders who overpromise and underdeliver. In his Winning Strategy, those characteristics are a sign of weakness.

Thus, when Mike couldn't get a satisfactory answer to the question "What's the point?" every aspect of his Winning Strategy was impeded. His entire being told him he was in an impossible position. He couldn't find the point; therefore, he couldn't act. He was afraid he would not be respected as a leader in his own eyes or in the eyes of others.

Being locked in his Winning Strategy paralyzed and blocked him from helping the chairman re-invent the company. Only when he could admit that it was okay for the company to tackle the impossible, that this was the scope of the game the chairman was playing, and that *he hadn't been playing this game of making the impossible happen at all* could he begin to act effectively. Until he could free himself from the notion that there was something wrong with either the chairman or with him, until he could recognize who he was *being*—a man driven by the need to be respected for leadership that doesn't overpromise and underdeliver—and until he could step outside the limits of his Winning Strategy, he couldn't move forward.

THE REWARDS OF EXECUTIVE RE-INVENTION

Striving to live beyond your Winning Strategy does not mean that your Winning Strategy disappears. You will always have it. But becoming aware of it and understanding how it works gives you options and power. You create a new relationship with your Winning Strategy by owning it. You will be able to have it, rather than it having you. You can allow it to work for you when you need it and step outside of it when you wish to go beyond its limitations.

The work of this transformation is painstaking and difficult. It is exhausting at first to try to look so carefully inside what drives you on a moment-by-moment basis. But the very exhaustion it produces is a signal that you are getting closer to an important understanding. It takes a lot of effort, on a daily basis, to keep the Winning Strategy satisfied; more often than not, when we feel exhausted, it's because we're fighting against ourselves.

The harder we push with part of our mind to unearth our Winning Strategy, the harder another part of our mind pushes back to keep it where it has always been, safely out of sight.

And yet in the long run, this transformation leads to less exhaustion. The more we can persevere, the more energy we have, because it is not drained by the need to satisfy our Winning Strategies. Peter Senge refers to this phenomenon obliquely in *The Fifth Discipline,* in his section on what he calls coping strategies:

> It can be very difficult to recognize these coping strategies while we are playing them out, especially because of tensions and pressures that often accompany them. It helps to develop internal warning signals . . . structures of which we are unaware hold us prisoner. Once we can identify them, they no longer have the same hold on us. This is as much true for individuals as it is for organizations.

You use your Winning Strategy every day, and you will continue to lapse into it, even after you go through all seven of the transformational stages of Executive Re-Invention. But the more quickly you can recognize it, the more skilled you will become in stepping outside it. Eventually, bells and whistles go off whenever your Winning Strategy raises its powerful head. Until you can learn to recognize it whenever it is engaged, you will not be able to free yourself from its limitations.

This exercise may help develop that understanding:

In a role play or mock meeting, *be* an extremely exaggerated version of your Winning Strategy. Like a bad actor, overdo all the things your Winning Strategy would ask you to do. As you overplay, "listen for" what aspects of your role play fit. If you win by "listening for" whether something is relevant, listen *incessantly* for relevance. If you listen for "What's the point?" let no event go by without being sure you understand the point of it. If you are a skilled facilitator, facilitate at all possible moments. If your goal is to be special, pursue specialness with all the naked power you can muster.

Obviously, this exercise can only be performed in an artificial situation, where exaggerations are forgiven. But it can be immensely valuable. Its purpose is to get the characteristics of your Winning Strategy so evident, in such larger-than-life form, that even when you finish the role play, you carry away a stronger sense of how your Winning Strategy works.

WINNING STRATEGIES IN ORGANIZATIONS

Organizations, too, have a Winning Strategy. It is a reflection of the Winning Strategy of the organization's leaders. Most of those leaders joined the organization, and remained there, in fact, because it was a hospitable environment for their Winning Strategy. It was a place where their Winning Strategy could flourish.

Depending on the business environment, the organizational strategy will work for or against the organization at any given time. At Chrysler in the 1980s, it worked. CEO Lee Iacocca was a leader at the right time and the right place. Judging from press reports, his strategy was: "Listen for dissatisfaction" so as to act by personalizing all concerns. Chrysler did exactly that, and its automobiles clicked.

Companies generally succeed in the proper environment if the Winning Strategy of the leader is in sync with the context of the external business environment. IBM was protected for years by Thomas Watson's Winning Strategy, in which sales and customer service took precedence while his competitors concentrated on technical concerns. This Winning Strategy made it possible for "nobody to ever get fired for buying IBM." But when the computer industry environment changed in the mid-1980s, the old IBM Winning Strategy posed immense problems for the new leader. Subsequent CEO John Akers had to deal not only with his own Winning Strategy but with Watson's, which was still operating within the context of the organization's culture. Any new leader coming into an organization with that sort of strong heritage, especially one built by a founder or former strong leader, faces a similar difficulty.

There are other difficulties as well. Each executive in an organization has his or her own Winning Strategy. These Strategies drive the executives to pursue personal desired outcomes that might not directly correlate with organizational goals. As executives struggle with their own need to succeed, their Strategies focus their attention on results, and not necessarily on the content of their projects. Thus, in many firms, while brilliant results occur everywhere, no one pays attention to the future of the company as a whole. Instead of creating a future, the major players are enmeshed in their own survival agendas.

If the executives could step outside of their own Winning Strategy-driven priorities, and focus instead on inventing and creating the best conceivable future, the company would experience its own state of "being" without a strategy. That would fuel the organization with extraordinary power, undiluted by conventional corporate politics.

Sometimes when managers in an organization are interested in the future and aware that a major shift must occur, the very senior leaders at the top feel threatened. But as I pointed out before, they are not necessarily aware of the Winning Strategy behind their feelings. *If they are in a position where they can't be pushed out, and they don't leave of their own volition, they will push the organization back to the point where they are again needed and feel power. They might say they are willing to do anything to help the organization succeed, but the Re-Invention process will be undermined.* Just like the rest of us, they have put themselves in organizations where they thought their Winning Strategies would flourish. If the environment changes, and their Strategies can't flourish, and leaving is not an option, they will force the organization to return to a place that allows their Strategies to once again thrive.

It is particularly important, in the Re-Invention of organizations, to make room for people who have vastly different Winning Strategies than the prevailing group. At first glance, it might seem to make sense for an organization to have compatible people, who listen and speak from the same place. But in 1965, IBM might have benefited greatly if only one senior manager had been heard saying, "Pretty soon people are going to have computers on their desks."

Here are some examples of organizational Winning Strategies that have helped the organizations in question succeed . . . and that, in some cases, have become obsolete.

Organizations' Winning Strategies:

	Listening for . . .	. . . so as to act by . . .	. . . in order to . . .
IBM	"What will keep us on a safe track?"	. . . figuring out rationally and communicating . . .	. . . be secure and protected, and avoid risk.
Intel	"How do we stay ahead?"	. . . innovating, combating, and gang-tackling problems . . .	. . . dominate, squash, or outflank competition, and avoid losing position.
Sun Micro-systems	"Where's the opportunity?"	. . . initiating, taking charge, and being "in their face" . . .	be first, and avoid loss of leadership.
A major New York bank	"Where or how are we at risk?"	. . . blunting or neutralizing the threat . . .	. . . lose as little as possible and coexist.
A chemical company division	"How do we stay ahead?"	. . . taking responsibility, communicating, and making commitments . . .	. . . secure the future and avoid being disempowered.

Next Stop: The Human Condition

You might feel that articulating your Winning Strategy doesn't go far enough.

It doesn't. It is only the first of a series of steps.

You may be wondering, "When do I get to break away from this Winning Strategy and find an alternative?"

That is the subject of the next transformation, step two.

Before moving on, however, please take a moment to hear one final admonition about step one. If you are serious about Re-Invention, then you must understand your Winning Strategy on a deeper level than a mere conceptual grasp. Knowing that you have a Winning Strategy is not enough. Having thought it through and recognized part of it is not enough.

If you are serious about Re-Invention, you should not only grow reflective enough to be able to distinguish your Winning Strategy, but you must begin to engage yourself in a new conversation with the world: one in which you have learned how to listen and speak differently, gracefully stepping out of your Winning Strategy at times and slipping in (against your will) less and less frequently.

The next stage of Executive Re-Invention will move you closer to that capability. It involves reflecting on what it means to be human: understanding the ramifications of the fact that you attach meaning and interpretation to everything that happens to you. Your perception has already gotten you in trouble, all your life, by keeping you locked within your Winning Strategy. Now let us look at the cultural context established by the human species.

In the process of Executive Re-Invention, the next step represents a giant philosophical leap, with enormous practical implications. It is time to make that leap.

CHAPTER 3

THE UNIVERSAL HUMAN PARADIGM

IMAGINE THAT you have just accepted a job on a new project with a group of people whom you've never met before. They've all worked together for months; you're joining this project as its newest person.

You arrive on the first day, and everyone is already there working. You walk in and say in a loud, cheerful voice, "Good morning." People look up from their work at their desks, and then they go right on doing what they were doing.

The same pattern continues as you go about your day.

When you arrive home that evening, your spouse (or someone else in your household) asks about the first day with the new group. "How was the day? What happened?"

What would you say?

Before we go on, either in the white space here or on a separate sheet of paper, take a moment to write down the first response that came to your mind.

What did you write? It might have been any one of a wide number of responses.

You might have written, "I wonder if they really needed me. They ignored me."

Or you might have written, "What a cold bunch of people! This is not a friendly group."

Or "Gee, those people were so dedicated that they couldn't even take time to greet me."

Or "This organization must demand that people keep their noses to the grindstone."

If fifty people took this quiz, there might be fifty different responses. Chances are, more of the responses would be negative than positive. Most people would interpret the group to have some sort of unfriendliness, ignorance, or even malevolence.

But are any of these interpretations, benign or not, correct? Is one meaning truer than another? You might argue that one interpretation is more plausible than another, but there is no way to tell what *really* happened—at least not until you go back into work the next day, correct?

Now it's day two. You go back to the same workplace. On this day, people start to open up and talk to you.

Right away, someone says, "I'm so glad you came back today. It was very difficult for us to get through yesterday. We really feel awful about it, but it's just kind of a tradition we have here. We do that on the first day with new people. You passed the test. Welcome to the group. We're excited to have you. How can we include you?"

At the end of that day, you go home, and again you're asked, "How was the day? What happened?"

What would you say *now*?

Once again, write down your first response, either in the white space here or on a separate sheet of paper.

What did you write?

You might have written, in effect: "I thought these people were strange, and now I know it. They wasted my first day and confused me the second day. It's hard to get inside the bunch and figure them out."

Or you might have written: "I thought they were cold, but now I see that they're actually very warm. They showed it in the way they apologized about that testing game."

Or perhaps, "Either they didn't want me in or I didn't fit or I was imposing on them."

Or perhaps, "I thought they were rude. Maybe I was off. They're not rude, they're silly. I can deal with 'silly.' "

Or, as one manager named Jim said when he took this quiz, "What the hell is wrong with these people? I'm in the wrong place or with the wrong bunch of people."

Once again, there might be a different response for every reader of this book. And in nearly each response, some form of "I thought they were . . ." would be present. If not explicit, it would be implicit.

No matter what you did on the second day, it would be shaped by your interpretation of the day before. And everything thereafter would be shaped, in part, by your interpretation, based on the first two days. Even though there may be many different interpretations, they all have one thing in common: Each person will take an action based on that interpretation.

If you had made a report that first day *without interpretation*, it would have gone something like this: "I walked in and said in a loud, cheerful voice, 'Good morning.' People looked up from their work at their desks, and then they went back to doing what they were doing." There would be nothing about what should have happened. Nothing about your expectations. No assumptions or conclusions about what it meant.

The idea that you respond not to events, but to your interpretations of them, is easy enough to understand as a concept. But on a day-to-day basis, if you're typical of most people, you don't distinguish between events and the interpretations that you give them. These two domains—event and interpretation—almost always get collapsed. You give your interpretation when you're asked, "What happened?" as if that's really what happened.

I'm not suggesting that you shouldn't give meaning to events. I'm saying that in itself any given event doesn't mean *anything*. It is simply what happened. But as human beings, we find it almost impossible to think about an event without assigning meaning to it. In fact, we spend a lot of time discussing "What does it really mean?"

Now, how did Jim "know" that when people don't talk to him it meant he was in the wrong place or with the wrong people? Where did his meaning come from?

His meaning came from the past.

Meaning, interpretation, and explanation all come from the past. Something happens in the present. ("Nobody talks to me at the office.") You interpret it and draw a conclusion about the way it is. ("People are hostile.") You take an action based on your interpretation and conclusion. ("I regard them with suspicion.") Your action validates the interpretation—or it doesn't. ("The next day they're nice to me.") If it doesn't, you make a second interpretation and draw a second conclusion. ("I'm in the wrong place with the wrong people.")

You repeat the entire cycle until you are satisfied that you have the right interpretation and conclusion. By that point, the original event, long since lost in the flow of interpretations, is part of the past.

The meaning you give that event ("I'm in the wrong place") is now an interpretation of something that happened in the past. The link between that past event and the present is based on connections you have drawn in your mind—more interpretations.

Any assumptions you make about your future possibility are also based on these interpretations. ("I can't stay here and be successful.") Thus, they are also based on the past—even if those past interpretations have nothing to do with current reality as it stands today.

No wonder it is so difficult to try to forge a future without dependence on what happened in the past.

THE VOICE WHISPERING IN EVERYONE'S EAR

A paradigm is a constellation of concepts and values shared by a community of people. The paradigm is an invisible cultural structure through which we see the world, a lens so transparent that we are unaware we are looking through it. Therefore, we are unable to see how it distorts our perceptions.

The most significant aspect of this definition, often unemphasized when people write or talk about paradigms, is the fact that it is shared by a community. *The larger the community, the more significant and all-encompassing the paradigm.*

One paradigm is shared by the largest community of all: the human race. This is the paradigm that I call the Universal Human Paradigm. It is a "master" paradigm, by which I mean that all other paradigms held by people are subsets of it.

In his novel *Ishmael*, author Daniel Quinn effectively describes how a master paradigm can work:

There's no need to name or discuss it. Every one of you knows it by heart by the time you're six or seven. Black and white, male and female, rich and poor, Christian and Jew, American and Russian, Norwegian and Chinese, you all hear it. . . . And hearing it incessantly, you don't listen to it. There's no *need to listen to it*. It's always there humming away in the background, so there's no need to attend to it at all. In fact, you'll find—at least initially—that it's *hard* to attend to it. It's like the humming of a distant motor that never stops; it becomes a sound that's no longer heard at all.[1]

What, then, is the message of this relentless motor? What themes do our culture, and our thoughts, continually whisper to us?

Before spelling out that message, let's look at how *you* conveyed it. Let's reconsider the story at the beginning of this chapter. As I noted there, there are many possible responses, and each is based on an individual interpretation of the scenario. All of those interpretations stem from the same fundamental unspoken interpretation that forms the basis for the context of the Universal Human Paradigm.

Something is wrong (or right) with the group. It shouldn't be that way (or it should be that way). The day didn't (or, perhaps, it did) turn out the way it should have. If the group was warm, devoted, or hardworking, that was good. The group was acting just as it should. If the group was rude, crazy, or curt, that was bad. The group shouldn't have acted that way. Something was wrong—possibly with you, possibly with the group, possibly with the whole organization.

Either way, the reality of the group was subsumed under your interpretation of what "should" have taken place.

The context of the Universal Human Paradigm, which colors all choices, decisions, and actions, is this:

There is a way that things should be.

And when they are that way, things are right.

When they're not that way, there's something wrong with me (the interpreter of events), with them (other people), or with it (anything in the world).

THE WAY THINGS ''SHOULD'' OR ''SHOULDN'T'' BE

You don't need to do anything to get into the Universal Human Paradigm. You inherit it, simply by being born as a human being. While Winning Strategies are unique for each person, every one of us shares the same Universal Human Paradigm. As humans, our ways of *being* are suffused with it. Our emotions are heavily invested in it.

It is the water in which all human beings swim; a driving force that colors all choices, all decisions, all actions. You only become aware of it when you start to interpret it.

Once again, the Universal Human Paradigm can be expressed this way:

There is a way that things should be. And when they are that way, things are right. When they're not that way, something is wrong with you, them, or it.

Our world is either consistent with that statement or not, but our interpretations are deeply consistent with it. Each person's life is full of what "should" or "shouldn't" be, and while these "shoulds" and "shouldn'ts" are constantly changing, they are continuously present. They reflect, at any given moment, what is right or wrong with you, with others, and with life itself. The natural state of being human means continuously comparing everything in life against the way that things "should" or "shouldn't" be. If things are as they should be, there is reason to feel triumphant and proud; if things aren't as they should be, something is wrong and must be fixed.

For example, we might say, "I 'should' be a senior vice-president by now," and feel quite unfulfilled and dejected. Or we might say, "I'm already a senior vice-president, and I'm doing even better than I 'should' be." We might say, "Marketing 'should' report to operations," or "The cost-to-sales ratio 'should' be less than 65 percent," or "I 'shouldn't' have to spend my time buried in hours of paperwork," or "My children 'shouldn't' be staying out until eleven." Whatever happens to us, we have a view of the world as the way it ought to be, against which we can judge it.

We see the fruits of this all the time in individual behavior. A manager does not speak frankly about bad news, because "the news 'shouldn't' be that bad." Skeptics don't disagree with the prevailing wisdom, because "we 'should' present a united front." People hire each other, reprimand each other, fall in love with each other, go to war with each other, and ask to work with each other based on what they feel the other person 'should' be, given their role and position—not based on what their own experiences tells them the other person *is being*.

Living this way, governed by one view after another of "the way things should be," feels quite natural. Nearly every human being lives that way. It almost seems to be hardwired into our minds. Indeed, the Universal Human Paradigm embodies a theory about reality that few of us see beyond. The Paradigm provides a "context," an overarching way of thinking that permeates our environment and shapes the actions and thoughts of everyone around us. We inherit it from the moment we hear our first conversations, and we pass it on to our children and other human beings with almost every phrase we utter. It's as if the entire human race were one big village of people whispering over and over the same message to each other, so that no one can help but believe it.

This context of the Universal Human Paradigm is the source of the Winning Strategies described in the previous chapter.

This is difficult to see at first. When you look at your Winning Strategy, you may not see any statement that "things should be a particular way" or that "there's something wrong with me." However, one of the functions of the Winning Strategy is to suppress awareness of this context and to keep it under the surface. Awareness of the Universal Human Paradigm, for nearly everyone, is innately disquieting. To continuously be in the presence of "there's something wrong" is uncomfortable. Therefore, one of the reasons you developed a Winning Strategy was as a survival mechanism—to dampen your awareness of this disquieting aspect of reality and to be able to survive in the midst of it. You took a sense from your Winning Strategy that you were in control, that you *could* make life turn out as it should—just as an addict gets a false sense of security from the addictive substance.

With your Winning Strategy, you "listen for" some question,

such as "What's the point?" or "What's really going on?" You are really "listening for" a more fundamental question: "Is the point what it should be? Should there be a point?" Or "Is what's really going on right? Is it wrong?"

Every time you exercise the "so as to act by" component of your Winning Strategy, you may think you're "taking charge" or "nurturing." But you are actually exercising what power you have, to compensate for what is not possible in that situation in that moment.

And the "in order to" component of your Winning Strategy? It's the future, which, if you can get enough of it, life will have worked out "as it should." And if life doesn't work out, you can at least devote your life to avoiding the parts you must avoid at all cost. That way, at least life won't work "as it shouldn't."

This chart shows how the form of the Winning Strategy is an expression of the Universal Human Paradigm:

THE UNIVERSAL HUMAN PARADIGM:

	Listening for . . .	. . . so as to act by . . .	. . . in order to . . .
Every human being	"What should or shouldn't be? What's right or wrong with me, them, or it?"	. . . compensating for what's not possible . . .	. . . control life, have it turn out the way it "should," and avoid having life turn out the way it "shouldn't."

If the notion of a Universal Human Paradigm is familiar to you (although you may not have called it by this name), then you may be tempted to dismiss all this as old news. However, unless you are a very rare person, that knowledge of the Universal Human Paradigm has not had any impact on your life. Your actions are still consistent with the Paradigm, even though you know it exists. You know it as a concept, but you still live as if you do not see the extent to which it affects every single action and choice you make in your entire life.

Since it's so universal, why be concerned about it? Because the

*Universal Human Paradigm, which we have learned from childhood
onward, hamstrings us in fundamental ways that affect our ability to
create the impossible.*

THE PERPETUAL ''MISSING DOT''

A good way to understand the Universal Human Paradigm is
to compare it to a popular game. Think of life as that familiar nine-
dot puzzle that is often used to show the advantage of "lateral
thinking"—although I want to use it for a very different purpose.
The object of the puzzle is to connect a square of nine dots with
four straight lines without taking your pencil off the paper.

If you are not familiar with this puzzle, and don't know the
answer, I invite you to try it now. See if you can draw four
straight lines that connect all of these dots.

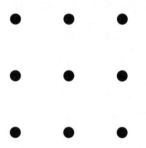

For most people at first, the solution is elusive. Our natural
tendency, as we draw the lines, is to stay within the border defined by the dots—the edge of the imaginary box they form. We
run through all the options until we get tired or bored or decide
that it is geometrically impossible to connect all nine dots with
only four lines.

On paper, the nine-dot puzzle can only be solved by becoming
aware of the artificiality of the edges of the box. Once we see that
the box is a limit we have placed on the puzzle—a creation of our
own perception—we know we can make the lines longer, so they
break through the walls of the imaginary box. Extending the lines

beyond the dots, we solve the problem by re-inventing the rules that our "strategy" for solving the puzzle had imposed on us.

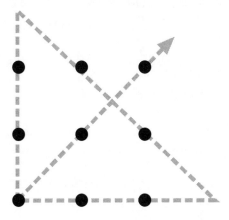

Once we know the trick, of course, the new awareness seems obvious. But it was not obvious before.

When it's used for lateral thinking, this puzzle is often compared to a particular problem. "To solve that problem, just step outside of the box." But suppose that problem encompassed your entire life? Suppose the puzzle were a limit that enclosed all human beings? Then it would not be so easy to "step outside of the box."

And suppose you were doomed to spend your life trying to solve the puzzle? Then you would go around and around, drawing lines. Each time, no matter how hard you tried, you would come up with one dot left unconnected. Each attempted solution would exclude one dot.

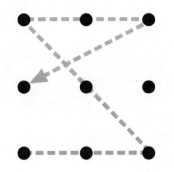

It would be a supremely frustrating—even a tragic—way to live. Every time you attempted the puzzle again, you'd be convinced that this time you had it! This time you'd finally get the dots all connected. Each time you thought you'd completed the puzzle, you would enjoy a moment of triumph. Then, inevitably, your attention would be drawn to the dot you had not connected. Once again, fulfillment had escaped you. Once again, it was time to start from scratch.

To live by the principle that "life should be some way" is to spend all your life playing an equivalent of the nine-dot puzzle. Every attempt to make life come out as it should seems like it will finally complete the puzzle and give you everything you want. (You will finally connect the dots.) "If you can only make vice-president," the Universal Paradigm whispers to you, "or move to another city, or consummate your romance, or win this election, *then* you will have the last component of success. *Then* you can relax."

But, of course, as soon as you make that last move, at whatever cost it takes, another dot mysteriously opens up elsewhere in your life. Because life never turns out the way it should.

You get better and better at playing the connect-the-dots game, and you reap success in the process. But every attempt leaves just one dot unconnected, one goal unmet, one significant aspect of life unfulfilled.

You can only solve the nine-dot puzzle by becoming aware of the artificiality of the limits of the box. Similarly, you can only break out of the dominance of the Universal Human Paradigm by increasing your awareness. The first step is the same as the first step in solving the nine-dot puzzle: to step out of your imaginary frame and look closely at the parameters of the puzzle.

"SURVIVAL" UNDER THE UNIVERSAL HUMAN PARADIGM

To survive is to exist in spite of adversity. Life under the Universal Human Paradigm is a game of survival that blocks you from your most cherished aspirations—and it's the only game in town. Let me explain how this dynamic works.

To begin with, any individual Winning Strategy is a set of personal techniques for playing the Paradigm's game, a game that might be called Pursue Life So It Turns Out the Way It Should. *The more you follow your Winning Strategy, the more you buy into the game. As long as you think you are playing the game effectively, you don't question the need to play it.*

Your experiences with your Winning Strategy lead you to accept the illusion that some people (those with more "successful" Winning Strategies) have control over life turning out the way it should while others do not have as much control. There are winners and losers. Enmeshed in your Winning Strategy, you don't see how everyone is caught up in the Universal Human Paradigm, all playing the same game: a game of reacting to the gap between what you have and what you think you should have, instead of creating the dream you really aspire to create.

Simply by playing the game, you buy into an implicit component of the Universal Human Paradigm: the belief that life itself is limited. Your only hope for surviving is to try as hard as possible to make life turn out the way you think it should. It's as if you're playing the nine-dot puzzle with more and more force and frenzy, frantically trying harder to reach the ninth dot without bursting outside the boundaries of your preconceptions. "I'll do what I really want," you say, "once I can feel secure about my job, my family, my home, my position, my power, and my prominence."

You will often see this dynamic echoed in organizational meetings. "Yes, we would love to re-create our goals and reshape our industry. But not yet. As soon as we get the stock price up, or the profits back, or the bottom line reoriented [or the ninth dot connected], we'll have the time and energy to think about new directions." This dialogue, or any similar sentiment, is simply an echo of the Universal Human Paradigm speaking through an executive's mouth.

If you believe (as the Universal Human Paradigm tells us) that all you need to do is "fix" the world and it will match the way it should be, then it's natural for you to think we need an edge, a strategy, or a tool with which to fix it. So you approve of any approach that seems to give you the edge in the short run. You continue in your mission to survive, by trying as hard as possible to make things turn out the way they should.

This helps explain why you can become so hooked on your Winning Strategy and so unwilling to let it go. By clinging hard to your Winning Strategy, you avoid the risk of accidentally embracing something that would make life turn out the way it "shouldn't."

Consider, in this light, some of the Winning Strategies from the previous chapter. Mike, when he listens for "What's the point?" assumes that things "should" make sense. If they don't make sense, he will be paralyzed. Caroline, in listening for "What's beneath the surface?" assumes that there "should" be an underlying, unsaid purpose. If it's not revealed out loud, she assumes that something is wrong with her for missing it. Instead of moving forward, she continues to search for hidden meaning that may not be there to be found.

This is the hallmark of a difficult, arduous life task. Survival now means more than keeping food in your body and a roof over your head; it means putting the world to right, over and over again, day after day. Since the world never matches the way it "should" be, you are inevitably disappointed. Survival comes to mean avoiding, and reacting to, the grief and misery you feel in your disappointment.

This sort of life is so difficult that all other goals must be put on hold for the duration, until you get the "survival problem" licked—until you get that ninth dot connected, until you feel you've measured up to the way things "should" be. Any attempts to make the impossible happen move rapidly to the back burner and stay there. Growing stronger in your mind and actions through the years, the Universal Human Paradigm keeps you from creating any new realm of possibility.

HOW YOU LEARNED TO COMPENSATE

Most people's Winning Strategies include techniques for helping you deal with disappointment. To recognize the technique in your Winning Strategy, especially if you are an American, you need only think back to high school and your teenage years.

Who did you want to be when you were in high school? Almost all of us can pick out someone we admired or envied on some level, someone who possessed traits that we didn't have but wanted—someone who was naturally one way, while you were naturally the opposite. Can you name that person and list the characteristics he or she had that you didn't? What was that person who you knew you could never be?

If you're typical, it seemed like that person was naturally good at *everything*. You had to work hard at your fine qualities, you were innately good at only a few things. But this person was a natural athlete, brilliant, good-looking, and probably wealthy to boot. Life had turned out for that person exactly the way it should turn out, and without any effort on his or her part. It didn't seem fair. But there was nothing you could do that would change the circumstances. You were born with your own array of athletic skills, intelligence, looks, family background, and wealth. Changing them was beyond your control. It simply was not possible. It was the way things were and you had to accept it.

When asked this question, even people who were the Homecoming Queen or the class president or the most popular student in school immediately come up with a name, someone who represented the perfect person, the complete whole person whom they knew they never could be. Sometimes it's an older sister or brother, or a parent, celebrity, or world figure like Jacqueline Kennedy Onassis. Someone who was a representation of the way they "should" be, which they could never really match.

One way or another, you began to develop compensatory powers to make up for your inability to be the person you knew you couldn't be. You set out to become skilled at something else, something you could control, that would compensate to some extent. You might learn to be skilled at providing things for people and helping them, or at understanding what was going on around you, or at humor, or at poise.

These skills are a further development of your Winning Strategy. Thus, your Winning Strategy, which developed much earlier, is the foundation of your identity as an adult, which jelled during your teenage years.

As your skills developed, you learned that you could move closer to what you felt life "should" be. The compensatory approach became a key part of your Winning Strategy, your pathway to success. Unconsciously, in the process, you became engaged in a conversation in which you found ways, every day, to say, "There's something wrong with me, them, or it, and it shouldn't be this way. But I can cope. I am surviving."

As part of that conversation, you accepted an interpretation: Some things were impossible. There were still great possibilities you could never be.

Of course, what you *really* began to compensate for in high school wasn't the fact that you didn't have the highest IQ or you didn't have your name listed in the High School Athletic Hall of Fame. You were compensating for your interpretation—your perception of your inability to win a particular game in life. When we meet old classmates later as adults, many of us discover that the inability that loomed so large in our perception was oblivious to everyone else. Yet it was dramatic enough to set the tone for your own Winning Strategy.

In the Universal Human Paradigm, there is always the need to blame whatever's wrong. Some people focus on blaming other people; others accuse the amorphous "it"—society and the world in general—for causing their problems. And some believe that the cause of their problems is themselves. Whether you look at "me," "them," or "it," the Universal Human Paradigm ("something's wrong") is always the context from which you take action. You work hard to improve yourself; you struggle to manipulate, charm, or maneuver around other people; you battle or seek influence in the institutions of the world.

The faster that you can make sure "it, them, or me" is heading in the right direction, the faster you can make things seem to turn out the way they "should," and the more in control of life you feel. When things are going well, you feel like you're winning the game.

THE UNIVERSAL HUMAN PARADIGM IN ORGANIZATIONS

I sometimes ask a group of people from the same organization to tell me "the way it *is* around here." I ask questions like these: What happens when someone new comes on board? What kinds of conversations do people have in the parking lots? When they are giving someone the real story on what's going on, what do they say? How do you make it here? Who are the heroes? How did it get to be this way?

We fill up flip chart after flip chart with their positive and negative responses: everything that's wrong; everything that's right; everything that should or shouldn't be; everything that has happened in the past. Each person present has his or her own view, so the result is a series of stories about the organization, often contradictory.

So we then start to ask ourselves: What do all these stories have in common? And, as with the varied responses to the scenario exercise at the beginning of this chapter, we find they share only one characteristic: All of them show that the organization is operating in a collective version of the Universal Human Paradigm. Everyone in the organization believes there is some way that its prices and policies "should" be. All of them are trying diligently to match the real organization with the ideal. But since they all disagree, implicitly and tacitly, about what that ideal should be, they all work diligently at cross-purposes.

Numerous interpretations operate within the context of these organizations. Each individual has his or her interpretation of what's happening, and each has a Winning Strategy in operation that is "listening for" certain messages. Can you see what this does to the dynamic of any management team? Each leader "listens for" an individual interpretation before moving forward; therefore, decision-making can get hindered and progress slowed or come to a halt as each executive waits to receive the message he or she is "listening for." All of this exists *on top of* the limits that are bound into the Universal Human Paradigm, the limits that focus attention on survival and make it hard to believe in making the impossible happen.

In the next meeting you attend, observe the context of the conversation held there. Are people speaking out of a sense of freedom and openness, in which they take a stand that what they want to create *is* possible? Or are they making one assessment after another, one evaluation on top of another evaluation? Is there an overall tone of disappointment and resignation because what "should" be happening is seen as impossible? Is the group operating from a limited set of options, left over after the impossible was discounted? If so, then they are also making choices, not for what they want to create, but for what they think the organization "should" be and what they feel is possible.

One group I worked with was in the process of a joint venture with a European partner, who was the major shareholder. The foreign group was waiting for the American group to fall on its face, but the Americans were extremely successful. However, their success started to cause problems in the joint venture because they were sending a message that said, "We think we're better than you." It would have made sense for the Americans to back down somewhat and to take some short-term losses, transferring some power to the Europeans in order to ensure the viability of the partnership. The Americans needed to give up the survival value that they found in their Winning Strategy of being the very best.

But they wouldn't retreat. They were concerned that if they slackened their pace, they would be dominated by their partners. "Since we want to keep our autonomy," their logic went, "we should always be producing great results. If we do not produce great results, we will have to submit to demands from our European partner. Only if we produce great results can we keep our autonomy." Transformation for this group only occurred when they recognized their fear was an interpretation, and transformed how "not being the best" occurred for them. As long as it occurred as a threat, they would never give it up.

The default context of organizations is the context of the Universal Human Paradigm: that there's a way things "should" be. When they are that way, things are right. When they're not, there's something wrong with me, them, or it.

Regardless of the innovation and creativity of employees, they are stifled because every manager is focused on making the organization get closer to "what it 'should' be." This "should" may be measured in the stock price, the market share, or the return on investment, but it takes on a power far greater than its business meaning. It becomes a mythic talisman, used to keep everyone focused on current problems and fixes. Regardless of the effectiveness of anyone's actions, results in this environment will not exceed the scope of what can be predicted. Quantum leaps and impossible outcomes will not happen.

The practices endorsed by most organizations are the practices that serve the old game of "keeping pace": predicting with reasonable accuracy what results are possible to achieve; bringing a group to consensus or alignment, so people feel "on board"; making feasible promises and delivering on them; creating visions, setting and reaching goals, and developing internal "change agents" who could spur others to improve performance.

All of these practices are designed to "predict and control" and are necessary when operating in a mode of improvement. They are driven, start to finish, by the needs of the Universal Human Paradigm.

An organization operating with a new master paradigm, the Re-Invention Paradigm, by contrast, develops an organizational context that operates from practices designed to "invent and commit," the practices necessary to operate in a mode of transformation: declaring the future rather than predicting it; taking a stand rather than generating consensus; making bold promises that you don't know how to keep; creating contexts; fulfilling new realms of possibility; and recruiting and developing catalysts for transformation rather than change agents.

The scope of results in this type of organization broadens immensely, encompassing anything that can be invented to which people will commit.

One of the ways that you can spot a transformed group or organization is to observe how people relate to each other. Their interactions are not based on personalities or on results; they are based on their commitments. Their personalities may clash, but when they declare a commitment to make something happen, they know that each of them will take that commitment seriously. If five different executives made a commitment to take a stand and act toward a particular future, their individual interpretations will be put aside.

Making this contextual shift that is a part of the Re-Invention process is not easy. It requires strength from a group of institutional muscles that we're not used to using, especially when organizations and industries try to re-invent themselves.

The software industry provides a dramatic example. Historically, computer software producers have felt they "should" be the fastest to release new products. That's how they stay competitive. There is never enough time to deal with process, to look for better ways to do what is being done, to get educated, to look at alternatives, or to improve quality—only to get the next release to market. Quality suffers, and only the most critical bugs end up getting fixed. When embarrassing problems come to public attention, as they did, say, with income-tax-preparation software in 1995, the industry producers simply vow to get the releases out even faster next time.

Alex, an ex-IBM executive anxious for a new way of *being*, is helping a Fortune 500 computer company manage a transformation. Hired for his ability to help integrate a newly acquired software organization into the structure of the company, he is heading the software engineering side of the business, which employs about one hundred people. He has made a commitment to create a world-class software development organization that produces high-quality software within two years.

Alex wants his organization to operate from a new context. The organization will value creating high-quality, usable, reliable software *from the beginning of the production process*, rather than operating from a context that values meeting schedules which jeopardize quality. Part of the declaration involved producing a zero-defects environment, which no software engineering firm, to Alex's knowledge, has ever achieved or will ever commit to achieve.

Alex believes the shift will improve the industry and software companies in numerous ways, including financially. "If you ship shoddy products just to get to market faster," he says, "it takes a long time to build up revenues because there are so many 'teething' problems in product infancy. For every ten software programs installed, you get five back, and you have to fix problems and handle issues about your reputation." Another shift is occurring as this transformation gets under way: The engineer, once viewed as an artist and hero, is gaining credibility as a professional. Alex says, "The typical software engineer got his job done by spending a significant amount of creative effort in off-hours, working late and over the weekend. More and more engineers are saying they are going to do something, and then they do it. They are making things happen in a reproducible way, without the heroics, sound and fury."

In the old context, reports from the field are viewed as interruptions, and companies only fix major problems; everything else piles up. In the new context, problems will no longer be interpreted as interruptions, but as opportunities to improve the quality of the product. For example, historically, if a product had a difficult-to-understand user interface, people often made numerous errors using it and reported their difficulties to the company. Companies deflected complaints by telling users it was their own fault for not reading the manual. This created an industry-wide interpretation that certain products were hard to learn. In the new context, when customers have difficulty with products, the problems will be viewed for what they are—problems—and they will be fixed. Calls reporting problems will be seen as interesting, because they will enable firms to optimize responsiveness to customers and they will provide feedback that will help firms enhance the rate at which products can be improved.

None of this can happen, however, unless Alex and his CEO, along with other significant senior managers, declare that it is possible and re-invent themselves to make it happen. An organization's context is not a place to get to; it's a place to come from, just as the Universal Human Paradigm is a place we come from.

That's why declaring an organization's context is different from writing a vision statement. A vision describes where the organization "should" go, and perhaps how to get there. A declaration of context is a statement that states what the organization is *being*, starting right now. For example, if you are a member of an executive entrepreneurial team, your context is *being* an entrepreneur. You don't propose a vision that you will become entrepreneurs later; you declare that you are already entrepreneurs. Then the actions you take are taken in the context of *being* entrepreneurial.

In the context of Alex's future, software engineering is declared to operate from a place where quality is valued along with fast cycle times. Operating in this context, it is possible that zero-defect products will be produced, without inflicting undue stress or demanding long working days from engineers. That would be a true transformation.

TOWARD THE FREEDOM TRAIL

The survival game established by the Universal Human Paradigm is the game that ultimately holds you back from making the impossible happen. Yes, the game is grounded in reality—according to one set of interpretations. It is true that some things can never match up to the way life "should" be. If you were born into a middle-class family in a small town in Ohio, then you cannot be transformed into the scion of a wealthy, upper-class family who grew up in a New York penthouse. If you graduated from a state college, you cannot go back and be a Harvard or Yale undergraduate. (You can go back to school in the Ivy League, but not as an eighteen-year-old.) You can be wealthy yourself someday, but you can never be from wealthy parents if your parents weren't wealthy. You cannot re-invent your past.

But you *can* invent a future that is not based on the past and is unrelated to the past.

You do this by separating yourself from the Universal Human Paradigm and its compensatory strategies. You become aware of an alternative approach to living in the world, an approach that is almost impossible to see at first, because the more prevalent and accessible Universal Human Paradigm hides it. But through that second approach, which I call the Re-Invention Master Paradigm, you can move beyond the constraints of your past success.

How, then, do we move to such a transformation?

If you have progressed through the past two chapters, you have explored your existing Winning Strategy and your existing relationship to the Universal Human Paradigm. While you have read about some conceivable alternatives to these pervasive ways of *being*, that is all you have done. You have not yet begun to develop your own alternative way of *being*.

The next step is acquiring the freedom to take the risks that accompany making the impossible happen. What stops leaders from taking these risks is the fear that such actions might result in serious consequences that could affect how life turns out.

Imagine that you already knew how everything in life would turn out. You still had free will, but you knew, regardless of which choices and decisions you made, what the final outcome would be. What impact would that have on your freedom to take risks?

The next chapter tests your answer to that question.

CHAPTER 4

"DYING" BEFORE GOING INTO BATTLE

Freeing yourself from the illusion that you can control life so that it turns out the way it "should"

JAPANESE SAMURAI WARRIORS, in reminding themselves of the inevitability of loss, used the phrase "Die before going into battle." This practice allowed a warrior to enter an episode of combat without the fear of death. He had brought himself through an experience of the acceptance of death ahead of time. He had forced himself to look at the fact that his death was a plausible outcome—indeed, an inevitable outcome eventually. In this way the warrior was able to fully give himself to his mission without concern for survival. He was completely free to risk everything. Such freedom made all the difference between defeat and victory.

The equivalent of experiencing "dying before going into battle" for today's leaders is to accept—*as if accepting a gift*—these statements:

Life does not turn out the way it "should."
Nor does life turn out the way it "shouldn't."
Life turns out the way it does.

When I say "life," I mean *your* life: the life of the person reading this book. And by "the way it should," I mean the way you most deeply hope life will turn out, the way you have always expected it ought to turn out in order to be meaningful.

To experience "dying before going into battle" is not merely to mock up a pretense at valor. It is to own your own death fully, to *accept* it. When you accept death, you are free to engage fully in life without compromise. When you accept that life does not turn out the way it "should," you are free to take actions that are not constrained by the need to control life so it turns out the way that it "should" (or, at the very least, to make sure life doesn't turn out the way it "shouldn't").

You must accept this "dying" before you can lead any form of Organizational Re-Invention, because you must be free to take the necessary risks in the face of threats to your survival. If you intend to play the game of Re-Invention seriously, then you must feel free to risk your reputation, your income, your position, and even your relationships, because all of these will be at stake. You will only take these risks when you recognize how, in the long run, you have nothing to lose.

You will have to accept that your career won't turn out the way it should and that your company's future won't turn out the way it should. Those threats will cease to hold you back only when, in the end, you see that they do not affect the outcome of your life. Like the samurai, you can face death today because you know that the outcome, in the end, is always the same.

Life turns out the way it does.

Years ago, a close friend of mine—a long-standing colleague and a passionate, charismatic leader who impressed people as being larger than life—died in an automobile accident on Pacific Coast Highway in California. The accident was caused by a boulder falling into his car through his open roof. He was hit on the head and killed instantly.

The shocking unexpectedness of his death moved me intensely. There was no way to predict or control that boulder. And it could just as easily have happened to me. A boulder could easily fall randomly on my own head at any time.

No doubt you have had a shock similar to this. You probably remember the new perspective it gave you on most of your ordinary, everyday concerns. Your priorities changed instantly. All of the concerns that occupied your attention before—a disagreement or dispute, an uncertain business risk, a family misunderstanding, a deadline or outside pressure—suddenly appeared trivial.

During the next few days or weeks, despite your grief, you were extraordinarily capable and self-possessed—extraordinarily focused on what was truly important to you. You were suddenly keenly aware of your own lack of control over what happens in life. And yet you were free to take actions that were previously considered too risky, because they might have led to life not turning out the way it "should."

The vividness of such incidents always fades after a while. Life takes over again, with its normal imperatives spawned by the Universal Human Paradigm—the idea that you should try to control your fate, to make sure your life goes the way it "should." And with this forgetting, you mislay the power that this shocking event had bequeathed to you.

Something similar happens to people who learn that they have a limited time to live. Once they accept the reality, a sense that they have nothing to lose permeates their lives. They become focused on the aspects of life most important to them. Questions such as "What would so-and-so think?" or "What if I failed that?" or "How can we get the such-and-such group on board?" are no longer important. These people possess a freedom to act, to engage in only the important aspects of life—a freedom that, despite their debilitating circumstances, is enviable.

What exactly happens in situations like this to provide people with the freedom to act?

And is it possible to live *all* one's life in the presence of that freedom?

THE END OF HOPE

So far, so good. You probably have a reasonably good understanding of what it means to "die before going into battle."

But can you induce the same lack of fear and lack of concern for consequences in yourself?

To produce the transformation necessary in this step, you must accept "dying" on a very deep level, one that goes far beyond merely understanding the concept intellectually. You must allow yourself to fully experience the hopelessness that naturally accompanies this acceptance. Accepting that *"life doesn't turn out the way it should" is the equivalent of an alcoholic "hitting bottom." You must go through a life-transforming experience before you can transform your relationship to the addiction and before you can move from denial to acceptance.*

This acceptance is the pathway for going beyond the Universal Human Paradigm. It is the only pathway that exists, because the Universal Human Paradigm, by design, is connected directly to the threats that you must learn to overcome.

So consider, *really* consider, what it means to make the statement "Life does not turn out the way it should."

There are at least three significant implications of this statement.

1. In the long run, your Winning Strategy will never completely "work."

You will never completely achieve the success that your Winning Strategy, all your life, has been designed to help you achieve. You will always be dissatisfied in your attempts to make the "in order to" component of your Winning Strategy come true.

As you may remember, the "in order to" component is the desired outcome of your life: the component that is most important to your Winning Strategy in the long run. It is the "way of *being*" that you believe, in your heart, would make you feel fulfilled—your most cherished dream and the avoidance of your worst nightmares.

Whatever means success to you—being the best, being valued and respected, avoiding being trapped, being in control, being needed, avoiding being forgotten or ignored, being known for who you really are, avoiding danger, being loved, or any other deeply desired emblem of success—you will never reach in a way that leaves you fully satisfied.

2. Your life will never be complete.

You remember the design of the Universal Human Paradigm, the way of looking at the world shared by every person alive. Something is wrong with life, says the Paradigm—something is wrong with you, or other people, or some "it," and life shouldn't be that way.

To be a human being is to devote your life to pursuing the ninth dot until you die. You are designed to always be in pursuit of the definitive accomplishment or expression of yourself which will let you be what you can't ever be: whole and complete and satisfied, unbroken and unflawed. Once you have attained great success, you will then pursue whatever you haven't yet attained—a great relationship, or family, or superb fitness, or contribution to humanity—whatever now represents the final achievement that will fully satisfy you that you have "made it."

But recognize this: You will never "make it."

In the long run, you will never get the ninth dot in the nine-dot puzzle and win the game that you've used your life trying to win. No matter how many times you succeed with your Winning Strategy and produce yet another successful result, you will never reach a point where there is "nothing wrong."

Paradoxically, it's often easier for people who are already successful to understand this. They have already tried, many times, to connect the ninth dot. They have already succeeded in gaining material goals: getting the job, marriage, wealth, or other goal that they thought would make them whole. But when they tell the truth, they are still dissatisfied and incomplete. "Is this all there is?" they ask themselves.

People who have *not* reached a particular level of success find it harder to re-invent themselves. It's too easy for them to believe that when they have enough money or status, they will still be incomplete. If you try to tell them, they will say, "Sure, it's easy for you to say that, because you've got it made." They, too, however, need only keep striving to learn: No matter how much you strive, you never connect all the dots of fulfillment.

3. You cannot control the outcome of your life.

I'm not talking about predestation. The individual events in your life are not predetermined. The actions you take during your lifetime may vary immensely based on decisions you make. But all that variation is irrelevant when it comes to affecting the final outcome. In the end, the outcome will be the same:

You will stay alive, with all the responsibilities and disappointments that life brings.

One day, you will die.

You will be ground up into ashes or lowered into the ground.

Someone with a shovel will throw dirt upon your face.

You will be, at that time, exactly as satisfied or unsatisfied as you will be.

In the meantime, life won't follow the pattern of the controls you are trying to put in place.

No one would argue with the value of fire safety precautions, such as an alarm system, a fire extinguisher, and emergency supplies. But no matter how many precautions you build into your home, you can imagine a fire engulfing it, a fire that will overcome every one of your precautions. Your fundamental commitment is to a safe home for yourself and your family, and you can never control the outcome enough to promise it with certainty. What happens to you will happen, and the amount of passion

with which you fervently wish to be safe will not be an influence—except in the way that you react to these events.

When athletes aspire to compete in the Olympics, they sacrifice years of their lives and put forth unparalleled effort. They
know from the outset that they may or may not make the team.
In a game where fractions of a second or fractions of a point
determine the outcome, anything from an injury to a loose shoe-
string to the weather could impact whether or not an individual
qualifies—and whether or not an individual wins. Prospective
athletes accept this lack of control, but it doesn't diminish their
passion for practicing, competing, or winning. It's part of the
rules of the game. They know that by investing less energy in
trying to control and manipulate circumstances, they have more
energy with which to compete.

". . . CATCH AS CATCH CAN . . ."

Some people ask, "Where is the proof that life will not turn
out the way that it 'should'?"

The proof exists in your life to date.

If you died at this moment, how would you feel about your
life? There is no doubt about the outcome. You would be satisfied in some ways and not satisfied in others. There would still
be one "dot" missing.

What if you had died ten years ago? The particulars might
change, but there would still be no doubt about the outcome.
You would still be able to distinguish areas that were satisfactory
and others that were not.

Now look ahead ten, twenty, or fifty years from now—to the
end of your life. There is *still* no doubt about the outcome. You
would still be satisfied in some ways and unsatisfied in others.
When you consider the enormity of what it means to "make life
work out the way it 'should,' " can you plausibly argue that you
would be any closer in the future than you have been in the past?

Life does not work out the way it "should" work out. It
works out the way it *does* work out. And this will remain true at

the moment of your death, just as it remains true during all other moments.

This does not mean "Life turns out the way it 'shouldn't.' " Life turns out the way it *does*. If your worst nightmares come to pass, the forces that bring them to pass will not include the fact that they're your worst nightmares.

And the degree of fervor with which you hope for the future will not be a factor in bringing that future to pass. In fact, the future that comes to pass will come regardless of how much you hope and expect it to come.

If you continue striving for life to turn out as it should, life will ignore what you think should happen. If you *stop* striving for life to turn out as it should, life will still ignore what you think should happen. Maybe you think you might try an aikido approach and stop *seeming* to strive for life to turn out as it should, while still secretly hoping it will. But life will continue to ignore what you think should happen.

Life pays no attention to what you require for life to be meaningful.

That's not the last of it. There's more.

You will never lose the Universal Human Paradigm, the whispering voice that tells you that you "should" be satisfied, that there "should" be nothing missing. You will always be driven to strive, to covet, to want the things you think you need. You will always be aware of being disappointed, of never quite getting there, of never quite filling in that ninth dot in the puzzle. Sammy will never stop running; the rat will never get out of the rat race; you will never arrive over the rainbow.

This is the understanding that Shakespeare placed upon the lips of Macbeth, when his own hopes begin to sour and he learns of the death of his wife:

> *And all our yesterdays have lighted fools*
> *The way to dusty death. Out, out, brief candle!*
> *Life's but a walking shadow, a poor player*
> *That struts and frets his hour upon the stage,*
> *And then is heard no more. It is a tale*

Told by an idiot, full of sound and fury,
Signifying nothing.

A more cheerful but equally stark rendition was penned by the American playwright Thornton Wilder, in the first act of his play *The Skin of Our Teeth*:

We've managed to survive for some time now, catch as catch can, the fat and the lean, and if the dinosaurs don't trample us to death, and if the grasshoppers don't eat up our garden, we'll all live to see better days, knock on wood. . . .

Each new child . . . seems to be sufficient reason for the whole universe's being set in motion; and each new child that dies seems . . . to have been spared a whole world of sorrow, and what the end of it will be is still very much an open question.

We've rattled along, hot and cold, for some time now, and my advice to you is not to inquire into why or whither, but just enjoy your ice cream while it's on your plate—that's my philosophy. . . .[1]

I invite you now to allow yourself to experience the hopelessness embedded in these bleak quotations.

THE EYE OF THE NEEDLE OF HOPELESSNESS

Allow yourself to come face-to-face with the inevitability of the design of being a human being and the inevitability of the outcome of your life.

One day, you will die.

You will be, at that time, exactly as satisfied or unsatisfied as you will be.

Your life will not turn out as you hope it will. There is no hope of life "turning out as it should." Life turns out as it does.

Leaders whom I work with sometimes reply, "It's better to

see a small speck of hope than to say from the outset that there's no hope." I disagree with them. As long as you see a speck of hope, you have not yet realized the fundamental bleakness required for complete freedom. People who cling to hope in this way don't take the actions they know they must take, because they fear the outcomes or consequences.

One place to see this is in parents' relationship with their children. Can you control whether in your lifetime one of your children will suffer and die? No. Those who do try to control fate, hoping they can prevent harm to their children, turn into overprotective parents. They become increasingly anxious about the gap they feel between the protection they think their children "should" have and the tiny amount of protection they can provide. So they limit their children from going outside at all and from many activities inside.

All of this effort to control makes it impossible for the parents to spend time *being* good role models of judgment and self-protection for their children. The parents lose sight of one thing they *can* do: to instill, in part by example, good judgment in their children, and to help them learn capabilities that will provide them with strength and power *in the face of whatever life may send their way.*

Just as most parents realize, sooner or later, that they have to trust fate with their children's future, leaders eventually realize that they have to trust fate before they can re-invent their organizations. But most try to control things first. They try to make sure that life will be "fair"—to their organizations, their employees, and themselves.

Who said life would be fair? What if the unfairness of life, and the ultimate disappointment of our individual lives, were simply part of the design of our species and its relationship with the rest of the world?

Assume, just for the sake of argument, that you accept that design. You recognize the cold void of life—you see that it has no safeguards or palliatives. You leave hope behind. You experience this "dying" in a visceral way, without faking it.

Where, then, do you go from here?

You have two choices: resignation or acceptance.

REACTING WITH RESIGNATION

Life shouldn't be this way, you can decide, but there is nothing you can do about it, except to play out your days as best you can. Like the Humphrey Bogart character Rick at the beginning of *Casablanca*, you can retreat bitterly to a locale where you feel temporarily safe.

There is a big difference between acceptance and resignation. To resign yourself to the future is to submit to despair, and take yourself out of the game of "making the impossible happen." You lie down and say, "Why bother?" There's nothing left but to wait for the time that you must go into the ground.

Many people, even intensely committed people, travel this route in the end. We hear their voices in politicians' statements: "I'm not willing to put my family through the political process, so my commitment to the country has got to fall by the wayside." They don't admit the possibility of re-inventing the political process, at least for their own campaign.

In business, we hear statements like this one: "I'm not willing to risk trying to make a difference, because people will think that I'm trying to make points with the boss. I'll lose the respect I should have from my colleagues." I know one corporate chairman who has resigned himself to not making a transformation, because it would mean putting more staff in his office. He doesn't want people to think the chairman's office is overstaffed when he's making cuts elsewhere. Other corporate executives I know would be more than willing to lead transformation efforts, except that they're afraid to risk alienating stock analysts and investors.

This form of resignation leads you back, inevitably, to the "continuous improvement" mind-set described in chapter 1. Like Rick in *Casablanca*, you are satisfied with improving life however you can: running your management competently and making gestures that do not bring too much attention. As I suggested at the beginning of this book, there is nothing wrong with resignation per se. But it will impede any effort you make to re-invent yourself and your organization.

ACCEPTING HOPELESSNESS — AS A GIFT

Accepting hopelessness means looking at "Life turns out as it does, not as it should or shouldn't" as a "design statement." It is a statement of the way that human beings are designed: hardwired to expect life to turn out one way or another, to seek that end throughout their lives, and never to get satisfied.

When you can accept that design, you have a different relationship with it. You're not trapped by it—"trapped" in the sense of trying to get out of it. You know that as a human being you are subject to it. That's the way that it is.

But you're not limited by it, either. Since that's the way that it is, there is nothing to lose. You are free to take any stand. To take any action. To fall on your face. To fail completely, regardless of the consequences.

Even if you fail utterly, well, you have *already* failed as badly as it is possible to fail, simply by being human. So you begin to think, "In that case, I'm going to do whatever I'm going to do, take the consequences, and play the game as fully as possible."

Accepting that you can't control the outcome is not the end of action—it is the opening for the boldest and most daring action. You can accept total responsibility for your choices and actions. You are free to play full-out in creating and implementing an extraordinary future for yourself and your organization.

You now know the outcome of your life. Life does not turn out as it should or as it shouldn't. Life turns out the way it does.

To accept something is to own it completely, to include it as a part of who you are. Acceptance gives you the opportunity, instead of giving up, to play with full engagement, free from the fear about how things will turn out.

Imagine that you are in a meeting room with ten other people—colleagues in a business meeting or travelers in an airport lounge. Suddenly, an announcement comes through a P.A. system. A loud, booming voice says, "Ladies and gentlemen, may I have your attention for a few moments? You are going to spend the rest of your life in the room that you're now in, with the people who are here with you. You cannot get out of the room, nor can anyone get in. Nor can you communicate with anyone outside. Food and anything else you need will be provided through conveyors. No one can escape. Thank you."

What would happen? Most likely, you would immediately begin to do everything you could think of to get out of the room. You would keep trying to escape until you had satisfied yourself that there was no way out and you could not alter the outcome. Then you would suffer through all the emotional stages that would naturally accompany such an experience.

Finally, you would accept that this is how your life turned out. That would take however long it took—days, weeks, months, or years. Once you fully accepted that this is it, that life turns out the way it does, you would have a choice about who you were going to be in the face of this life. One choice you would have would be to take on the seemingly impossible mission of creating an environment of possibility and opportunity, regardless of the circumstances, from which to lead yourself and others to design and implement an extraordinary future within that room.

You could take that choice, but only if you gave up hope of escaping. As soon as you thought there was any hope that you could get out, that you could change the outcome, your efforts to create an extraordinary future within that room would cease to be meaningful. If your jailers wanted to foil your efforts to create an extraordinary future, all they would need to do is to keep leaving you illusory hints about how you might escape.

As human beings, we are all in such a room together. There is no way out. There is an illusion, however, that you can control the outcome.

For this transformation to affect you, you must see through that illusion.

There are many wonderful examples of people who have accomplished owning something when, either by birth or through an accident, they did not have all of their limbs. When the condition can be accepted as the way it is, it's not a limitation. If these people are extraordinary human beings, it's not because they were innately gifted, but because their acceptance of their condition made them extraordinary. Once they began to accept themselves, rather than protesting, reacting, or compensating for it in some way, they began to operate beyond the limits of their circumstances.

"Security is mostly superstition," said Helen Keller. "It does not exist in nature nor do the children of men as a whole experience it. Avoiding danger is no safer in the long run than outright exposure. Life is either a daring adventure or nothing."

Many people are afraid that when they reach this state, life won't mean anything. There won't be any purpose to life if it's all going to turn out the way it does. And, in fact, they are correct. Life will be meaningless.

The experience of life being meaningless is the eye of the needle, ready for you to go through.

But the fact that life is essentially meaningless doesn't mean anything. All your hopelessness and despair at the idea of life being meaningless stems from the idea that life "should" be meaningful.

Who said life should be meaningful?

Your purpose in this transformation is not to *intellectually* understand that life is meaningless but to allow yourself to *experience* it.

You must design for yourself, as often as necessary, experiences that compel yourself to "die before going into battle"—experiences that compel the basic meaninglessness of life to hit you in the face.

You may ask, "Where are the exercises to lead me through this step?" But giving people exercises is too constraining. It is much more effective to learn on your own to generate the experience as you deal with everyday life.

No matter what's happening to you—a divorce, an enormous work-related event that has you on the line, a deadline, a crisis, a catastrophe—remember the same thing. No matter what you do tomorrow, and no matter what anyone else does, *all of us* are going into the ground eventually, with dirt thrown on our faces, satisfied as we are and unsatisfied as we are.

Speech makers trying to get over stage fright are told to imagine that everyone in the room is naked. I suggest that when you walk into a group, try imagining that everyone in the room, yourself included, is dead, in the ground, with dirt on their faces. Remember that you have nothing to lose.

This discipline of practice feels unfamiliar at first, but the skill improves with time. One can achieve mastery at it.

You must recognize, down to your core, that you have no control over the outcome of your life. This is how it turned out. This is it. You know the outcome: You will be just as satisfied as you are now. And you will die. They will throw dirt on your face. And that will be it.

Then allow yourself to come through the eye of the needle of hopelessness. If it's going to turn out the way it does, why not pursue anything and everything in the meantime? Thereby you lose the "fear of death"—or, more accurately, the fear of loss of authority, status, and approval. You can invest yourself in what's really important, as if you didn't care about the risks or the outcome—because you already know what the outcome is.

Nothing you do can alter the outcome. You will still be unwhole and incomplete. But nothing else will alter the outcome, either.

In the meantime, you can provide a different quality of life for your life. You can take on making the impossible happen, knowing all the while that *even if you do that*, you still will not alter the outcome. You will *still* go into the ground incomplete and unsatisfied, flawed and broken.

I sometimes call this process "getting to zero"—reaching a state where you do not interpret events as being "better than they should be" or "worse than they should be." Events are simply what they are.

LEARNING TO HIT BOTTOM WITHOUT GIVING UP

Few stories of people "hitting bottom" are as moving as what happened to the inventor, philosopher, and writer Buckminster Fuller. What makes his story unique is *not* the circumstances of his fall, or even the dramatic turn of his recovery, but the unusual direction he took when he bounced back up.

It happened in 1927. Fuller had started a family and built up a construction business in Chicago. He had worked as hard as he could, and at first it was a success. But then his four-year-old daughter died, he began drinking heavily, and then he went bankrupt. He later blamed the bankruptcy on his own naïveté and a series of betrayals by business associates. The bankruptcy left him bereft of confidence in himself, his associates, and his ability to provide. One day he stood at the edge of Lake Michigan and asked himself, "Am I an utter failure? If so, I had better get myself out of the way, so at least my wife and baby can be taken over by my family and they will do the best they can with them. Am I going to be a drag on them, or is there possibly any reason I can see why I ought to go on?"[2]

Years later, Bucky talked about this as the moment he accepted himself as a "throwaway." He would never make it in conventional terms. His life was over. Standing at the edge of the lake, he realized he was at a "jump-or-think basis." Since he had nothing left to lose, he might as well begin thinking, for the first time in his life, by discarding everything anyone else had ever told him and drawing conclusions only from his own experiences. He would never know his own significance, he realized, but, as he told himself, "You do not have the right to eliminate yourself. You do not belong to you. You belong to the universe." He would set up the rest of his life as an experiment. He would see what kind of difference an average individual like himself—a person who had never excelled in school, had failed at business, and had no particular strengths—could make in the lives of his fellow human beings.

For the first time in his life, and for the rest of his life, Buckminster Fuller was free. He let go of the need to earn a living: He and his family would be supported either by luck or by the returns that came naturally from his experiment. He let go of success; he never thereafter evinced concern for any position of prominence. He even let go of speech; for two years after his epiphany, for all the hardship this caused his wife, he did not use words. "I thought I would see if by doing that I could force myself back to the point where I would really understand what it was I was thinking." He held on only to his experiment, and to the increasingly wide-ranging and intellectual ideas about geometrical form, systems thinking, and industrial evolution that made his reputation.

Some of the most powerful fiction involves the same understanding. There is the moment, for example, in Mark Twain's *Huckleberry Finn* when the teenage hero realizes that he must make a full commitment to helping the runaway slave, Jim, escape. If he does this, however, he will not just be seen as worthless by his entire community, but will be relegated in the eyes of God (or so he has been told) to everlasting torment. He writes a letter betraying Jim and then tears the letter up. "All right, then," he says, "I'll *go* to hell." At that moment, Huck Finn hits bottom. And yet that moment is arguably the beginning of the transformation of his life.

TELLING YOURSELF THE TRUTH

Hitting bottom leads to holding a new type of conversation with oneself as a result. Here are the elements of that conversation.

If you indeed have nothing to lose, then who are you to be? What choices do you have between now and the time you go into the ground?

We covered this question once before, at the end of chapter 1. And we will cover it again, in chapter 6. But for now, consider it an opportunity to tell yourself the truth about your aspirations.

Having acquired the ability to "die before going into battle," you now have the opportunity to choose to play a different game—a game other than survival—with the rest of your life. It is very important that you see this as a game worth playing, regardless of the outcome. Is the game and everything that goes with it—everything you have to learn, all of the struggling, victories, and losses—worth playing? Would you play it even if you knew it wouldn't turn out the way it should?

You'd better love the game itself because that's all there is to be engaged in between now and when you go into the ground.

How much of your life is engaged in activities related to your work? If you are typical of executives, that amount would be well over 50 percent. That represents, over the next ten or twenty years, a substantial amount of time.

What do you want to use that time for? It takes time and perseverance to ask that question truthfully. Many people don't allow themselves to ask it. In the face of what they feel they have to do, they don't seem to have the time to think about what they want to do. But because you have reached "point zero," what you feel you have to do is no longer a concern. So I invite you to look at the question freshly.

What *do* you choose to use your life for?

In the next chapter, on declaration of possibility, we look more closely at how that opening is created, and how to embrace it.

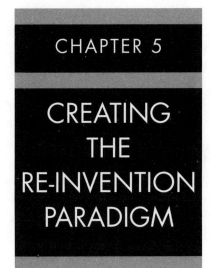

CHAPTER 5

CREATING THE RE-INVENTION PARADIGM

Acquiring the capacity to make the impossible happen

THE MOVIE *Rudy* tells the story of a blue-collar youth growing up in a steel-mill town on the Great Lakes who creates a new order of life for himself. We first see Daniel "Rudy" Ruettinger (played by Sean Astin) as an eager ten-year-old making a solemn declaration: Someday he will play football for the University of Notre Dame. That declaration establishes a context for his way of *being* throughout the rest of his life.

In the eyes of most people, however, Rudy is disqualified before he begins. He is far too small physically to match anyone's conventional image of what a football player should be. During the course of the movie, everyone (except his best friend, Pete) tells him that the dream of playing for Notre Dame is impossible. They tell him he isn't good enough, and they dismiss his athletic skills; in the meantime, he trains and works out incessantly. They say he isn't smart enough to get accepted into Notre Dame, and in fact it takes him two years of determination and dedication at a community college, and three rejections, before his transfer to that university is accepted. They say he isn't rich enough, that he should work in the local steel mill as his father and brothers do. In fact, he doesn't have the money for college, so he works at the mill for four years until he saves enough to cover his tuition.

"Dreamers are not doers," he is told. But Rudy spends his life with this dream at the center of his way of *being*. After he enters Notre Dame, he joins the walk-on practice squad—the closest he can get to the team. Battered and bruised daily by the varsity linemen who use him as a human dummy, he holds on to his dream. He has resolved by this point that his declaration involves running onto the playing field with the team, wearing the gold helmet of the Fighting Irish.

Rudy's guts, good nature, and raw determination impress many of the people who meet him during the course of the film, including legendary Notre Dame coach Ara Parseghian, who promises Rudy that he can "dress"with the team on the field for just one game before he graduates. But Parseghian retires before he can fulfill his promise, and in the fall of his senior year, with only a few games left, Rudy's name does not appear on the players' list.

This setback propels Rudy to hit bottom. For the first time, he feels himself on the brink of defeat, ready to throw in the towel and quit. "What good is it, if it doesn't produce results, if it doesn't mean anything?" he says. His friends point out to him how much he has accomplished, despite the fact that he didn't make his goal: He is set to graduate from one of the top universities in the country, despite his blue-collar background. He has made one of the All-American teams, despite his size and lack of athletic prowess. And his determination has become an inspiration to his teammates and to his friends at school.

In the film, Rudy's disappointment propels him through a "passing through the eye of the needle" experience: accepting, finally, that life does not turn out the way it should. He decides to return to practice, to finish out the year, doing his job 100 percent, *being* a Notre Dame football player, and knowing that his impossible dream is not going to happen.

When he returns to the team at the end of the movie, he finds his name on the players' list, after all. He dresses for a game. From the stands, his father and brother see him wearing the uniform with the team. Then the impossible happens. With less than a minute to play, the quarterback, against the coach's call, throws a touchdown pass, enabling the defense to come back on the field. Under pressure from the team, the coach allows Rudy to play. In the last seconds of the game, Rudy's family watches from the stands as Rudy sacks the opposing quarterback. The team carries Rudy off the field on their shoulders.

The film is based on events that actually took place twenty years ago. Since Rudy, the Notre Dame football team has never carried another player off the field.

You may or may not think Rudy's goal was meaningful. That's not the point. His life story provides a dramatic example of the need for making a declaration. Having made the declaration, Rudy had the power of the stand he took, to stay in action regardless of the circumstances, to move the possibility he declared to a reality. With this kind of power, the kind of power that is not encumbered by the habitual ways of thinking of the past, he was now capable of handling everything life threw in his path.

DECLARING THE FUTURE

The previous chapter involved transforming your relationship with risk-taking—from having risks occur to you as a threat to having risks occur as "nothing to lose." When that transformation is complete, you will have freed yourself from the Universal Human Paradigm.

The next transformation is to invent a new master paradigm—the Re-Invention Master Paradigm—discovering its possibilities as if nobody had ever discovered them before.

Inventing a new master paradigm is accomplished with language: specifically the speech act of declaration.

A declaration is an act of speaking that brings forth a future the moment it is spoken.

In addition to the basic form "I declare," there are other forms of declaring, such as "I pronounce," "I proclaim," "I say," or "I stand for the possibility." **For a declaration to be authentic and have the power to create a future, one element is essential. The person who speaks the declaration must have authority in the arena in which he or she is declaring.**

When a judge says to a convicted criminal, "I sentence you to five years in jail," he speaks from his or her authority to make that declaration. The world of that convict is altered during the moment those words are spoken. When a priest, minister, rabbi, or justice of the peace tells a couple, "I now pronounce you husband and wife," or when an employer says, "You're hired," a new future is created by those acts of speech.

But those declarations have no power if they are spoken by people without authority. The convict is not sentenced by the declaration of the victim. The couple is not married by the declaration of friends. Only certain people within organizations have the power to hire you. Similarly, if a department manager in a worldwide corporation says, "I declare a paid holiday across the organization for all employees on their birthdays," his words would be ignored. Yet if that same declaration were spoken by the chairman of the board, the future would be different.

A DECLARATION OF POSSIBILITY

The new master paradigm that you are about to invent is rooted in a particular type of declaration: a declaration of possibility. A powerful declaration of possibility can move the forces that alter the world. From the moment it is spoken, this declaration lays the groundwork for action in a new realm: a specific realm of possibility, which you define, that did not previously exist as possible.

The new realm of possibility you declare is founded *solely* on your stand for that possibility—without precedent, argument, or proof. Said another way: A declaration of possibility brings "what is not" into existence as a possibility.

As with all declarations, to make an authentic declaration of possibility, you must have authority in the arena in which you are declaring. That arena is: *What you say is possible, and not possible, in your future.* So imagine that anything to do with "what you say is possible and not possible in your future" is gathered together in one arena. Who has authority over everything in that arena?

This is actually a trick question, like "Who's buried in Napoleon's tomb?" The answer to that question, of course, is Napoleon. So who is the authority in the arena of what you say is possible and not possible in your future? The answer, of course, is you. *You have total authority* with regard to what you say is possible and not possible in your future.

While this may seem self-evident, it is extremely important to understand that in the past *you have not taken this authority.* As a function of your Winning Strategy and the Universal Human Paradigm, you have given away your power to determine what is possible or not possible in the future. You have given over this power to the past. Heretofore, for you, "what is possible in the future" has always been determined by "what has been possible so far" (along with some improvement). Anything impossible in the past has been impossible in the future.

You are about to break through that barrier. You will reclaim the power you have given to the past.

In essence, that is what Rudy Ruettinger did. Rudy had no authority over the Notre Dame football team policies. He did not have authority to declare he would dress and play for Notre Dame. Only the coach had that authority. But Rudy, like you and me, had complete authority over what he said was possible in his future. He could declare the *possibility* of dressing and playing for Notre Dame. His declaration, naïve as it might have seemed, recognized that an individual's personal authority can carry a person quite far.

A significant declaration of possibility can be remembered for years, if not centuries. The Magna Carta was a declaration; in posting it, the feudal lords declared that the king could not have absolute powers over local communities. Mahatma Gandhi transformed himself from a workaday attorney into a catalyst for his country's future by declaring the possibility of the British walking out of India. The Wright Brothers fulfilled the declaration of possibility, that human beings can fly, which had been made since antiquity. Half a century later, it took only a decade to fulfill a declaration of the possibility that a human being can walk on the moon.

In the history of groundbreaking businesses, declarations for new realms of possibility often play a prominent role. Shortly after he invented the telephone, Alexander Graham Bell made a formal statement that this new sound-transmitting device would be the cornerstone of a comprehensive communications network between all citizens who wanted to take part. The declaration of this possibility paved the way for American Telephone & Telegraph's Bell System. In the 1970s, William McGowan of Microwave Communications, Inc., built his business by declaring the possibility of having the right to connect to the Bell System—a declaration that eventually led to AT&T's divestiture of its local phone companies. 3M's statement that "25% or more of our profits each year come from new products," considered one of the cornerstones of that company's success, is nothing more nor less than a declaration of possibility which prompts the company, every day, to continue investing in innovation.

Much of the personal computer boom can be traced back to several declarations, made during the 1960s and 1970s, about the possible impact of this then-potential tool. For example, Alan Kay, one of the key inventors of the graphic user interface of Windows and Macintosh operating systems, declared that it is possible that a personal computer could be as easy to work on as a piece of paper. This, in turn, would make it a communications medium, instead of an arcane technological tool; and "then the very use of it would actually change the thought patterns of an entire civilization."[1]

Sir Colin Marshall of British Airways consciously used the power of a declaration of possibility when he said that British Airways would be the world's favorite airline, at a moment when it was clearly one of the worst. Stepping down as chairman of Motorola in 1982, Robert Galvin said Motorola was to be the world's premier company. Managers snickered. He countered with, "Why not? Someone is going to do it. Why not us?" This commitment has since become the "future" of Motorola. One of its highly important Senior Executive Projects is to create a road map to accomplish that future. The list of examples could go on and on, including virtually every household-word corporation.

And it could include your organization.

During the last few years, I have worked with a very successful business unit in a leading multinational chemical company (which we'll call the Fisher Chemical Company here). The unit, which manufactures dyes, is so innovative, and so far ahead of the rest of the corporation in profits and performance, that its managers do not bother to benchmark competitors or other business units in that company. There is no one they consider worth benchmarking.

One day, the business unit's senior executive, a fifty-one-year-old manager named Claude, decided to push his people as far as they could be pushed.

"We are on the top of the pile here," he said to the members of his senior team. "There is no place else to climb. Let's cut the umbilical cord to everything that's helped us gain success in the past. Let's commit ourselves to achieve something we think is impossible."

To begin, he conducted a one-day seminar for the key people in the unit—all senior management personnel and those reporting to the management committee. At the seminar, each person reported his or her interpretation of the elements that contributed to the success of the unit; two of his or her best contributions; two approaches or tasks that weren't successful; and a description of what would make work exciting ten years hence.

At the end of the day, the group made a declaration: In the future, they declared, when consumers think of dye, they will instinctively say "Fisher," just as consumers say "Kleenex" when they think of tissues.

Managers of an industrial enterprise, such as a dye manufacturing business unit, would not ordinarily aspire to make their product name a household word. Part of Claude's job involved helping to lead the group away from its fear that it would fail. The team had to admit the possibility that they could fail. They had to say, in effect, "So what?" to this possibility of failure. They had to take a stand that they would put everything they had into becoming a household word, knowing that whatever the outcome might be, the effort was worth committing themselves to it.

Suddenly, they were no longer *being* industrial company managers. They no longer kept a rigid boundary between their manufacturing, research, and marketing departments; to transform their dyes into a household-word operation, these groups would have to work together through informal as well as formal channels. And they no longer followed established industry practices—even their own practices—which had been based around being an industrial supplier. In every aspect of their jobs, they now asked themselves, "Will this help Fisher Chemicals become a household word in dyes?"

CREATING THE RE-INVENTION PARADIGM

Getting beyond the limits of your Winning Strategy and the entire Universal Human Paradigm requires reclaiming the power you have given to the past: the power to determine what you say is possible or not possible in the future. This is accomplished by a series of three specific declarations which bring into existence a unique realm of possibility—a new master paradigm designed for making the impossible happen, the Re-Invention Paradigm.

Henceforth, this is the new master paradigm from which to express your leadership.

The first two declarations create the new Re-Invention Paradigm. The first creates a new *future* for you as a leader. The second provides a new source of power in the face of *present* circumstances. The third declaration is the context for the new paradigm. It frees you from the constraints of the *past*.

The first declaration: "I declare the possibility that 'what is possible' is 'what I *say* is possible.'"

With this declaration you reclaim for yourself the power (to determine what's possible in the future) that you had formerly granted to the past. In the past you had said that "what is possible" was "what is predictable," based on the evidence, experience, and research of your life up to that point. You break out of the limits of your Winning Strategy. You acquire the power to play a leadership role in the game of making the impossible happen.

Before operating from this declaration, you automatically related to the future according to the guidance of the Universal Human Paradigm. Which means:

- Events take place.
- You interpret those events.
- Those interpretations determine what you are willing to declare possible, which in turn shapes the limits within which actions can occur.
- Those limits, in turn, affect the scope of the results that can be produced.

Once you are operating from this declaration, the future is invented. What you say is possible determines what is possible. Your actions, and the results they produce, are a reflection of the possibility you declared.

You may doubt that such a circular, seemingly tautological declaration can make a difference. But it does.

Suppose that two people you know, named Fred and Sally, are continually pressured by money troubles. They never seem to have enough. Not only do you hear them talking about their lack of funds, but you see it in their demeanor, in their attitude, in their way of *being*. Indeed, the statement "There is never enough money" represents the way they are *being*. And this ongoing conversation with the world remains the same whether the money in their savings account triples or quadruples.

Moreover, Fred and Sally have become convinced that it is impossible for them to exist in any other way. "We were born with money troubles," they say, "and we will go to our graves with them—unless, of course, something impossible happens."

Now suppose that Fred and Sally make the declaration: "We declare the possibility that what's possible is what we say is possible," and declare the possibility: "There is no scarcity of money."

This shifts the boundaries of their future. Fred and Sally may have taken financial planning courses without success before, and this part of their past (which in turn was affected by other legacies from their past) may have helped convince them that they would always have money troubles. Now they recognize that it is possible for them to shift their way of *being*, so that the financial planning courses do them some good. The way they are *being* now with regard to money is "there is no scarcity of money." This is now the context—the environment—for their actions with money. When Fred and Sally took financial planning courses in the past, they did so operating from the context "there is never enough money," and the results they produced from the financial planning courses reflected the context—"there is never enough money." This time, the same actions—taking financial planning courses—are being taken inside a new context, a new realm of possibility that did not exist before—the possibility "there is no scarcity of money." Now there is an environment in which taking financial planning courses can actually make a difference.

An outsider would recognize the possibility immediately— after all, many people with less income than Fred and Sally manage to live without perennial money troubles. But it only matters, for Fred and Sally's purpose, that *they* recognize the possibility themselves. And they will only reach this recognition after they make a declaration about their own influence over the possibilities of their own future.

The second declaration: "I declare this possibility: 'Who I am' is the stand I take."

With this second declaration, you create the possibility of a new way of being *for yourself as a leader.* The phrase "who I am" (in the declaration) refers to the way you are *being.* Heretofore, that has meant the context of your life: oriented toward survival, expressed through your Winning Strategy, and inherited from the Universal Human Paradigm. This declaration displaces that way of *being* and makes room for a new way of *being* that is a function of the commitment that you are willing to make.

Power in the Re-Invention Paradigm is generated from a commitment to an "impossible future." When you commit to this impossible future, you are "taking a stand." People often misunderstand what taking a stand means. It doesn't mean being resolute, stalwart, or grimly determined. It means committing yourself to continuously act consistent with the possibility you declared, from the moment the declaration is spoken, regardless of the circumstances.

Once you declare a specific impossible future (this happens in chapter 6), your way of *being* now operates in relationship to that declaration. Your Winning Strategy no longer dictates your action. Any action is part of your repertoire, including altering the way you are *being.*

After this stand is taken, and the commitment is made, then all the deterrents of the past—interpretation, historical analysis, and fear—are no longer deterrents. They are now something that exists, about which you are informed, while you take actions to move the possibility into a reality.

The Apollo space missions offer a wonderful example of this type of commitment. From the moment that John F. Kennedy said that America would put a man on the moon, the entire country, in effect, took a stand and made a commitment. Every deterrent along the way, including Kennedy's assassination, became a signal—making the country even more determined to fulfill that commitment, and guiding the process of doing so. Six years and two presidents after Kennedy's death, the commitment was fulfilled.

The third declaration: "I take this stand: 'There is no such thing as right or wrong and no fixed way that things should or shouldn't be.' "

This declaration is the context for the Re-Invention Paradigm. It displaces the Universal Human Paradigm context ("There is a way things should be, and when they are not, there's something wrong with me, them, or it").

The most important word in this declaration is "thing." It signifies that constructs like "right," "wrong," "should," and "shouldn't" have no intrinsic validity or substance. They are not "things"; you cannot depend on them to remain stable. They are only and always interpretations from the past, and they never reflect what actually happened. You can't point to a thing called "rightness" or "wrongness," or a thing that represents all the ways in which things "should" or "shouldn't" be.

Instead, you are declaring the possibility that henceforth you are relating to everything that happens primarily as something that happened—without any meaning added. You are declaring the possibility that henceforth you do not relate to an event as whatever interpretation or explanation or conclusion you drew, based on the past. You do not relate to it as "the event happened the way it should" or "the event happened the way it shouldn't." You relate to it as "the event happened."

By declaring "no such thing as right or wrong," you are not renouncing your ability to call some specific aspect of life "right" or "wrong." For example, in parenting, it's part of your job to determine for your children whether particular actions are "right" or "wrong." Without those guidelines, they could get hurt. But you can set those guidelines with the knowledge that there are no "right" or "wrong" absolutes. Each of these guidelines is technically a declaration that you have made. You know that you are assigning that judgment of "right" or "wrong," rather than thinking that the object of "rightness" or "wrongness" really is right or wrong. When they are old enough, your children will make their own declarations (just as you did) about what is right and wrong (perhaps knowing, thanks to your influence, that they, too, are assigning those judgments).

You still experience sadness, grief, or loss as well as happiness, joy, and elation. But these emotions are something you *have*. They do not determine and shape your actions.

This perspective enables you to move ahead. If you declared the possibility of becoming CEO of your organization, and someone else gets the position, all that has happened is that so-and-so was named CEO. It doesn't portend anything about you, them, or it. Now you can return to the declaration you took a stand on, "becoming a CEO," and ask, "What actions do I take next to move this forward to a reality? What's missing and essential right now?"

A grave setback occurred during the production of this book. Under a very tight deadline, specified by the publisher, I hired a talented editor to help me put the manuscript together. He was someone I knew well, and I looked forward to working with him. But just as he was about to begin work, he was involved in a freak automobile accident where a piece of glass flew into his eye. The injury put him out of commission long enough to keep him from working with me.

Under the Universal Human Paradigm, I would have been consumed with one type of concern: There was definitely something "wrong." It "shouldn't" be this way. My friend "should not" have been hurt. My concern for him aside, I would have held an image in my mind of the manuscript as it "should" have been written, with both of us together. "Why did this happen?" I might have asked. Et cetera, et cetera, et cetera.

But operating from the Re-Invention Paradigm, standing in the context that "there is no such thing as 'right' or 'wrong' or 'should' or 'shouldn't,'" I was only concerned with taking actions in response to what happened.

There were three concerns in front of me. First, I was committed to complete my book by its deadline. Second, the deadline was still imminent. Third, my colleague was hurt. At the same time that I moved into action, to offer assistance with anything he might need for recovery, I moved rapidly to take action on my book project. What could I do to make the possibility of the book's completion real? What was missing?

My publisher and I, searching together, found that a consulting editor—one of the best in the business—who had been unavailable when we first approached him (back before my friend came on board), suddenly became available. Because the deadlines were so tight, he could not handle the job alone. He enrolled another editor, whom he knew from other work, to help him. With my attention focused on taking action into "what was missing," I could take the necessary steps to quickly move through all of the stages involved—contracts, briefings, background, et cetera. Within one week after my first editor's accident, the two new editors were both fully engaged in working on the manuscript.

Of course, my immediate reaction, like anyone else's—both to my colleague's injury and to the interruption of this project—had been "Oh no." But **power is determined by the *speed* with which you can declare something possible and move that possibility to reality.** My capability in moving forward was affected by the strength of my declaration—"There is no such thing as right or wrong or should or shouldn't"—only what happened and what actions there are to take for the future.

TAKING A STAND

Taking a stand is a declaration of possibility that allows something to move forward from "existing as a possibility only because you said so" to "existing as a reality where it *is* so in the world."

While people often talk about taking a stand for something, they often simply mean "being resolute." The term is rarely used with rigor. The elements that make taking a stand an act of transformation are little known and infrequently applied.

Taking a stand, in fact, involves five essential elements:

1. The stand generates a unique kind of certainty.

This is not "certainty" in the usual sense of the word—it does not mean being sure that an outcome is predictable or inevitable. Instead, when you take a stand, you are certain of your persistence and continued capability in the face of risks and quandaries. You base your certainty on the willingness to "live in a question," rather than needing to know the answers.

When you have taken a stand, you do not need to know in advance how you will accomplish this possibility. You trust that you will be open enough, questioning enough, and capable enough to handle whatever needs come along during the course of your commitment.

Rudy Ruettinger never knew in advance how he would handle all of the hurdles between him and his purpose. Yet he was certain that he could handle whatever he faced—whether it was taking a test, finding a way to pay for living, or facing opposition from his family.

Similarly, at the Fisher Chemical Company, Claude's dye group leaders were certain that no matter what issues emerged during their new effort, they could ask the right questions. If the group couldn't find its solutions using one methodology, they were confident that they could uncover other approaches. In fact, the group began its work by designing projects for each of its members that deliberately represented a stretch from known practice—a problem without an obvious solution. This turned out to be a terrific way to involve new people.

2. There are no explanations, evidence, or proof in this arena.

You can't explain or justify a stand. If you precede your statement with the word "therefore," you are no longer operating in the arena of taking a stand.

You don't take your stand "because" it fits with some proof or precedent that *this* is the preferred declaration of the moment. You take your stand because this is the stand you take.

Rudy had no evidence or proof that he could make his dream a reality. All precedents were totally against him. He could not say, "I know other small, mediocre student athletes, with lack of tuition money, who have made the Notre Dame football team; therefore, I will do it, too." Instead, he said in effect, "I will do this—whether or not it has ever been done before."

3. There are no justifications.

No stand is justifiable. When you follow your statement with the word "because," you are no longer operating in the arena of taking a stand.

You do not need to justify your purpose: You do not take a stand because it's the right thing to do, or because it must be done, or because the world will be a better place.

Rudy had no justification. There was no real reason why his dream should become reality, beyond the point that he wanted it with his entire being. He could not say, "I deserve this because I have worked hard and waited years."

Similarly, Claude and his Fisher coexecutives could not say *why* they wanted their dye to become a household word. But that made the goal no less important to them.

4. There are no prescriptions.

There are no rules of behavior, textbook solutions, or formulas for what to do or how to do it. Each person who makes a declaration must find his or her own unique way of acting toward the commitment and filling in the missing pieces.

Claude's group developed its own unique marketing methodology. Every step of the way, they identified what key components were missing from their image of their desired future. They created new projects on the spot to fulfill those missing needs. Each step of the way, group members had the confidence that they would know what they needed and could meet the needs in time.

Similarly, Rudy had no plan for reaching his goal—no career path that another student might adopt. Each step of the way, he did what was necessary at the moment, whether it involved starting at a community college until he could produce the necessary grades, applying for admission again and again, demonstrating his tenacity at Notre Dame in the tryouts, or pleading his case directly to the head coach.

5. There is a commitment to take action.

When you take a stand, you make a commitment to move the declared possibility to a reality, regardless of the circumstances. This requires making a series of bold promises and fulfilling them. Without this commitment to act, the possibility you declared will never be transformed from a possibility to a reality, and it will go out of existence over time. (This is the focus of chapter 7.)

Declarations are deliberately purposeful. They are always made in relation to your commitment to provide what is missing for the declaration to become real. That is what gives them credibility. Offhand, casual, or whimsical declarations have no power, because they are not relevant. You don't make declarations that seem to defy the laws of nature or physics, unless you are willing to do everything possible to test those laws. I could declare, "It is possible for me to balance Buicks on my pinkie," but the declaration would be meaningless—even if it is theoretically true. I could declare it possible to fly from my rooftop in Texas to Ohio without benefit of a vehicle. This would be meaningless, too, *unless* I was willing (like the Wright Brothers) to devote everything I had to providing the missing elements. Perhaps someday, someone will invent a personal jet propulsion capsule, or some similar technology, for single-bodied human flight, but it will take the same total commitment that the Wright Brothers devoted to flying.

Both Rudy and Claude's group are notable not just because they quickly moved into action, but because their commitment remained active over the course of years.

All five of these elements involve courage—a kind of existential courage where you must stand on your own, bringing forth yourself and the future from nothing. Standing on your own doesn't necessarily mean standing alone or without support. It does mean standing on your own with nothing from the past or the present to prop you up. Taking a stand takes work, commitment, and discipline. But above all, taking a stand requires the courage to come from nothing into all of the forces resisting an impossible future.

Having taken a stand does not guarantee success. Don't forget, you have already acknowledged that there is no such thing as a "right" or "wrong" future. The possibility of surprise and the lack of control do not lessen your commitment. They merely mean that you accept, as a gift, the reality that things work out the way they do. Taking a stand determines who you are *being* and what you are committing yourself to, while life is working out the way it does.

DECLARATIONS IN ORGANIZATIONS

During one of the Executive Re-Invention sessions, we found ourselves talking about how unlikely people sometimes become the people who raise new possibilities within organizations. You may recall Mike, the retail executive whose Winning Strategy included listening for "What's the point?" After he revealed his Winning Strategy for himself, he told this story:

"A young man was looking for his niche in the company, and he appeared at my door every morning with ideas on photo processing. At the time, we had 6 percent share of the market, and I thought he was a nuisance. I kept sending him away, but he would always return with new charts and ideas. This went on for three months, until he finally wore me down. 'Okay,' I said. 'I'll give you money.' Well, the guy tripled the performance he said he would show. After three years, we had 40 percent of the market share in the Southwest, simply because he didn't let me stop him."

This young man had obviously made a declaration and was committed to having his ideas become reality. He would not give up. However, beyond his extraordinary perseverance and gritty tenacity, there are a number of fascinating elements to this story.

Mike recognized that his own Winning Strategy had acted as

an impediment to the declaration in this story. He didn't hear this fellow's possibilities because they didn't fit into his existing Strategy of listening for "What's the point?" He continually considered the idea in the context that it was impossible. If prompted, Mike might have articulated the unsaid premise he followed this way: "There's no possibility of getting much more than 6 percent of our share in this market." End of discussion. End of meeting. End of possibility.

In retrospect, Mike had to ask himself how many possibilities might have slipped by him because, instead of banging on his door time after time, the person involved was whispering them only once. Or, to make the question more general: If the organization is to become open to possibilities, how must the relationship between leaders and subordinates be tranformed?

Inevitably, this question will arise in some form as people begin to take stands. As with Mike's case, it may emerge when ideas begin to come forth from people at lower levels. Or it may emerge when people at the bottom take seriously a declaration made at the top.

Jack Welch, the CEO of General Electric, is best known for the power of his declarations: that all GE businesses would be number one or number two in their markets and that the leadership of the company would be "transformed." It's interesting to note that Welch's declarations are most effective when GE employees feel that the senior executives back them 100 percent. When employees have doubted the sincerity of or commitment to a declaration, on the part of Welch himself or the business executives, the effectiveness of the GE declarations has dropped off. This dynamic may lie at the root of some of GE's "ethics crises" of the 1980s and 1990s.

Sadly, most CEOs never make the declarations that the organizations need someone to make, and for which they are the candidate with the most authority in the arena of the entire organization. When a reengineering effort takes place without a declaration of what transformation is possible, the effort can't possibly succeed, because the thousands of people involved have no common understanding of its purpose—of what the effort is meant to accomplish.

Several years ago, my partner and I consulted with a manufacturing plant where the top executives had made a commitment to guaranteeing safety. There were 200 to 250 workers who
handled the machines on the factory floor, and all of them had
to declare their commitment, and live that commitment, or the
senior executives' commitment would be powerless.

The plant had a dismal safety record, which had negatively
affected morale. The workers were resigned to conducting their
jobs, day and night, among substandard conditions and a down-
right threatening environment. Most of these men (they were
nearly all men) had worked at the plant for their entire lives. For
years, each of them had gone to work every day hoping that he
wouldn't be the next one to get hurt—but believing, in his heart,
that sooner or later his luck would run out. There was a tremendous amount of history from which these people needed to free
themselves before they could create any possibilities.

First we engaged them in an extensive process of completing
the past. Then, as part of inventing a new future, the workers
and managers declared together that they were committed to the
possibility of a totally accident-free plant. Both sides took their
commitment seriously. Both sides backed it up with participation
and action. It was incredibly moving to watch the workers, during the next few months, as they brought this possibility into
reality, especially when they experienced setbacks. But the problems, which were inevitable, were a subplot in the overarching
drama of transformation.

Having made the declaration, the workers heroically brought
it to pass. They maintained their commitment throughout the
process. After new safety measures and systems were in place,
they went for months and months without an accident. Then a
huge accident occurred. However, by that time everyone could
see the accident as an anomaly—merely something that happened, not proof that their commitment had been mishandled.
The accident didn't invalidate their efforts. They found the cause
of the accident and made sure it could not take place again.
And they went for an even longer period of time before another
accident occurred.

Normally, when a group has worked hard to get to "zero

accidents" and stayed there for a long time, if an accident happens (and eventually it will), they are devastated and invalidated. It is hard for them to start all over again. But this transformation altered who the workers were *being* about owning everything, beyond mere concern about reaching a goal. They were now committed to being able to maintain the context of "no accidents," regardless of the circumstances.

HONING THE DECLARATION

It may take several meetings working and reworking many different versions to generate a declaration that transforms your world. For example, I worked with a top-level executive (I'll call him David) in the communications and entertainment industry whose declaration transformed both his life and his industry.

David's industry was moving into multimedia and new types of entertainment technologies, and his company needed some creative breakthroughs. David believed that he personally had developed a creative direction that would work. There were snags: David didn't feel he had the technological expertise to develop a new product on his own. And within his company, ideas were not supposed to come from the management side. Executives at his company did not lead through creativity. Yet creating a new product was the game that most excited him.

David frankly admitted where his creative impetus came from. "I always admired Ernie Kovacs. His early television comedies had great purity of form because they combined truth and humor. TV was relatively new and the rules of the game were not yet established. Today's media are not yet defined, but everyone knows they will be pervasive and extensive. However, there are not yet rules to the game. No one knows what will constitute success. It's a grand opportunity, to re-create what Ernie did in the 1950s."

I talked over the implications with him, and David's interest level increased. "Presently, the company has me in a well-defined role," he said, "and to get away from that I would have to create a future that is different than the present. It's very appealing and sounds like a lot of fun."

Thus, David framed his first declaration this way: "In my re-invented future, I would be responsible for new forms of entertainment, emphasizing humor as a subset. It would be a matter of my being involved with a separate division that created as well as produced the first hit product for this new medium, and I might even be the star of one of the shows."

But the declaration didn't feel right. David felt he was hampered without the help of his technical people. He couldn't see how he could create alone. I reminded him that he could always find someone who had already invented a product and build onto it, rather than being hampered by a need to manage all the pieces. Managing all the pieces was part of his normal Winning Strategy, and he would not be able to operate that way in this game.

He also realized that, once he entered the game, he would have to stop waiting for a signal to begin. If the company he worked for wasn't interested in having him take the creative lead, he would go to another company. Even if he kept his job, he was now a free agent, loyal to a game that was larger than his company. He was like a writer with a script; if a studio turns down a script, the writer takes it to another studio.

"I declare that in a year," he said, "I will develop a product that no one will say no to," he said.

I said, "That's not a declaration, David. That's a promise. It can be incorporated into your declaration, but it's incomplete in itself. *The declaration you generate creates your way of being.* Who are you *being* in this declaration?"

He said he was *being* a spontaneous source of innovation, on both the technical and the creative sides. I pressed him further. "I remember you talking with me about finding a person to run a division. When you were looking for a person to do that, what were you looking for?"

"The expert," he responded.

"Could you declare yourself an expert?" I continued.

"I'm not sure in what," he said, "because multimedia involves fields in which there is no developed expertise at this point."

"That's right," I said. "So what could you declare yourself an expert in?"

"I guess I could declare myself the expert in these new applications," he said.

"Yes, and your being an expert is a reality that does not currently exist. From this declaration, you could take actions consistent with being an expert in those fields. Your promises would flow from that."

David framed his new declaration in three pairs of statements and promises: "I declare the possibility: I am the source for the vitality of new technologies in the entertainment industry. I promise within two years to bring a new product to the studio that knocks people out.

"Second, I declare that I am a person who stops at nothing and I promise to allow myself to fail on any project.

"Third, I declare that everything needed to fulfill this possibility exists or can be created, and I promise to be open to any and all ideas and partnerships that can move things forward, regardless of past experiences."

FROM DECLARATION TO DESIGN

I am closing this chapter with an invitation. I invite you to make a bold declaration of possibility regarding yourself as a leader.

Most of us forget that we have this power, because it is so easy to lose sight of the results of declarations. Once possibilities become realities, a paradox takes place—the actuality becomes self-evident. It becomes hard to remember that there was a time when no one thought a state could be run on democratic principles, or no one thought computers would be owned by individuals. "Of course human beings can fly," we say. "Of course, humans can walk on the moon. Of course, photocopiers, telephones, vaccines, and cameras can exist." It becomes difficult to grasp the point that these realities weren't always perceived as possible. That's the way transformation works. Once you alter the way something occurs, it's hard to realize that it wasn't always the way it is now. You forget that once it wasn't obvious that it would be this way.

History changes through declarations. Only through your declarations can you begin to alter the context in which you live. Only declarations allow cultures to give birth to a new way of being. *Only declarations allow you to transform the world.*

By declaration and the stand you take, you have the level of commitment that is necessary for Re-Invention. Next, you design a new game, from the future, standing in the new master paradigm, the Re-Invention Paradigm. This game will be the vehicle for building the muscles of being an extraordinary leader and operating from the mode of transformation.

Since everyone's future is different, there is no step-by-step plan in the next chapter, but rather a plan for developing a plan. It's up to you to recognize the components that are needed for the game you want to play. And it's up to you to design the game in a way that will draw all those components together, in a manner that creates a realm of possibility in which you can express your leadership by using your professional life to make the impossible happen.

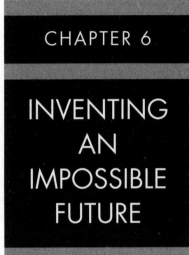

CHAPTER 6

INVENTING AN IMPOSSIBLE FUTURE

Creating a new game that redesigns you as a leader

I NOW INVITE YOU to take the opportunity to be the architect of your future. This transformation leads you to design a new "game" for your life—an invented future, constructed with rules, principles, and a designed scoring system, in which the stated purpose is to reach your "designated (im)possibility." Based upon your design, this game will shape your choices and actions, while life "is turning out the way it does." The game will redesign you as a leader.

You have already declared that "who you are" is "the stand that you take." The next step is to create a *specific* stand—a stand that is large enough in scope to replace the game of "surviving" that you have played, in the past, through your Winning Strategy. It will be interesting enough to devote your life to fulfilling.

This stand becomes your "impossible" game in life. What's the relationship between the stand and the game? Once you take this stand, you will have embarked on the game; indeed, designing the stand you take is a key part of designing the game.

As you play the game, it will alter your identity. To make the impossible happen, you give up the old identity that was built around your Winning Strategy. You constitute yourself, not as a new "person," but as a future larger than a person—as the future of your organization, industry, or country. You begin to relate to yourself as: "Who I *am* is the future of my enterprise." What you mean is that, although you remain a human being, you can now call upon qualities, talents, and capabilities that are not simply a product of your personality. When you are *being* the future of your organization, you are *being* what Martin Heidegger called a "clearing" in the world: an opening in which an invented future can crystallize. Over time, others will quite naturally relate to you as this invented future, rather than as a personality.

LEADERS ARE THE ''CLEARING'' IN WHICH THE FUTURE HAPPENS

What does it mean to *be* a clearing, or an opening?

Consider the case of Vince Lombardi. When he led the Green Bay Packers, he reached a point where he was no longer *being* Vince Lombardi. He was *being* the future of the Green Bay Packers. This meant more than simply "caring" about the Packers or doing his job effectively. All his actions stemmed from an embodiment of the future of the team and the community that supported it. "The Green Bay Packers," he declared, "are not just the people who play, but the ticket sellers, the peanut vendors, and the people in the stands."

What made Lombardi powerful was the stand he took. He was *being* the stand that "his team were champions." His per-

sonal identity was no longer driving his actions; instead, the future of the Green Bay Packers, and maybe the future of
professional football, drove his actions. Thus, he became a clearing—an opening for action—for the people who worked with
and for him. For those people, from the players to the staff to
the community leaders, that clearing was bigger than any fear of
discipline or resistance to change. He did not have to get people
to "buy in," nor did people need to be "paid off" or feel obliged
to act; instead, action favorable to the Green Bay Packers found
a resonant welcome in the environment created by Lombardi's
way of *being*. People could show up as bigger than themselves—
they, too, could relate to themselves as the future of the Green
Bay Packers, and naturally take actions consistent with that future.

Leaders are memorable for the "clearings" they create during
their leadership. John F. Kennedy is remembered today, not for
his presidential policies, but for the opening he created, which
galvanized other people into being active participants in public
life. The line "Ask not what your country can do for you; ask
what you can do for your country" was powerful precisely because it echoed his way of *being*; had most other presidents made
the same statement, it most likely would have fallen flat. The
maker of that statement, and others like it, had become a "clearing" for the future of the country. When he spoke lines like that,
people heard *themselves*. They heard Kennedy say what they had
been thinking about, or feeling, or trying to say, but had never
quite been able to articulate. Ronald Reagan, with very different
values, generated a similar kind of clearing. Like Kennedy's, his
presidency is remembered not necessarily for his policies, but for
the openings for actions that it created and inspired in others.

Jack Welch, the CEO of General Electric, is a clearing for
bold and daring leadership to naturally show up around him. A
large number of successful CEOs of other companies are veterans of General Electric, and they all talk about working with
Welch as a primary influence. It wasn't what Welch told them or
showed them that still moves them years later. It's the way he
embodied the future of General Electric when they were around

him. In the clearing he created, they related to themselves as powerful, and able to act in bold and daring ways.

The German word Heidegger used for "clearing," *Lichtung*, means literally a clearing in a forest. Heidegger used it deliberately because it conveyed a sense of "opening." A clearing is an opening in the world of dense, conflicting interpretations—a place of light and simplicity.

The clearing is created by your listening. You are always "listening from" the stand you have taken to be the future of your organization, the country, education, government, or your industry. This listening functions as a kind of gravitational pull. When you are a clearing for a particular future, you will find that everything around you shows up as related to some concern or commitment associated with that future.

A highly successful marketer with whom I have worked (I'll call him Rob) discovered firsthand what it was like to become a clearing. He worked for a large apparel manufacturer, and his speciality has always been building brand names. But in the past, he had had a Winning Strategy of listening for "How do things fit?" so as to act by "acting personally to deliver the goods" in order to be "appreciated and valued." "I thought I always had to be the best," he later said, "and I relied on myself to manipulate all the moves." An athletic, charismatic, obviously bright man, for years he had always been seen as "the guy with the answers," and few other people seemed to shine around him.

But during a boom season at his company, he realized that, no matter how capable he was, he *couldn't* do it all himself. The implicit credo of his life's survival, "If you want something done right, do it yourself," kept him from expanding the scope of his interest beyond a certain scale; and now his company was demanding that he develop five new businesses. If he wanted to make them work, he would have to create a game that would make him become a clearing for *others'* leadership.

Using the techniques that I will describe in this chapter, Rob designed a game that would require him to operate outside of his identity and embody the stand that everyone has the capacity for leadership. To be sure, he "did" some specific things differently: He hired better people and allowed them more freedom to do their jobs. But the significant difference came in the way he was *being*: People suddenly found that they were eager to provide him with whatever his businesses needed. People now gravitate to him because they recognize that he doesn't just *believe* in developing them; *everything* about the way his businesses operate embodies the idea that they will be developed as people.

Rob sees an earlier version of himself in one of his protégés, and he is enabling his protégé to grow and prosper in the light of Rob's clearing. "I had a major breakthrough with him," Rob said. "I kept trying to get him to play a bigger game than being the guy with all the answers. That was very uncomfortable for him. But now he's president of one of my businesses. He needed a designer, someone for sales, and a marketing person, and I was pushing him to hire the best people, which he eventually did. He learned to create an environment that is now drawing the most knowledgeable people in their areas."

Note that, in Rob's case as in all cases, the new game he adopted replaced the old game of his Winning Strategy. "My Re-Invention," he later said, "is from being Rob the valuable executive to being Rob the valuable leader. I was able to create such a competitive edge that it was invisible to the people I was competing with—and, to be perfectly candid, invisible to me. I thought everyone thought the way I did. Only in recent years do I realize how other people didn't intuitively understand what I was talking about. I thought we were all interested in building brands, but they were interested in building the business."

An invented future is a game that your Winning Strategy would never allow you to play. The game Rob created began by declaring himself the future of the apparel industry. In that clearing, he declared that the possibility "building brands replacing building businesses" could be a new context for the industry. To play this game, he had to demystify his own success, and to create many other leaders as good as, or better than, he is at building brands. He could never have engaged in this game from inside his Winning Strategy. He had to re-invent himself to operate beyond it.

You will know that you have become a clearing when the kinds of problems you have to deal with, and the kinds of conversations you have, are altered. They will no longer have to do with your Winning Strategy but with the stand you have taken. Once he had taken a stand that the British will leave India, Mahatma Gandhi's problems no longer involved his survival or his personal wants, needs, or concerns. Instead, the problems around him all had to do with the game he designed, such as keeping the possibility alive for others, mounting campaigns, and designing nonviolent strategies.

The kinds of requests that people make of you, the kinds of promises that you make, the reasons people come to you, the invitations you receive, and the areas you spend your time with will all be different when they are shaped by your invented future. Instead of seeking you out for the talent associated with your Winning Strategy, people will start coming to you for concerns connected with your invented future. For example, if you are a clearing for "the future of education," over time people will start thinking of you and education as the same. When serious conversations regarding education are designed, your presence and participation start to occur as essential. In uncanny ways, like a teeter-totter gravitating toward equilibrium, people and events will be attracted to the clearing that you have become, because around you there is an opening for people to take action to make the impossible happen in the area of education.

Take an airplane flight, and a casual conversation with the person sitting next to you will trigger a unique approach, one that you haven't thought of before, to fulfill your "designated impossibility." Open a book, and you will flip to the page that gives you "what's missing." Talk to a janitor, a stockholder-gadfly, a creditor, or a government regulator, and you will hear gold in their comments—opportunities that would never occur to you listening from your Winning Strategy or from your interpretations of those people.

When you are being a clearing for the future of the organization, you'll find that you no longer need to threaten or bribe people to get them to buy in to your program. They won't need to buy in to the future because they'll feel it's theirs; by being a clearing, you've created an opening for them to hear themselves in your speaking and "own" the future. Indeed, one of the primary tasks of leadership is the creation of a future that calls people naturally to action. Anything less is insufficient to make the impossible happen.

Thus, as a leader operating in the mode of transformation, the fundamental question for you is: "What kind of a clearing are you being?" Your actions, and the actions of those you lead, will be correlates of that clearing.

Are you a clearing for an "impossible future" for your organization? Is your way of *being* providing an environment in which the people around you are enabled to find new openings for action and are free to be engaged in making an impossible future happen?

GENERATING A CLEARING FOR YOURSELF AS A LEADER

To generate a clearing, you speak "yourself." This is a very different act than speaking *about* yourself. It's made with a kind of speech act called an "expressive"—a form of declaration that lets others know who you *are* in regard to a specific issue or relationship.

Everyone uses some expressives quite frequently. For instance, if you are joyous on behalf of someone who has just had a graduation, marriage, promotion, or appointment, you will utter the expressive "Congratulations." It expresses that joy to them, acknowledges their accomplishment, and takes the stand that you support them. When you say that, they know who you are *being* about their accomplishment, and can relate to you in that way.

"Thank you" is an expressive that lets someone know that you feel gratitude. "I forgive you" expresses your pardon for a specific offense or injury. It lets the other people know that, with regard to this specific matter, you renounce any anger or resentment. It lets them know that you are ready to "give as before," with regard to them. On the other hand, the expressive "I curse you" lets people know that who you are *being*, with regard to them, is a desire for evil or misfortune to come their way. All of these declarations present who you are, calling forth yourself as a possibility.

In the context of your "designated possibility," the game you are creating is too complex for a simple expressive like "Thank you" or "I forgive you," which *implicitly* expresses who you are *being*. The game calls for being more explicit. This can be accomplished by using an expressive that begins, "Who I am . . ."

You always create a clearing with an expressive that brings forth the arena from which you will generate the stand you take. The expressive might take the form "Who I am is the future of . . ."

Here are some examples:

■ The CEO of a Canadian business, a man whom I'll call Stephen, generated a clearing with the expressive "Who I am is the future of politics." He declared the possibility "Politics provides the foundation for people to take responsibility for having their lives work" as his "impossible" game worth playing. Stephen was already a successful entrepreneur, but had no background in politics. His time was all tied up in running his business, and he still needed the income from it.

Part of playing the game, for Stephen, involved taking a step he would never have considered before: turning the business over to his wife. She had never run an enterprise, but she became quite successful at it; running the business unearthed capabilities in her which had never come to the surface before. Now, free to engage himself full-time in politics, Stephen was able to bring his capacity for Re-Invention to bear on those parts of the political process that hamstring or restrain most would-be politicians. For example, he deliberately ran his first campaign, knowing that for various technical reasons, *he could not win*. He saw the election as "a place to learn from"—an experience that would bring to the surface everything he and his staff had to master if they would win an election. This meant not just plotting his own path, but generating a clearing that would attract other people's willingness to put learning above winning.

"We were seriously attempting to fail brilliantly at everything, and that game is fairly attractive to people," he said. "It's tough to fail brilliantly at everything, to push everything over the edge. And we didn't get everything pushed over the edge, but we sure got a lot of it done. Interestingly, I don't think any of the people who were active in that campaign fell off the wagon after we lost. Unlike most politically active people, they stayed on to help develop the next one."

Stephen's campaign is built around an initiative to convert much of the political party structure into a more grassroots-oriented, volunteer-driven form, in which political parties are vehicles for conveying ideas, rather than for consolidating power. "So instead of three or four parties," he says, "we may end up with three hundred or nine hundred parties, or four thousand parties, each holding ideas. A political person wouldn't represent only one of those parties, but a number of them." Gathering the steam for creating that sort of more adaptive political system is a challenging, but very compelling, game indeed.

Stephen made this declaration in 1989. On June 8, 1995, five years after he began his game, he was elected to Parliament in his province and three weeks later was named to the high-level post of Minister of Education and Training—an unusual appointment for a new member.

▪ Joseph, a senior vice-president of human resources, when invited to speak of himself as a clearing for the future, said, "Who I am is the future of human resources." He designed a game around the possibility: "Organizations worldwide demonstrate that people are the competitive advantage of an enterprise. He committed to make this happen not just at his own company, but, by extension, his company would be an example to, and a prototype for, all companies. He declared that using his professional life engaging in filling that specific realm of possibility was a game worth playing.

Since 1991, the game led Joseph to switch jobs several times. He is now the head of the human resource function at a multinational company. The group has committed to creating a future based on the idea that "people are the company's most important resource"—not just as a rhetorical slogan but as a principle of the design of the company.

■ Edward, the managing partner of an entertainment industry CPA firm, with many clients who are celebrities, generated a
clearing for himself, beginning with the expressive "Who I am is
the future of entertainment management." At the same time, he
declared the possibility: "Well-known performers and athletes
use their star status to make a difference in the world." He became a clearing for clearheaded conversations about how entertainers could wisely spend their time and money to acquire the
most leverage. As a result, he has attracted people looking for
powerful relationships with their business adviser, relationships
in which they can mutually consider not just how to manage their
money but how to make life choices. He's become a coach for
his clients. Around him, people get in touch with the part of
themselves that wants to make a difference.

■ Jerome, the chairman and CEO of a telecommunications
company generated his clearing with the expressive "Who I am
is the future of my organization," meaning that his way of *being*
would embody the future of his particular company. In 1990 he
declared the possibility: "This company is the premier company
in the industry, continually breaking new ground, and sustaining
a role as the model for using new technologies effectively." Every
choice he makes about whom he hires, how he promotes people,
and where he allocates investment is determined by what will
fulfill that realm of possibility. That is the only game he is playing.
As a result, he (and his company) are continually making moves
that are "out of the box"—completely unexpected in terms of
past practices—and they have become a model for other companies.

CREATING AN INVENTED FUTURE

Don't be misled by the term "game." These games are not
trivial affairs, but vehicles for your ongoing Re-Invention as a
leader who makes the impossible happen.

If you are the player in such a game, you are completely committed to it, and willing to shift your way of *being* to match what

the play requires. Results and scores are kept and you pay careful attention to them. But your attention is focused not on gaining the best score, or making sure that the game produces the right results. Instead, your attention is creative. You create not only your play but the parameters of the world you play within.

That's why I use the word "design" to describe your role in the game of Re-Invention. The idea of design suggests that your choices will reverberate over the next weeks, months, and years, to influence what is possible—in the same way that the design of a building influences what activities take place there.

Between now and the end of the game, instead of your life being occupied with the problems associated with making sure your Winning Strategy prevails, your life will be occupied with the problems associated with your invented future.

Before you begin designing this new game for yourself, it is important to understand how creating an inventing future (by declaring a realm of possibility to fulfill) is different from setting and reaching a goal.

Goal-setting is fundamental to the mode of continuous improvement. *A goal is a place to get to from where you are.* You are driven to reach it for some "in order to" result: in order to beat the competition, have the stock price go up, or be the best, perhaps. Whatever the goal may be, it represents an outcome linked to some key element in your own, or your organization's, Winning Strategy. Ultimately, of course, it is linked to the Universal Human Paradigm's "in order to" component: to control life so it doesn't turn out the way it "shouldn't," and does turn out the way it "should."

Unlike a goal, a realm of possibility is not a place to "get to" from the present. It's an invented future to "come from" into the present. An invented future is unrelated to the past. It has no "in order to" component. It is not oriented to producing an end result, but to fulfilling a specified realm of possibility. In fact, if you fail, it doesn't matter. It's irrelevant. It still moves the possibility forward. (Consider how unconcerned Stephen, the Canadian entrepreneur-turned-politician, was about losing the election—or, for that matter, subsequent elections—as long as he continued to move forward the possibility: "Having politics provide the foundation for people to take responsibility for their lives." That is the game that he's playing, not winning elections or keeping constituents happy.)

You engage in the possibility for its own sake, simply because you said you would. You declare it a game worth playing, regardless of whether you succeed or fail. Indeed, it is unlikely that you will succeed, since the scope of your game is intentionally designed to probably be very large. Consider the ramifications of each of the games described earlier: re-inventing a profession, transforming a technological company's practices from top to bottom, reshaping the form of a nation's politics, altering how people are regarded in corporate cultures everywhere.

Even if you succeed in fulfilling the realm of your impossible future, life will still turn out the way it does. The game will not get you the "ninth dot." It will not make you whole, complete, and satisfied. When it's all over, and they put you into the ground and throw dirt on your face, you will *still* be flawed and broken, and you will *still* be as satisfied and as unsatisfied as you are.

So what will the game get you?

Playing the game, you will be free to live and work in an environment of unlimited possibility, rather than in an environment of inherited options. You will have the capacity to use your professional life as a leader who makes the impossible happen by engaging in actions of the highest risk. Re-inventing yourself into an impossible future doesn't alter how life turns out. It alters who you are *being* and what is available, while life turns out the way it does.

THE DESIGN OF *YOUR* GAME

You invent an "impossible future" by creating a specific realm of possibility and declaring that fulfilling this specific realm of possibility is the game you are now playing in life. You further declare that you are no longer playing "life" for survival, but for making the impossible happen.

In other words, you take on commitments that may occupy you for the rest of your life.

Everything, from here on in, depends on what you are committed to creating.

The rest of this chapter, and the two chapters that follow, present the three remaining transformations that constitute Executive Re-Invention, and allow you to invent your future, operating in the mode of transformation. The game you invent out of the transformation in *this* chapter is the vehicle from which you will develop the mastery you need as a leader who makes the impossible happen.

▪ First, make sure you are standing in the presence of the three declarations described in chapter 5, the declarations that together free you from the Universal Human Paradigm:

"I declare the possibility that what is possible is what I say is possible."

"I declare the possibility that who I am is the stand that I take."

"The stand I take is: 'There is no such thing as right or wrong and no fixed way that things should or shouldn't be.'"

▪ Now move to take your specific stand and put the game in motion.

Are you ready to complete the expressive?

"Who I am is the future of . . ."

Are you ready to complete the declaration of your "designated possibility"?

"I declare the possibility that . . ."

You will return to these speech acts when necessary, during the course of your game. This is because you must create the Re-Invention Paradigm anew each time you operate from it. Since this is an act of creation, it does not persist. It must be continually brought into existence. Just as you were born into the Universal Human Paradigm as part of your heritage, you will inevitably wake up each day into its game of survival (trying to control life so that it turns out the way it "should"), as played through your Winning Strategy. It may be appropriate, especially at the beginning, to reiterate your expressive and declaration, almost as a ritual—when you walk into your office for the first time each morning, for instance—to bring yourself back into the transformational mode, from which you are playing your game.

■ Finally, make the game real by making an initial bold promise—a promise that stretches you beyond the limits of your present reality. This is the first of many you will make during the course of the game. Some bold promises are five-year or ten-year promises; others are of a shorter duration.

The bold promise is the answer to the question *What is the focus of your attention in the game you are playing?*

During this game you will always be in action. You won't take action on fulfilling the declaration of possibility itself. The game is intentionally designed so that the realm of possibility you declared might not be fulfilled in your lifetime. It is so large in scope, and so sweeping, that it certainly can't be handled all in one gulp. It is handled by making a series of bold promises, and taking action, again and again, to fulfill them and make new promises, standing in the future that you have declared.

In chapter 7, we will learn more about the power that comes from making bold promises. For now, it's important to recognize that your initial promise is made without fear. You construct it before you know the obstacles you will encounter. There is no question that you will encounter obstacles. The obstacles are all an opportunity to develop your muscles of transforming an impossibility to a possibility and a possibility into a reality. The obstacles are part of the game.

You may remember Mike, the chief operating officer whose story was told in chapter 2. Mike had to give up his old Winning Strategy to accept the four business goals that his CEO had dictated: high-quality products, low prices, a great working environment, and no increased spending. In his mind, those goals acted like four different constraints on ways that the company could profitably "win."

Engaged in re-inventing himself, Mike came to a point where he could make a declaration: The chairman's four goals were not self-contradictory. It was possible to achieve all four.

But having declared that possibility the game, what bold promise could he design?

"I promise we will earn $60 million this year," he said,

"within the perimeters set by the CEO's four goals. We'll do it with high-quality products, low prices, a great working environment, and no increases in spending."

That language, with its boldness and specificity, verified Mike's commitment and put the promise right up in everyone's face, especially his CEO's. (More examples of bold promises will follow throughout the rest of this chapter and in chapter 7.)

■ Throughout all of these stages of designing the game, bear in mind five key design principles:

PRINCIPLE #1: ASSUME YOU WILL FAIL AT THIS GAME.

Ask yourself: Would I play this big new game of making the impossible happen even if I knew I would fail? If the answer is no, then don't play. Because you *might* fail. You cannot be certain of the outcome.

Remember: Your game will not turn out the way it "should."

You will wholeheartedly play to win. The only way you can play any game authentically is to play it to win. But you know, in advance, that it will turn out the way it does. Your survival will not depend on winning. A championship tennis player doesn't know if he or she will win each major tournament. Stephen did not know he would win his 1995 election; Joseph did not know, when he committed to re-invent the role of human resources, that it would lead to resigning his current position.

Like any champion, when you lose a tournament or a series—fail to deliver on your bold promise—you will continue to play, and you will continue to reap rewards from playing the game. Besides various material rewards (if you design the game's structure appropriately), these rewards will include the pleasure of playing at 100 percent, the thrill of not knowing what is going to happen next, and the enjoyment of spending your life engaged in something you are passionate about.

Leadership always includes knowledge of the possibility of failure. In this type of game, that provides a remarkable degree of confidence. If you operate with an acceptance of failure, you will remain confident no matter what happens during the course of the game.

You still play "to win," of course, as without that, there would be no game at all. And there is always a scoreboard—you kept the bold promise or you didn't. You check the scoreboard when the whistle blows on the bold promise. But the game never ends. You calculate the results and debrief on how you "played." What's important, because you said so, is that you move the possibility forward. That allows you to immerse yourself in the challenge and pleasure of your game, regardless of the impediments you encounter or the circumstances that you must include. They are all opportunities for building the muscles of making the impossible happen.

PRINCIPLE #2: SOMETHING WITHIN THE GAME HAS TO BE MORE IMPORTANT THAN SOMETHING ELSE.

Every game must have some guidelines to determine when it is finished, how it can be won, and what measurements will determine if you have won. Above all, the guidelines determine what aspects of the game are the most important—to you, and eventually to the other players.

Whoever invents the game determines the guidelines and measurements. They are created when the inventor declares them. And as with all games, people who enter make a tacit agreement to play by those guidelines. For this reason, everyone playing must have a clear understanding of what is expected within the game.

The point of devising guidelines is not to win. The point of devising guidelines is to give your game some definition and form of measurement that illuminates the characteristics that you have decided are important. In golf, for instance, people take a stick and hit a small white ball into a small hole. When the ball goes into the hole, that shot becomes important; it is more important than a shot where the ball didn't go into the hole. It is more important to hit the ball accurately than to hit it with high speed; it is more important to get it into the hole than to get it further from the starting point.

There is a rule in golf that whoever gets the lowest score wins. However, that rule is merely an expression of an important guideline designed into the game: that it is important to hit the ball into the hole with as few strokes as possible.

Guidelines in the games of business are often equally indirect. A factory manager sets a guideline about safety, not just for fear of safety lawsuits, but because a good safety environment attracts behavior that promotes morale, quality, and cohesiveness on the job. A retail store entrepreneur might set a guideline about store cleanliness, not to keep the merchandise clean, but because cleanliness reflects more fundamental values about attracting customers—the guidelines the store owner set as important for that game.

These are valuable guidelines, but they do not involve Re-Invention. They merely continue the business's existing game. And to produce the valuable, but not transformational, state of continuous improvement.

Players in sync with the game will automatically discard old games and old rules; they will often recognize that these rules are simply designed to produce more of the old organization's game. "We don't need to keep track of such-and-such anymore," they'll say. "It isn't important for what we're doing now."

That is why, if you are serious about Re-Invention, I suggest that you avoid thinking of the guidelines you design as "rules and regulations." Those words imply a standardized, rigid set of dictates, and they draw people back to playing the old games. When you are inventing a new game, there is no standard set of rules and regulations to follow. Every game is different and unique, as determined by the bold promises you create. For example, a multimedia production company might make a bold promise to produce a groundbreaking product in an impossibly short amount of time. Then, to turn that promise into reality, they might create conditions for fulfilling the promise, such as these: "The product must be seen as significant. No production or design delays are permitted. Only a six-week debugging period is permitted (compared to the six months we typically require), but the product must be released bug-free. We'll know we're successful if we garner great reviews and word of mouth. We'll also know we're successful if it makes our own hearts sing to boot up our prototypes."

This set of rules ensures that before a single line of programming code is written, or a frame of multimedia film is shot, the team will be thinking through what the product would need to have to make their hearts sing. Those features are more important than, for example, being available on a variety of different technical platforms. (Being on a variety of platforms would be nice, but it's not part of the guidelines they set.) The impossibly short deadline will force the team to invent ways that they can focus their attention, moving beyond the methods that the multimedia industry has produced in the past.

Obviously, anyone working on the product will follow the guidelines, but so will reviewers, store buyers, and customers. They will all judge the product according to the declaration the group made, back in the beginning, about what they had promised to produce. Customers, hearing the declaration about the product being groundbreaking, may indeed find ways to use it that the product makers never anticipated.

As you create measures, keep checking on whether this is truly a *bold* promise. If measures begin to reflect only what's "doable," you need to give the promise a grander scope, or in some way make it more difficult.

Since 1975, I have been participating with a group of people who created this possibility: "a world without hunger." I, along with several million other people to date, accepted the invitation to play in that game. The bold promise is "to end the persistence of hunger and starvation on the planet by the year 2000." The creators of the game declared that the measurement for determining if the game had been won would be the infant mortality rate. They set a level that very few countries had achieved, and declared that by the year 2000, if the infant mortality rate fell below that level in all countries, the bold promise to end the persistence of hunger and starvation on the planet would be fulfilled.

The people who developed the promise were not concerned with finding the right measure, or the best measure, but one that would establish the credibility of the game, and most important, would create a sense of urgency by confronting the specifics of the promise.

As I write this, the year 2000 is rapidly approaching, and the time frame for the bold promise is in sight. The promise will be fulfilled or not. The people who invented the "impossible future"—a world without hunger—and declared fulfilling that realm of possibility their "game worth playing" while life is turning out the way it does, will invent the next bold promise. This game has provided its executive leaders and key players—who since 1975 have been and are being "the end of the persistence of hunger"—the opportunity to spend their lives continuously engaged in making the impossible happen. For these leaders—many of whom have become, through their participation in the game, some of the best-known and most respected experts on hunger in the world—it is their full-time life game.

In addition, the game's other players include millions of people who play a support role of contributing time, money, and resources. And the players most certainly, and most importantly, include the hungry people throughout the world who courageously fight for the end of the persistence of starvation each day of their lives.

PRINCIPLE #3: THE GAME YOU DESIGN MUST BE CURRENTLY IMPOSSIBLE, AND YOU MUST BE PASSIONATE ABOUT ENGAGING IN IT.

Why have you chosen this particular game? Why have you designed it in this particular way?

The main criterion is your passion. Since you are the reason for this game, it depends on your full commitment to it. It doesn't have to be significant or noble, but it must be worth the whole of your life. You do not enter the game when you go to work, and you do not leave it when you go home. Nor do you sacrifice your private life to it. You design it in such a way that it encompasses both your work life and your private life, and makes both into aspects worth playing.

The game is now your opera. It becomes the context for everything else you do. You play it, in particular, every time you speak and listen. It replaces the survival approach to life, the approach dictated by your Winning Strategy.

When they are compelled by a Winning Strategy, people spend their entire lives doing what they think they "should" do. They become good at some job or skill, often by drifting into it, and then end up with so much invested in it that they stop thinking about other possibilities.

Wouldn't it be better to spend ten or twenty years in pursuit of something that impassions you? Something that gets you out of bed in the morning, something that invigorates you and drives you forward?

Not long ago, a senior executive from a Fortune 500 corporation attended my program. He was in charge of a huge division, to which he was extremely committed. He wanted to take it into a future that was nontraditional for this corporation. He was one of the company's youngest senior officers, and one of the best results producers, but his ideas met tremendous resistance from the chairman, the board, and the CEO. When he became clear about the game he wanted to play, he realized that it was not a game that anyone at his company was interested in playing. In fact, he saw that it was not appropriate for this organization to play the game at that particular time.

Prior to his discovery, he had not thought at all about leaving the company. His Winning Strategy was centered around loyalty and stability. Now he understood that, as long as he remained at this company, he would not be free to create the game he was most committed to playing. He also realized that the organization would best be served by having an executive in his position who was excited about the organization's declared game. Much to the astonishment of every one of his colleagues, he took early retirement. Within a year, he became the CEO of a smaller home improvement company, which allowed him to develop the game that was now at the center of his focus.

You are the only person who can determine which game is worth the focus of your life. You should not restrict it according to what anyone else thinks you should do, or by such arbitrary factors as your age, gender, physical attributes, or feasibility as a player. Although this game becomes the center of your *being*, it doesn't have to be a game that saves the world. It must be a game that compels you to enter into a realm that you currently think is not possible.

It should also be fun to play. You are playing to win, because that's the nature of the game. But you have chosen to try to win *this* game because it is intrinsically enjoyable. You bring the same attitude to the game that people bring to backyard football, soccer, or softball. You may play hard to win and devote hours to practice and strategy. But you don't seek any outcome from winning; there's no prize money or esteem involved. You play for the pleasure, the thrill, and the excitement of the game itself.

In addition to being driven by fun, you are also responsible. If you are designing a game to re-invent an organization, then you must take on solo responsibility for designing the game. The guidelines do not have to have the approval, or even the participative input, of anyone else in the organization, except the leader who is imposing the game onto his or her organization or division.

The reason is accountability. Someone must be held accountable for designing the parameters of the game. Only one person is ultimately accountable for the future. That is the person who says, "This is where we're going." If you are the leader in this game of Re-Invention, then that person is you.

That doesn't mean that you are right, and it doesn't mean that you aren't going to make mistakes. It simply means you are in charge of designing this future, whatever the outcome might be. You do not make your design decisions by following the consensus of other people's opinions. Anytime you have a place where the entire group says, "Well, we're all accountable," I promise you that no one is accountable. When Rosa Parks refused to give up her seat, she didn't consult with anyone else. There were people on the bus who were not in agreement with her. But she made her declaration and put herself in action. History was made as a result.

What role, then, do other people play?

An organizational game cannot be played alone. Everyone involved in the game must understand what is important. Each must make his or her own commitment to it. People will be responsible for their own activity as they play the game; everyone must understand the guidelines that will determine his or her play.

Commitment to a game is not like commitment to a vision. A corporate vision, in particular, is generally a static image. Once crafted—even if crafted through some sort of shared vision process—it remains as a statement, to which people feel they must pay lip service. It stands outside of the day-to-day life of the firm, like a lofty pronouncement of the way life at the firm "should" be—a way of life we know will never be attained.

A game, by contrast, is an environment in which people are immersed. Anyone can commit themselves to it, because they are not committing to an outcome or a statement about how life should be. They are committing to a set of guidelines for play today: "When I go to work, I will operate in such-and-such a way, shooting for such-and-such a result, with such-and-such a standard to tell me if I have succeeded." If the game is not won, people do not feel the sense of failure and cynicism that overtakes them when, inevitably, they do not realize their vision.

At one of my seminars, a woman executive from the telecommunications industry talked about the vision for the future that her organizational leaders had worked so hard to craft. Wouldn't that vision help them re-invent the future of the company? I asked her how many people worked there. She said there were five thousand managers and employees.

"And how many of those five thousand people can't wait to get out of bed in the morning because of their commitment to that vision?"

Her answer was about fifty.

"Fifty's pretty good," I said. "That's a lot better than most organizations." But it meant that 99 percent of the people in the company, who might be able to meet some of the organization's goals and objectives, were locked in by the vision that was supposed to have liberated them.

A vision is inevitably couched as a demand: a request that cannot be refused. A game, on the other hand, if it is designed effectively enough, offers fair rewards for innovative play. People can choose to play or not to play. If the game is designed for Re-Invention, it will reward people who re-invent themselves. Transformation in an organization won't take place until a leader is totally committed to designing and playing such a game that other people want to play, or finding other people who are passionate about playing the game the leader designed.

If you design a game within your organization, you will remain ultimately accountable for the game, but accountability will expand to include other people. If you have a large number of players, teams will most likely become involved, and they will become responsible for certain parts of the game plan. Within each team a specific person must be designated as being accountable, just as you are accountable for the overall plan. One person on each team must be accountable for making sure that the team is contributing to the possibility of the whole being fulfilled.

This accountable person is not necessarily in charge of the team. The accountable person is the voice of the team, making sure that communication is open and excellent, both within the team and with all other people inside and outside the organization. "Accountability," in this context, means making sure that everyone understands the guidelines. If this team has developed a game of its own within your game—if they are beginning to create their own guidelines, to move themselves toward a Re-Invention in their arena—then someone must be accountable for informing the rest of the players, so everyone is aware that the game has taken on a new dimension.

PRINCIPLE #4: THE BOLD PROMISES YOU MAKE SHOULD HAVE CHALLENGING TIME FRAMES.

Every promise has a beginning, a middle, and an end. At a certain point in time, the whistle blows, and that promise is either fulfilled or not. If it is, you create the next bold promise. If it isn't, you . . . create the next bold promise.

In the course of playing the game of fulfilling the realm of possibility you created, you will fulfill some bold promises and fail to fulfill others. Either way, engaging in these promises moves the possibility to a reality, regardless of the outcome. (I will discuss this more fully in chapter 7.)

Setting the time frame of your bold promise is very important. I often suggest that executives set a five-to-ten-year period for fulfilling a significant bold promise—enough time to move, but not so much time that you are tempted to slide into the old way of doing things.

Choosing an "impossible" time frame is an elegant, easy way to make a bold promise.

Yet the time frame also has to be the most empowering you can imagine. It must empower the game's players to make the game into a vehicle for Re-Invention. It must help them measure the progress of the game. It must allow time for the appearance of "breakdowns"—problems that produce opportunities for Re-Invention.

If you create a time frame of one year for a promise, it will engender one set of possibilities; a five-year time frame will produce a different set of possibilities, even with the same promise.

In chapter 5, I described how a business unit at "Fisher Chemical" made the declaration that " 'Fisher' is the household word in dye manufacturing." Claude, the accountable executive, initiated the game with a bold promise: "We will make Fisher a company that everyone else benchmarks, within one year."

He could have chosen any time frame; he considered five years and one year. Making Fisher a company everyone benchmarked in five years, he ultimately decided, was too conceivable. It could be done, within the existing capabilities of the group. They could accomplish it without having to re-invent themselves. However, fulfilling this promise within *one* year seemed to be outside the business unit's existing reality. The one-year time frame pushed at the limits of what the group could achieve.

Once Claude and his colleagues made their bold promise and chose the one-year time frame, they faced a different and more challenging set of obstacles than they had before. They moved immediately to identify impediments. The impossible nature of the time frame had, in effect, made them "die" before they joined into this battle. They all had confidence that they would be able to overcome their impediments and continue to identify and conquer additional obstacles as needed.

It is still not certain, as of this writing, whether Claude will fulfill the promise or not. Either way, he has been extremely pleased with the design. He claims, "We are transforming the business. Not only has it become very profitable, but it has a high cash generation, and I know that in five years, we will more than double the size of the present cash generation. It's really become a moneymaking machine. And not so long ago, I would have said that I was in a very secure, no-risk, but not very exciting business because of the segment in which we were selling. But now I say, 'Hold on, we're in the game.' And it's rapidly becoming very exciting."

PRINCIPLE #5: THE GAME MUST BE LARGE ENOUGH IN SCOPE TO HOLD ALL OF YOUR OTHER ACCOUNTABILITIES INSIDE IT.

This principle reminds you that you are creating a game of very large scope, in which every aspect of your game will fit.

Consider the case of Joseph, whose game was designed from the possibility of "people being acknowledged as the competitive advantage of organizations"—not just at his own company but everywhere. After completing Executive Re-Invention and stepping outside his Winning Strategy, he spent six months in his current organization, trying to make this redesign of human resources happen. During this time, he was playing a game from within the declaration of possibility that applied only to his existing company.

However, it gradually became clear that his organization was not interested in that game. They did not want a re-invented H.R. department; they wanted a traditional, personnel-oriented function. More important, he did not want his game's impact to be limited to one company. The game that compelled and excited him had to do with all of business culture.

Putting his job security at risk as part of this game, Joseph replaced himself with the kind of H.R. executive who was aligned with the actual intention of the organization. Then he went out on his own as an independent consultant. He began working with senior human resources executives at a variety of organizations, looking particularly for those who could echo his own commitment to a new future for the function. He became extremely successful at this, and was very excited to be spending all of his time fully engaged in fulfilling his "impossible" game. Soon, he was approached with the opportunity to head up the function at a company that was much larger than the company he had left, where the CEO was looking for exactly the same sort of future for human resources that Joseph championed.

Joseph hadn't anticipated returning to a corporate post, but he was pulled in that direction because it meshed with the future he was committed to. He recognized that if he wanted to move forward the possibility of "people being acknowledged as the competitive advantage of organizations" *most* quickly, he could take his most effective actions from a post at an influential company where he could design and implement H.R. of the future as a model for other organizations. He is now engaged in introducing the transformational mode into the company.

An invented future limited to one organization, one venue, or one region may well be too small in scope. Who you are *being*—the clearing you are for leadership—is *being* the future of your industry, organization, association, or country. Examples of clearings generated by executives with whom I have worked include:

"I declare: 'Who I am (being) is the future of education.' "

"I declare: 'Who I am (being) is the future of politics.' "

". . . the future of local government," "the future of organizations," "of my state," "of human resources," "of management," "of collaborative partnership," "of fitness," "of new technology in the entertainment industry."

The purpose of the game is to provide you with parameters for taking effective action; and the wider the scope, the broader your realm of possibility will be.

CHAPTER 7

BUILDING THE BRIDGE BETWEEN "POSSIBILITY" AND "REALITY"

Implementing your impossible future

DURING MY CAREER as an adviser to actors and entertainers, I had a client who had found himself stuck in his career. He was well known, and he got lots of parts—which to many actors would be an enviable sign of success in itself. But he was having trouble landing what he really wanted at the time: a lead role in a television series. He was continually considered for leads in situation comedies and adventure stories. In every audition, however, he would come down to the wire but wouldn't quite get the part.

I was perplexed, so I talked with a number of people for whom he had auditioned, and I sat in on several of the auditions themselves. The next time I met with him, I excitedly told him that we'd had a breakthrough, and I now knew what action he needed to take.

"Great!" said the actor. "What stopped them from casting me in a lead? What did they say?"

"You don't have any talent. You're not very good," I said. I explained that the casting agents and directors I'd talked to had been very clear with their perceptions of him. He was fine for smaller parts, because he was charming, graceful, athletic, good-looking, and naturally witty. He had shown, through a long career of small parts in films and TV, that he was reliable and hardworking. But the casting people considered him "lightweight"—he didn't have the talent, stature, and presence needed to carry a show. I told him all of this with a broad grin and then I concluded triumphantly: "Isn't this great?"

He scowled at me. "Tracy, give me a little more, please, than just 'Isn't this great?' You've just told me that the people who count in this business say that I have no talent. What am I supposed to do now?"

He went on to say that this news meant he would never work. His dreams and his career were over. He talked at length about how there was something wrong with *him*. After all his years of working and all the acting classes he had taken, he still hadn't acquired the talent he needed. Then he went on to talk about how there was something wrong with *them*—"It's the fault of the Hollywood system and the casting agents. Somebody who they think is a lightweight can never get a break!"

Finally, he calmed down and looked at me.

Well, that's one way you can look at it," I said. From the Universal Human Paradigm, all of his ranting made sense: Things "shouldn't" be that way, and there was clearly something wrong with him, the casting agents, and the whole entertainment industry. But then I suggested that we look at things from the Re-Invention Master Paradigm, in which everything is a conversation.

What actually had happened? Somewhere during the course of his career he had declared the possibility of his being a rich and famous celebrity. He had taken a stand, committing himself to that possibility of his future. And then he had made a *request*: "Will you accept this offer of my talent?" Each audition had been an offer of talent for a particular role.

The talent he was offering for lead roles was declined.

Everything else he had concluded—his dreams being over, his myopia about his career, the shortcomings of the industry—was an interpretation, including the agents' explanation for declining his offers (their statement that he had no talent).

Rather than having him continue to react to the interpretations, I suggested that he relate to "what had happened" from the future for which he had taken a stand—being a rich and famous celebrity—and take an action to move that possibility to a reality.

I recommended the following actions:

First, that he make a promise to himself: not to engage in any conversation about what was wrong with himself, the other people, or the industry.

Second, that he make a request of me: to support and help him in dealing with the situation from the perspective of the future.

Third, that he stand in his "impossible future" of being a rich and famous celebrity, and declare that talent (as the casting agents and directors defined it) *was not necessary*. He would be a rich and famous celebrity without *needing* the talent that he didn't have.

Fourth, that he not interpret the judgment of "lightweight" as something that shouldn't be, or as something he should fix, but that he accept it instead as something he could *perfect*.

At the time he made this declaration, the idea that this could happen for him occurred to him as impossible—even though he could find lots of evidence of rich and famous celebrities who had once been told they had no talent and who, in fact, even agreed they had no talent.

Standing in that possibility, he then made another promise to himself. It was a promise about his future actions. Henceforth, when he went into an audition, he would operate differently. He would no longer struggle to do the best acting job he could and offer his talent as the reason for giving him the part. He could now see that he didn't have the talent to pull that off.

Instead of offering them his talent, he would offer them his personality—his charm, his likability, everything that they had said made him too "lightweight."

He perfected his charm and likability during the months that followed. When he went back for auditions, he continued to make his new offer. It was accepted more frequently, and he got larger and more visible parts than he had ever gotten before. Within a year, he landed the lead in a series. The series ran for years. Then he went on to films, and the actor's name is now a household word.

He would agree that he still has no more acting talent than he ever had. But he does have talent for landing big roles, for projecting his attractive, likable personality, and for being a celebrity. Acquiring these new talents became possible by breaking the addictive cycle of interpretation.

THE ADDICTIVE CYCLE OF INTERPRETATION

If you have taken yourself through all the transformations of this book thus far, you are ready to play the game: to go into the world, or into your organization, and begin laying out parameters for yourself, milestones to live up to, and ways to bring other "players" onto the field.

Stop.

Before you can proceed, you must break an addiction. All human beings have this addiction; it is a component of the Universal Human Paradigm. You have had it all your life, but you probably never had any reason to care about it before. It never threatened your success or your goals. But now that you are playing the game of your life, trying to make the impossible happen, this addiction threatens to trip you up and block you at every move unless you can come to terms with it.

It is the *addiction to interpretation.*

Consider your response whenever something happens in the present. You automatically assign a meaning (an interpretation, explanation, or conclusion) based on the past.

You've already seen example after example in this book. If you did the exercise at the start of chapter 3—the story about walking into a workplace on your first day there, saying "Good morning," and having people stop, look at you, and go back to what they were doing—you assigned a meaning to that story based on your own experiences of the past. When asked, "What happened?" you offered a response like this: "They don't want me to be here," Or "They don't know what they're doing." Whatever your response was to that question, it represented your *interpretation* of what happened, not what happened.

After you wrote your response to the exercise, you turned the page and moved on. But in real life, when an event takes place that demands your response, you are always drawn to operate under the Universal Human Paradigm. Thus, you get "hooked." Your interpretations snag your emotions in some way, without your consciously realizing it. This happens even if you have a "game" developed and even if you are committed to the concept of Re-Invention.

Being "hooked" in this way, like any addiction, leads you to take actions that serve the addiction foremost. Those actions are always based on your interpretations from the past and serve your interpretations. Imagine that the scenario in that exercise actually did happen to you when you began a new job. Imagine that this occurred to you as "being snubbed." Imagine that you were addicted to your interpretation. When you went into work the next day, you would take some action based on your interpretation. You would *have* to react to what you said their action meant. The addiction, and its effect on who you were *being*, would not let you rest until you did. You might bring up the fact that you felt snubbed; you might act standoffish yourself; you might try to approach people individually; or you might make some demands based on what you thought you would need to endure the strange behavior that your interpretation told you was there.

Your own actions would then be interpreted by the other people in the room, and they would assign meaning to those new actions. Everyone would react under the Universal Human Paradigm and create new actions in response. Those new actions would lead, in turn, to new interpretations . . . and more new actions . . . and before an hour has gone by, perhaps, you and your colleagues at work would be enmeshed in a continual addictive cycle, always reinforcing itself, always based on what has occurred before, and thus always rooted in the past—an addiction from which it seems like there is no escape.

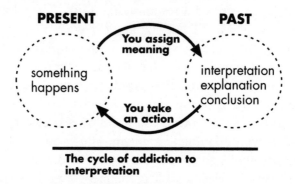

The cycle of addiction to interpretation

If left unchecked, this cycle will continue to pull you out of operating from the Re-Invention Paradigm. It will throw you back into a mode of operating from the Universal Human Paradigm and your Winning Strategy.

Suppose you have declared the possibility of a new kind of breakthrough product. You take a stand, committing yourself to making the product a success in a specified period of time. You produce a prototype and show it to investors and decision-makers. Then you receive the news that they will not fund your product.

What happened?

You made a request. (You offered your prototype.) The request was declined.

Here are some events that did *not* happen: The product was rejected. Something was wrong with the project. Something was wrong with the investors. Something was wrong with the business environment. Those are all interpretations you made up.

Once you react to those interpretations, you are hooked into an addictive cycle. Using your Winning Strategy, you frantically try to "fix" the product, the investor relationships, or the environmental trends, and then try to make sense of the "results" of those efforts. Additionally, you will then be thoroughly anchored in the past, no longer operating from what you declare possible but likely to base your decisions on what market research, investors' opinions, or your own company's history tells you is possible.

As soon as you are pulled into the cycle of interpretation, you are no longer standing in the future. Your actions are no longer shaped by the declared possibility that led you to develop the product in the first place.

Suppose that someone you respect came to you with "bad news"—the equivalent in your business arena of the message "you have no talent" in the acting arena. "The products this company produces are not very good." Or "Your reputation is fairly low in this business." Or "You really don't have the skills to make that engineering breakthrough."

In making the impossible happen, and operating from the Universal Human Paradigm, you interpret such bad news— analyze its validity and what it means—then take an action shaped by your Winning Strategy to fix, correct, or improve what you have determined is wrong with "you, them, or it." Depending on your Winning Strategy, you might try to get another opinion: "Maybe the bad news hasn't really taken place." You might procrastinate dealing with it, waiting until a better day. Or, like the actor in that story, you might be tempted to move into resignation and despair. Or you might try harder, and more forcefully, to overcome what you see as "obstacles."

By contrast, in the mode of transformation, operating from the Re-Invention Master Paradigm, you consciously break the addictive cycle by recognizing that "bad news" never happened. Nor did "good news" happen. They are both interpretations about what happened. They are meanings you gave to what happened, meanings derived from the past.

Transformation always begins by breaking the addictive cycle of interpretation and distinguishing what happened from your interpretations about what happened.

What did happen? Someone has made some form of a request or promise. In the "bad news" example, what happened is someone offered you (an offer is a form of a request) their assessment of your company's products, your reputation, and your skills. If you don't react—there's something wrong with me, them, or it—you might simply respond by asking if they have any specific request of you regarding the company's products, your reputation, or your skills. If not, they clearly just wanted to "speak their mind—their point of view," and this needs no response other than perhaps social politeness. If they do have a request, you can respond appropriately.

In the Re-Invention Paradigm, what happens—whether generated by you or someone else—is always and only a conversation: always and only a request or a promise.

THE BRIDGE FROM POSSIBILITY TO REALITY IS A CONVERSATION FOR ACTION

The next two transformations of Executive Re-Invention are designed to break the addictive cycle by transforming the way that "action" occurs to you. Your vehicle, once again, is conversation. In the same way that in chapter 5 you moved an "impossibility" to a "possibility" with the speech act of "declaration," you now move a "possibility" to a "reality" with two new speech acts: requests and promises. Together, they constitute the elements of a conversation for action.

Gradually, the concept of "action" will shift for you, so that it no longer means a series of activities to accomplish. It will now mean "a series of committed requests and promises."

REQUESTS: QUERIES THAT GENERATE COMMITMENT

Both requests and promises bring forth the future as a commitment. When you make a request, you generate something in the future as a possible commitment. And you seek a committed response from a person who has the authority to deliver on that commitment.

Your purpose in making a request is to move a specific possibility forward to a reality. You give a name to that possibility and invite one or more people to commit themselves to it, in some form.

Consider a simple request such as: "I request that we meet for lunch on Friday at noon." Even that request brings forth the possibility of a commitment in the future, to a lunch meeting. Making the request *in itself* is as much of an action as stepping over the threshold of the restaurant. Indeed, in terms of the effect it has on the future, making the request is probably a more significant action—whether the request is granted or not.

The power of a request stems in large part from the fact that a request isn't a representation of an action but is, in fact, an action in itself. Most speaking is representational. When you say, for example, "Here is a table," a table does not come out of your mouth. A word that represents a table comes out of your mouth. But when you say, "I request that we meet for lunch on Friday at noon," a request—not a representation of a request—actually comes out of your mouth. At the moment the request is made, it brings forth the possibility of an action in the future.

When you make a request, you are not trying to persuade, convince, or enroll others into doing what you want them to do. You are taking an action to move a declared possibility to a reality. You add velocity in moving the action forward by making requests and not reacting to the responses.

Suppose you request six people to join you in your game, and present to them the possibility that you see, letting them know your conditions for joining your team—what is expected of them to produce, how much time it will take, what resistance they can expect to meet. Suppose five of those people decline. You are in a better position to move the action forward, by continuing to move on—presenting the possibility to new people and making your requests of them—rather than going back and trying to convince any of the decliners to change their minds, pressing them to think about it differently or bargaining with them. Even if you are successful in convincing them, the one person who willingly accepted is going to be far more powerful in moving action forward than the other five whom you talked or pressured into acceptance.

What allows people to authentically accept a request? The assurance that they have the authentic opportunity to decline. In reality, anyone can always decline any request. Some kinds of requests, such as demands or requirements, have serious consequences when they are declined. Others, like invitations, only have the consequence of a lost opportunity when declined. It is important to distinguish between these forms and to recognize the power inherent in the ability to say no to any of them.

With the freedom to decline a request, both people are empowered. If you know that others can authentically say no to you, you feel much more comfortable making requests of them, and you also feel free to make many and/or unreasonable requests of them. Conversely, when they accept, you know they really own their acceptance because they have the freedom to decline.

Once you integrate into your way of *being* the knowledge that anyone can say no, it will begin to change you. You will begin to ask for more, which can be a huge departure from your previous way of operating. *Executives, in particular, are often hampered by the false notion that the less they ask for, the more powerful they are.* They think of making a request as a plea for help rather than the powerful tool that it is.

If you don't think you need to make requests, if you don't need to ask anybody for anything, you are playing a very small game.

You are also playing a small game if you only make the requests you think will be accepted, rather than what you actually want or need.

In business, requests might include:

"I request that you commit now to buying this merchandise."

"I request that you endorse this initiative with your signature today."

"I request that you provide training to the customer service representatives in my department, at no extra charge, within the next two weeks."

"I request that you be responsible for accomplishing this task by the fifteenth of next month."

And many others. There are an infinite number of possible requests.

One common type of request is an *offer*, in which you present something and request that someone accept it on the terms you propose. You might offer someone your time, your support, your proposal, your idea, your product, your candidacy for their job, your deal, your service, or your help. In each case, the act of making the request invokes commitment from the other person and makes it clearer what the future "designated possibility" will require.

A request always involves four elements:

■ *A committed speaker.* If you are making the request, it must come from a committed stand. You must be extremely clear about the commitment, because it shapes the way the request is worded, which in turn affects the ability of the listener to respond effectively. You shortchange your own power if your request does not reflect your own commitment.

A senior marketing manager named Diane made a request to the vice-president for training in her company. She was frustrated because she thought the salespeople in her company were only interested in their bonuses. Her commitment was strong, she said: to find better ways to delight customers. She wanted the salespeople to focus on customer service, even after a sale was completed. So she requested extra training in customer service.

The training director, who had authority in this area, declined her request. He said it was too expensive. At the same time, he asked Diane to suggest some additional alternatives.

Diane took two weeks to investigate options and write a reply. In her mind, however, this was an exercise in going through the motions to appease him. No other solution was possible—only a massive training effort.

At first, nothing got accomplished toward Diane's stated goal, because she had not operated from a clear commitment. Her commitment to customer service was muddled, because she was also committed to her preferred method for improving it: training. When she became aware of those conflicting commitments, she requested a meeting with the vice-president for training, to discuss customer service. What would move them forward in that area? What could they align on to accomplish that aim?

Instead of adversaries, the request made them into collaborators, starting with the more precisely articulated, more fundamental commitment that Diane's second request came from.

■ *A committed listener.* The listener must be someone who can do something about the request. If the person you are speaking to does not have the authority to grant your request, then you are not operating from a place that will move you to the future.

A writer named Robert spent years making unfulfilled requests trying to get a teaching post at a university near where he lived. Robert was qualified, and he had always relied on the technique (part of his Winning Strategy) of asking for referrals from people whom he met. Once before, he had landed a terrific teaching job, at a university far away, through personal acquaintances, and the approach made more sense to him than what he called "going in through the front door"—calling on the head of the appropriate department cold.

He had a well-articulated request that made it easy to say yes. But he continually made it to the wrong people—to faculty members in the wrong department, or to faculty members who did not have the authority to create a new adjunct teaching post, and did not feel capable of taking his case to the people with authority. Ultimately, Robert's request could not be granted until he decided he was committed enough to go in through the front door, to find the person with commitment and authority, and make the request directly.

■ *A specific set of conditions.* Even a simple request like "Meet me for lunch at three o'clock on Friday" carries a full set of specific conditions. Both parties must be able to get to the restaurant. A certain type of dress will be appropriate. Lunch may require two or more hours, or it may be constrained to thirty minutes. All of these conditions are either explicitly or implicitly contained in the request. If they are imprecise or ambiguous, then the request will be ineffective.

■ *A deadline or time limit.* At least one of these conditions must involve the time element. This must be specific: not just "by next week" or "as soon as you can," but "by 4 pm Friday of next week." The listener must know exactly how much time there is to fill the request, and the speaker must know the point in time at which he or she can clearly determine whether the request has been fulfilled.

If the requests do not contain all these requirements, then they do not bring forth a committed response, and the action does not move forward. Unless all of the conditions are clear, there is no sure way to determine if the requests have been fulfilled or not.

How many times have you requested something of someone—a report, for example—and received something back that did not in any way fulfill what you had in mind? Somewhere between your request and that person's fulfillment, some of the conditions were not met as you had intended them. Requests with clearly worded, specific conditions ensure that the listener is, in fact, responding to the same request that the speaker intends to make.

"WHAT ARE YOU ASKING FOR?"

As the speaker making a request, it is your responsibility to make sure that the listener can hear the possibility in your requests and offers. It is your responsibility to structure the conversation so that the listener accepts or declines the request that is actually being offered or requested, rather than declining or accepting a request that he or she *thought* was being offered, or a request that was not even presented.

Thus, unless you are clear about what you want and what you don't want, the listener cannot give a committed response. Make sure your request is unambiguous. With ambiguity, neither you nor anyone else can tell what is really happening. You and your listener can only draw conclusion after conclusion without being sure of the facts.

A lot of work goes into clarifying your requests. The more precise and sharply phrased your request is, the greater chance it has of being heard correctly. Consider the different flavors of each of these ways of saying "I request," and the different possibilities each of them creates:

"I beg of you." This phrase connotes charity and entreaty. To "beg" literally means to ask with earnestness or to ask as a charity. You "beg" for help. Thus, you wouldn't say, "I beg of you," to people you know casually. It presumes that the listener already has a commitment to you.

"I beseech" is even stronger; it suggests an earnest or urgent request, to someone whom you may not know well. ("Implore" carries the same flavor.) When you beseech people, you do so from the stand of a common principle that you believe (or hope) you share with them.

"I urge" is equally strong, but it carries the connotation that you are making the request, in part, for the other person's own good.

"I ask that you." This word connotes *lack* of flavor, except perhaps for a desire for information. As the *American Heritage Dictionary of the English Language* points out, "ask" is the most neutral word you can use in making a request; It can stand in for many other "request" words. That makes it useful when you want to avoid weightiness or too much specificity in making your request. (Consider the difference between "I ask you to provide me with an advanced copy of your review" and "I beg," "I invite," or "I demand" that you provide me with an advanced copy of your review.)

"May I inquire" (for instance, "May I inquire what your background is") often suggests a request for information, but when you "make an inquiry" it goes deeper. An inquiry is a request for the fundamental roots of information: the experience, attitudes, or reasoning that have led someone to make an assertion, or the full history and ramifications of a situation.

"I insist." Insistence is also a request, in which (as the speaker) you make it clear that you will refuse to yield if the request is declined. This ups the ante of the request. "I demand" is even stronger, and "I order" is a request made from a position of authority. The language of demand implies that declining the request will have grave consequences for the listener. If those consequences are not enforceable, then the demand is called "empty."

When you say "I invite," you are implicitly requesting someone's participation. It is always a request for establishing a relationship, even if only a brief one.

"I admonish" is a negative request. You admonish someone to request that they remember a responsibility or danger that they would otherwise forget.

To "warn" is stronger. In effect, you are saying, "I request that you desist, for your own good." Warnings of something that might happen are requests; warnings of something that *you* might do are promises.

"I forbid" or "I prohibit," like "I demand," implies that the speaker has power to enforce the request, or that there will be serious consequences in declining the request.

"I offer." This is one of the most significant and most common forms of requests. When you make an offer, you present something for acceptance or rejection. (The word derives from the Latin *ob ferre*, meaning "to bring something to someone.") You implicitly ask, "Will you accept my offer?" If it is not accepted, that doesn't mean the offer is "wrong"; it means that you have learned that this offering will not be accepted by this listener at this time.

Most people are not used to thinking so seriously about the *form* of what they say. Therefore, they come off as "bad communicators" or reluctant or vague, simply because they haven't put the time and effort into thinking through exactly what they are trying to request, and how to word the request.

Ask yourself what you really want. Many times, people are so sure they can't have what they want that they don't ask for what they want.

George, a junior executive in charge of pricing in a retail establishment, declared the possibility of building a flexible pricing system, coordinated throughout the chain, in a way that no one had ever thought feasible in the past. He had requested, and been granted, the opportunity to be accountable for this. One of the missing components needed to fulfill this possibility was to be in direct communication with all of the people involved in pricing, both in stores and in purchasing, around the world.

But George felt he had a serious problem with Lee, his boss. George had tried repeatedly, always in vain, to get Lee to change the conditions of his job, so that he could move the new system forward.

When he talked about his story, George could not describe, except in the vaguest terms, what he really wanted from Lee. First, he said he wanted Lee "to be involved." Then he wanted Lee to "get out of micromanaging." Then he said he wished Lee would "have a dialogue with me."

If you think each of those requests sounds like incomprehensible jargon, then you agree with George. He knew he wasn't being clear. But it took him many renditions, peeling back each layer of what he *thought* he wanted, before he was finally able to bring himself to articulate what he really wanted from Lee.

"I'd like to have the accountability and the responsibility that my job description calls for."

And when he put *that* into even plainer English, it turned out that George wanted Lee to give him the final word in his specified area (pricing). When other executives came to Lee with a pricing question, George wanted Lee to refer them to him. He wanted Lee to refrain from getting involved in pricing questions, except at George's request. In effect, he wanted Lee to delegate not just the formal "pricing" title but the informal position and all the authority that went with it.

But Lee had no way of knowing what George wanted, without a precise request.

And when George finally articulated the request, in a conversation with me, it felt a little scary to him, because it put him out on a limb: "I want to urge Lee to declare that I am fully accountable for managing the delivery of profitability. I would design and manage the strategy, and he would endorse it." He paused, and then said, "But this is such a big request that I don't know if it's fair for me to request it of him."

"George, at this point," I said, "we're only talking about what *you* want. Have you ever said any of those things directly to him?"

"Yes, but I don't know that I've said it clearly."

"Have you ever made those requests of him in the specific way you just did?"

"No."

As part of his job *and* his commitment to re-inventing the organization, George is responsible for making the request clearly, in a way that lets his boss understand what is being asked for and what is being offered.

Lee's job is to accept or decline the request, based on whatever grounds are important to Lee. George can try to second-guess Lee's criteria for accepting or declining the request, but those guesses will always be interpretations. In the end, the responsibility for making that judgment remains with Lee.

Yet George must make the request, not knowing how Lee will respond, risking his security, his relationship with Lee, and possibly his job. That's the only way the conversation can move toward George's "designated possibility." There is only one way that George can avoid the risk, and that is to avoid making the request in the first place—in which case George has made it clear that avoiding risk is more important that moving toward his "impossible future."

In the Re-Invention Master Paradigm, you design your conversation to ensure that your requests will be heard. You can do this only when you realize that you have no control over the outcome. No matter how well you phrase your request, it may be denied. If it is denied, that will be a denial of your request. You will move from there to making another request.

In fact, either way, you will move on from there to make more requests and promises. For instance, suppose Lee accepted George's request. That would only be the beginning. Other requests and promises had to follow: How would George be held accountable? What promise would he make regarding pricing in the future? What role would Lee play? How would they communicate with each other about details? What time frames would George operate within?

Timing is vital in making a request. If you move into action too soon, there will not be enough support for possibility because the speaker and the listener will not be connected to the same commitment. There must be enough background conversation to ensure that both parties are willing to play in the same game.

Thus, for example, in my conversation with George, I next asked him, "What would be important for you to say about your position before making your request?"

"I think I need to clearly express to Lee that I am committed to his priorities for the company."

"But what else haven't you done?"

"I haven't made my requests in a way that links back to his overarching strategy for the company, so he knows that we're playing the same game."

Don't you think it would be extremely powerful if you told him that?" I asked. George had never created a background of relatedness between the commitment that generated his request—the commitment to an innovative pricing system and Lee's commitment for the organization to lead the industry in communications technology. He had never made it clear what he brought, along with his request, that would give Lee a reason to grant it.

At first, George hesitated to spell this out, because he thought it might come across as patronizing. He felt that he and his boss already understood each other. Often, when people have been working together for periods of time, they assume they don't have to create a background from which their commitments are related. They can depend on the history of their relationship. However, the history of their relationship is no doubt based upon interpretations (of each other and of events that have happened) and will inevitably draw them back to the addictive cycles and to their Winning Strategy.

Thus, before making a request, you must create a background of relatedness that supports the possibility. If George goes to Lee, his vice-president, and starts making requests without a background of relatedness—without connecting to Lee's commitment—it is likely that Lee won't be able to hear anything George is saying. Lee will hear only his interpretations of what George has said in the past, and not the possibility that George is offering.

A background of relatedness is rooted in the shared commitment that all the principal players have for the work you conduct together. If you are approaching the board of directors of your organization with a request to invest in reshaping of your own department, a powerful place to begin is to make it clear how your request is specifically related to moving your mutual commitment forward.

To create a background of relatedness, you begin by *"listening for"* that mutual commitment. Whenever two people work together, each party makes constant statements, implicit and explicit, about what is important to them. Those statements might take the form of assertions or declarations, requests and promises, or responses to your requests and promises. Each tells you something. You listen for those statements in the actions of the other person, find the aspects that resonate with your own commitment, and then build those into your request. You might say something like, "I'm here to speak to you about the future I see for this department. I am starting from the position that my department must be, will be, and is a significant conduit by which the organization accomplishes its mission for the next five years." When you say that, the board members should hear themselves speaking in your statement. If they don't, then you have not spoken from the background of relatedness that you share.

People assume that they don't have to create the background of relatedness; that it will automatically be there. The Universal Human Paradigm tells us, after all, that they "should already know how committed I am, and I shouldn't have to tell them." But all they have as a background so far is their interpretations of what you have said and done to date. If you don't create a background of relatedness, you will be limited to that background. From that context, you may feel as George did about Lee—that you can never get your request across and understood.

Creating a background of relatedness is one example of how each conversation in the Re-Invention Paradigm is an act of creation, with both players starting at zero. The two players can only create a new context by articulating it freshly—being specific about the language they use and making sure that important features of that background are spelled out. George may back up his request with specific assertions that operating this way, with his own full accountability, will benefit not only himself but Lee, the other employees, and the whole department. He might need to buttress the request with a promise that makes his commitment clear to Lee. "Lee, I recognize what you need for someone to fulfill this position completely," he might say. "Within six months, I promise to meet whatever specific criteria you establish—or I will return to my old role."

Keep complaints out of your request. The re-invented future holds no space for complaints. Complaints create a clearing for no possibility. They focus on what you think "should" be happening, with no responsibility for what actually is happening. If a situation arises in which you would normally complain, discover what needs to happen, go to the person who can do something about the situation, and make a request—which will either be accepted or declined.

If your request is accepted, move the action forward with more requests and promises, as they seem to be called for. Legitimate requests and promises are never seen as greedy, because people can see that they're being made in the service of the "impossible future," which is presumably designed to benefit the organization as a whole. To discover the velocity with which you are moving any "designated possibility" forward to a reality, look at the number of conversations for action you are engaged in.

Specifically, how many requests and promises have you made in that area to date? Half a dozen? A dozen? Several dozen? How many more can you think of and make? Have you considered sending a request to hundreds of people via E-mail or voice mail? Have you called all those you know in your personal network of support to share the possibility you declare and invite them to look for any opportunity that they see to contribute? The more requests and promises that you are engaged in, the faster the possibility becomes a reality.

Obviously, if the boss says yes, the context of George's position in the organization will change completely. But what if Lee declines his request?

When They Say No

If you are clear about what you want to happen and what you are requesting and promising, then simply by making the request you shift the context in which you are operating. Strange as this may seem, this is true even if the request is declined.

It doesn't matter whether requests are accepted or declined. It doesn't matter if they are declined with vehemence. A clearly worded request always moves things forward, even when it is declined. Simply by making the request, particularly if it is a well-thought-out request, you have put yourself in a better context from which to raise other requests, or make other promises, related to your "designated possibility."

Consider George's current ambiguous, uncomfortable relationship with Lee. If George can't make his request clear, that relationship will remain uncomfortable. He might have powerful, wonderful conversations with Lee about unrelated matters, but the next time some event brings forth the pricing authority issue again, George and Lee will be faced with the same ambiguity.

With a clear request, the relationship between George and Lee is re-invented. The context and conversation change, and the level of understanding deepens. This is true whether Lee accepts the request or declines it.

The decline of a request is, in fact, a committed action. *Declines move action forward as powerfully as acceptances if they do not become embroiled in interpretations.* Declines bring hidden issues to the surface. If you are not fixated on the outcome of someone saying yes, the awareness of these hidden issues will help you to play the game of making the impossible happen.

Suppose Lee says no to George's request. Then suppose that George does *not* get pulled back into the cycle of interpretation, where his next action will come from the past. He does *not* interpret Lee's no to mean something. Instead, he returns to the original stand he took, the possibility he declared of building a new worldwide pricing system, the possibility that generated his original request. Standing in that possibility, George generates a new request or promise. He might request that Lee tell him what the conditions would be for accepting his request. Lee might respond by telling him what those conditions are. Then George might promise to fulfill those conditions. Or Lee might respond by saying, "I'll have to think about it." Then George can respond by requesting the opportunity to check back with Lee in a couple of weeks.

Or Lee might respond that, under no conditions will George's request be accepted. This is important information. If you are in a similar situation, this declination tells you not to waste time going in that direction. Instead, return to the original declaration, your "designated possibility," and make another request or promise in another direction.

It's important to remember that you have made a commitment to fulfill the possibility, not to fulfill the possibility "in a certain way" or "the way you want to." George's request for full accountability was one possible route for dealing with something that was missing: being in close relationship with all of the people in the pricing area. Returning to his original possibility, George now looks to go in another direction to accomplish that end. If you find out that your requests are continuously declined, and you are frequently told that there are no conditions under which they will be accepted, that always moves you forward toward your commitment. It brings to the surface the lack of alignment between your interests and commitment and the interests and commitments of the people you are working with. Both of you would be served by having a conversation about that and taking actions—probably parting company—that would forward each of your commitments, rather than continuing to work together.

Manipulating people to say yes when the acquiescence is not sincere, well informed, or made in response to a clear request does you no good at all. A yes that you have earned through some deceit or finesse about your real intentions does not let you take the action implicit in your request. In fact, it restricts your freedom to access all the possibilities. Henceforth, you will not be able to act in any way that might threaten the lie you told, in effect, to get your manipulated yes.

A city dweller named James learned the problem of the manipulation approach when he wanted to build a rooftop garden on his apartment building. He knew that gardens were not permitted, but he requested that an exception be made. He claimed he wanted to build the roof garden to enhance the living environment for himself and his neighbors.

James tried to make the request more palatable by politicking. Before he approached the planning board, he requested the help of one of his neighbors, hoping to garner support. But the politicking backfired. A request requires a committed listener, someone who can do something about the request. James's neighbor had no power to approve it and was, it turned out, the opposite of committed. James only succeeded in getting his neighbor entangled prematurely. Then not only did he have to deal with the planning board, but he also had to deal with his neighbor's vehement opposition.

Ultimately, James's plans were never approved. His actions to manipulate and "finesse" the results wasted everyone's time and didn't help him progress on his path. He aggravated himself and alienated his neighbors. He would have been better off being clear about what he wanted—in part because that clarity would have helped him see the limits of his own request.

Remember, in order to be a committed speaker, a person has to be dedicated to the original "designated possibility"—in James's case, to enhance his living environment. James was more committed to being right about the way that he wanted to enhance his living conditions (specifically, to build a roof garden) than to fulfilling the possibility that he said he stood for. Thus, James became hooked in a game of "I want things to work out the way they should—my way." He is now playing a game of "How can I get them to give in?" He is no longer operating from the future or any declaration of possibility.

Suppose, instead, James had made a commitment to live in a better environment? The roof garden would be only one route, not *the* route or the "right" route. Once he found his first plans thoroughly blocked, he would be able to see that as a starting point from which to reconsider his whole game.

Under the Re-Invention Paradigm, you want to know as quickly as possible if you are going to be declined. Thus, James's first question to the planning board might have been: "Under what condition, if any, can I receive approval to build the roof garden?"

If he had gone to the planning board first, he might have discovered the worst-case scenario: His plan would not be accepted. With this knowledge he could test his commitment to live in a better environment and see what other possibilities he could declare. For instance, he might have made the declaration that he wanted to find a new place to live.

James might have been able to succeed at getting a roof garden through manipulation. Eventually, he might have been able to delude, threaten, cajole, bribe, or otherwise put pressure on the board. If he did, he would have been operating out of his strategy to get people to do things his way; he would not have been operating out of his commitment. His achievement would have represented the successful implementation of an option, rather than participating in a game of limitless possibilities. The roof garden would have become another sort of game, in which winning took precedence over all other concerns—including James's desire to build the kind of life he most wanted.

PROMISES, *BOLD* PROMISES

A promise is the second speech act in a conversation for action. Like a request, a promise is an action that brings forth a future as a commitment and moves the possibility forward to a reality. *It's important to remember that only requests and promises move possibilities to a reality.*

When you make a promise, you bring forth a particular future, as a commitment. You always make a promise to a committed listener, even if that committed listener is only yourself.

Consider a simple promise such as: "I promise to meet you in the restaurant at the park on Friday at noon." Even that promise brings forth a commitment in the future, of your presence at the appointed time and place.

As with making a request, making the promise "I commit to be there" is as much an action as seating yourself in the waiting area of the restaurant. Once again, a promise is not a "representational" speech act. When you say the words "I commit," a commitment comes out of your mouth. You are not *talking* about the action of committing. You are acting. You are committing. And, just as requests are significant whether they are accepted or declined, making a promise is a significant action, whether the promise is accepted or not.

In business, promises might include:

> "I promise one case of our product at your company's standard price will arrive tomorrow morning at ten."
>
> "I promise to buy all of the components you can deliver by the end of this quarter at a 10 percent discount of our normal price."
>
> "I promise to invest 50 percent of my department's entire budget in this research endeavor for one full year, beginning July 1."
>
> "I promise to vote against this measure and to do everything in my power to defeat it, beginning now."
>
> "If I am not satisfied by the end of the month with the outcome of this project, I will fire you at that time."

And many others. There are an infinite number of possible promises. Note that each has a very specific time commitment; as with requests, the conditions of a promise should be explicit.

Note also that the last two examples are threats. A threat is a form of a promise.

In each case, and in every other case, the act of making the promise invokes your commitment and makes it clearer what the future "designated possibility" will require.

In making the impossible happen, action is always and only a speech act, and always and only a request or promise.

In moving a possibility to a reality, there is no set order as to which comes first—a promise or a request. However, I recommend beginning with a bold promise, because it creates urgency and makes fulfilling the possibility an immediate priority.

The boldness of the promise is important. A bold promise is a promise that you do not know how to fulfill and that, predictably, you could not fulfill within the specified time frame. Bold promises dramatically shorten the time it takes for a possibility to become a reality.

Whom would you prefer to work with? A partner who cautiously made sure that every promise he or she made could be fulfilled easily? Who never made a commitment to anything significant? Or would you prefer a partner who made big, monumentally exciting promises? Who, despite a full commitment to all of them, never quite managed to bring them all to pass, but who, even when promises were not kept, still produced results way beyond the results produced by the cautious, feasible, reliable promises?

Wouldn't working with the second partner, the one with the monumental promises, be a far more exhilarating way to live? Wouldn't working with the second partner provide you with far stronger resources for making *your* "designated possibility" happen?

If you are keeping all your promises, then your promises aren't big enough. They can only produce results that you know ahead of time you can produce. If you are not making promises that are bigger than you can keep, I'll wager that you are bored.

When you make a bold promise, you are also agreeing to stay in communication about your progress. You have made yourself accountable to the person who is receiving your promise.

I've told the story of Mike, the retail chief operating officer who promised his CEO that he would deliver $60 million in earnings. When he made that promise, Mike realized that $27 million would be a predictable amount to promise, one he could easily deliver. Forty-five million was a stretch, but he could do it. But he promised $60 million. Taking on such a promise would definitely require him to make the impossible happen.

However, before he made the promise, he had to create the possibility from which he made it. He had to declare that it was possible to deliver $60 million, and he had to request accountability for himself. Additionally, he put a time frame on the promise. And he made additional requests. His promise was not conditional on them, but they helped support him in fulfilling his promise. He backed his declaration up by laying out some of his plan.

"I know the numbers don't indicate that $60 million is possible," he said, "and that $45 million is as far as we can stretch, but I think there's an opportunity here for us to forward our common commitment of being the retail store of the future. I plan to enroll each of the store managers in this venture and get each of them working from a place of being extraordinary within the next six months. I request your support when we encounter the problems that will inevitably arise as we proceed forward."

This was the foundation of his conversation for creating a background of relatedness—a necessary part of the support for his promise.

I recommend that you include as many supports as you can think of when you are designing the conversation in which you make your promise. Additionally, it is important to be aware of the other person's listening. How would Mike's chairman hear him? Considering in advance how your words will be received helps to design the conversation in the most effective manner. For example, if Mike had delivered on an "impossible" promise before, reminding the chairman of that fact would be a key part of the support. Similarly, if Mike believed that the chairman considered him a poor performer in the past, then his background support would need to include reasons why Mike's track record would not be a debilitating factor this time.

The promise is the tool you use to put your words in action. If you promise something, you are saying that you will do everything you need to do to live into your promise. All that counts is your word.

Thus, as with requests, the way you phrase a promise is critical. Different forms of phrasing a promise convey different nuances. Each form has its own flavor and ramifications. Each represents a different style of commitment. For example:

"I accept" is a promise to receive something that has been offered to you, or a promise to fulfill a request that has been made to you.

"I pledge" or "I vow" is a solemn, binding promise to do

something, give something, or refrain from doing something. You would never make a pledge or vow casually; the words imply a strong degree of earnestness and commitment.

"If you do X, then I will Y." A threat is a promise to inflict harm or injury. When you threaten someone, you are making a grave, considerable promise. A serious threat can be a powerful tool within the Re-Invention Paradigm if it comes from the context of your "designated possibility." For example, "If your product does not fulfill our new needs, then you can count on us not to renew our contract."

"I contract" or "I agree." These words are used to make mutual promises, in which your promise and your listener's promise are contingent upon each other. You may want to be explicit about what happens when one party breaks their promise. Is the other party still responsible to fulfill theirs?

"I guarantee." In this very powerful form of a promise, you assume responsibility for the results. If the results do not live up to the conditions you set, then you offer to set them right.

"I swear." Often attached to a declaration, this word invokes a promise that the declaration is true.

"I concede." Here you have promised to acknowledge or grant status to something you have been reluctant to admit in the past.

"I authorize." In this form of a promise, you give permission for the listener to act in an arena where you have authority. For instance, a city agency can authorize your company to construct a building. "I permit" serves a similar purpose in less formal circumstances.

AFTER A PROMISE IS MADE

When you make a promise, there are three possible outcomes.

■ You can keep it—that is, you can fulfill the conditions of the promise on time.

- You cannot keep it. When the due date for the promise is past, the promise has not been fulfilled.
- You can revoke it. Revoking a promise is taking an action, at the moment that you recognize that the promise will not be fulfilled by the specified date. You declare that your original promise will not be fulfilled, giving the person you made the promise to as much notice as possible, so that person can deal with any consequences or inconvenience your revocation may have caused.

In all cases, as with accepting or declining a request, no meaning is added to keeping, not keeping, or revoking a promise. It's just what happened. What follows is, as always, returning to the "designated responsibility," asking "What's missing?" and taking the next action.

What if, in the end, you don't fulfill your promise? Then you don't fulfill your promise. It doesn't mean you are "good" or "bad." Promises don't have anything to do with good or bad, with "should" or "shouldn't."

There may, however, be consequences to not keeping or to revoking your promise. You must take responsibility for those consequences. You are responsible for taking action around your inability to fulfill the promise. The recognition that you aren't "good" or "bad" does not absolve you of the responsibility. In fact, the only reason to revoke a promise is that revocation is the responsible thing to do, and you fully accept the consequences.

There are actions to take after a promise is revoked or not fulfilled. These actions might include offering an apology for what the other person must deal with; making either a new or different promise, to help ameliorate the results of not fulfilling the first; offering to fulfill any requests the other person might have that would reduce the inconvenience for them.

That last action, offering to fulfill the other person's requests, creates an opening for *that person* to ask for a reduction in price, to specify some special consideration, or to let you know that there isn't any inconvenience. In this way, you do not destroy the background of relatedness. In fact, your offer can create an opportunity to build an even stronger background of relatedness.

A good example is bankruptcy. In essence, the bankrupt company says to its creditors, "I am revoking my promise to pay for services I agreed to, and I understand this is a problem. I apologize and I request that you delay taking any action. I am making a new promise that within three months we'll begin payments. I request that you accept our promise."

Some creditors will say yes and some will say no. The bankrupt company understands that the creditor must do whatever it must do. The promise wasn't revoked lightly, and the bankrupt company will deal responsibly with whatever choice the creditor makes.

In contrast to the Universal Human Paradigm, under which we tend to blame people who revoke promises, nothing personal is involved in a bankruptcy under the Re-Invention Paradigm. If you are the creditor and you are counting on payment, you need to focus your energy on the action you need to take to keep yourself solvent and to move toward your commitment, not on venting your feelings toward the person breaking the promise.

If you are the creditor, you may have to come up with an entirely different source of revenue to support your commitment. Under this Paradigm, the reason the promise was revoked is irrelevant. Feelings are irrelevant. The action that you are going to take to forward you is the only thing that is relevant.

If you make no committed effort to live up to your promise, however, then you have broken your word.

When a promise is made to you, assume it will be kept, rather than doubting the person who made the promise. Doubts are a part of conversations for no possibility. When you show doubt, the other person has much less room within which to keep his or her promise. If others promise the impossible, help them in their commitment by asking what you can do to support their commitment. Ask them if they have any requests that will help you support them in fulfilling their promise.

THREE QUESTIONS AFTER SOMETHING HAPPENS

With your knowledge of requests and promises, you can now react differently to events that happen to you. Instead of occurring for you as the "causes" of "what's right" or "what's wrong" in your life, actions can now occur for you as "requests" and "promises" that come your way. This gives you a great deal more freedom in the way you respond to them.

The key is in the speed with which you shift out of the Universal Human Paradigm. Being human, you cannot stop yourself from interpreting what happens. In the first moments after an event, you will inevitably think, "Such-and-such happened. It happened just as it should." Or "Such-and-such happened. There is something wrong."

But can you then move immediately to keep that interpretation from throwing you off balance?

Question #1: "What happened?"

The answer to the question "What happened?" is always "A conversation took place."

In other words, someone made a request or a promise. That request or promise has no meaning in itself. It is not "good" or "bad" for you. You intentionally do not assign any meaning to it. You merely note any interpretations, explanations, or conclusions that occur to you as something that "you have."

You then ask the follow-up question.

Question #2: "What's missing?"

In the case of the actor whose story opened this chapter, one obvious answer to this second question would be: "Acting talent" or "More acting talent." But that answer, if you look at it closely, actually answers a different question: "What's wrong?" or "What's missing here that 'shouldn't' be missing?"

The property of "talent" is missing only if you assume that the actor "should" have talent. Answers like this throw you back into trying to "fix" yourself, or the world, or other people, so that you, it, or they have "what 'should' be there." In fact, the actor didn't *need* acting talent as long as he was willing to make a different type of offer.

In the Re-Invention Paradigm, the question "What's missing?" is never about what "should" or "shouldn't" be there. When you ask, "What's missing?" you ask, in effect: "What does not exist that is essential for your 'designated possibility' to become a reality in the context of the game you are playing?" In an organization, for example, you might look to what systems, structures, work relationships, or policies do not exist that are essential to move your "designated possibility" to be a reality. In the actor's case, "what was missing" was an alternative offer *besides* acting talent.

Sometimes "what's missing" is a request that you need to make. In the case of a manufacturer with a prototype who can't get funding, "what's missing" would be a request to the investors, asking them what they needed in order to fund the product development.

"What's missing?" is then followed by a third question.

Question #3: "What's next?"

The answer is always "Take action from the future." Make a request or promise that moves your "designated possibility" (the game you created) forward into a conversation that is taking place in the present.

When that request or promise is accepted, declined, or countered, then make another. And another. And another. Until the invented future, the possibility that you are *being*, occurs in the world as a reality, for you and other people.

ACTION UNDER THE RE-INVENTION PARADIGM

You can "have" your interpretations, instead of acting from them as if they are the "truth," or an event that "really" happened. You can say, as with the actor, "I am interpreting my rejections at auditions as a statement that Hollywood can't appreciate my acting. This feeling I have, this thought, this interpretation: This is something I have. I see that I have it. Now what action do I take? What's missing from the future I want to create? What request or promise do I make next?"

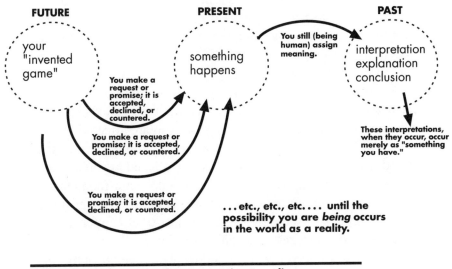

FUTURE   **PRESENT**   **PAST**

your "invented game"

You make a request or promise; it is accepted, declined, or countered.

something happens

You still (being human) assign meaning.

interpretation explanation conclusion

You make a request or promise; it is accepted, declined, or countered.

These interpretations, when they occur, occur merely as "something you have."

You make a request or promise; it is accepted, declined, or countered.

...etc., etc., etc.... until the possibility you are *being* occurs in the world as a reality.

How action occurs under the Re-Invention Paradigm

Or, in a business context, you need to say something like this:

"I have concluded that the lack of investor response to our prototype means that something's wrong with our R&D people, or else our investment brokers. This is the conclusion I've reached. It might or might not be a valid conclusion, but it is not the 'truth.' It is an interpretation of the past. Now, standing in the future, what do I declare is possible regarding this prototype? What's missing to fulfill this possibility? What action do I take? That is, what request or promise do I make next into what's missing?"

Each time you operate in this mode, you are transforming your relationship with action. It occurs less and less as a "series of activities" and more and more as a "series of committed requests or promises."

As you will see in the next chapter, operating in this mode also transforms how you relate to problems. What makes a situation into a "problem"? It is the interpretation that there is something "wrong" with what happened and that whatever happened shouldn't have happened. For example, you only have a problem that the investors declined to fund the product if you add the interpretation that "they should have funded it, and there's something wrong with what happened." When you take away the interpretation, there is no longer a problem. There is just what happened: The investors declined to fund the product. There is no meaning to that event.

This process of having events occur to you without meaning attached is what "getting to zero" looks like on a day-to-day basis. It affects you in the same way that you are affected by the awareness of life as empty and meaningless: You end up in the ground, with dirt thrown on your face, as satisfied as you are and as unsatisfied as you are. "What happened," on a moment-to-moment, hour-to-hour, day-to-day basis, is similarly irrelevant to the final outcome. "What happened" is just what happened.

Given that awareness, the only question is: What's next in the impossible game you've invented to play while life is turning out the way it does?

CHAPTER 8

WHAT ATHLETES AND PERFORMERS KNOW ABOUT BEING EXTRAORDINARY (THAT EXECUTIVES DON'T)

SUPPOSE YOU closed this book right now and started to tell a story about your life from now until the moment you die—the moment that they throw dirt on your face and your life turns out the way it does. What would that story include?

What would you do differently, if anything, in the moment after you closed the book? In the events at the office tomorrow? In events next week, or next year?

This is an unusual question, because most people are not used to thinking seriously about transforming their action after reading a book. You already know that transforming your action as a result of a book is difficult—maybe even impossible.

Let me then make a declaration and a promise.

I declare the possibility: The transformations necessary for Executive Re-Invention can be produced by reading this book and using it as a coaching tool.

I invite you to make the same declaration, and I promise that the transformation from this chapter will give you the where-withal to fulfill it.

CREATING A LIFELONG PRACTICE

Everything starts with practice.

The seventh transformation of Executive Re-Invention, and the focus of this chapter, involves your relationship with practice and with "being extraordinary."

If you are like most of the executives I work with, some of the transformations in this book have sunk in—that is, they are now part of who you are *being*, and they are shaping your thinking and your actions. Others are more difficult to absorb, and they have not completely sunk in. You may recognize or appreciate them on a conceptual level, but they are not yet reflected in your day-to-day operations.

These transformations reinforce each other to the extent that (no matter how valuable you may find them individually) the power they provide to make the impossible happen is only available when you incorporate *all* of the transformations as part of who you are *being*.

That includes this last transformation in the area of practice—to embrace practice as the pathway to attaining a level of competency at making the impossible happen, and to continue to refine it throughout a lifetime. In short, you develop a way of *being* the practices, not just *doing* them.

When you engage in this transformation, you shift your relationship with "being extraordinary" from occurring as a function of natural talent, opportunity, and circumstances to "being extraordinary" occurring as a function of practice.

Henceforth, when you see an extraordinary performance of any kind, your first thought will not be about the natural ability, luck, family connections, or training the person has had. Your first thought will be something like this: "A lot of practice must have gone into that feat!"

When this transformation is complete, practice will no longer occur to you as a means to an end. Practice will occur to you as the essence of beginning. You will be aware that practice is part of daily life, even for someone with mastery over a craft. An actor can't step onstage until the character is developed and the lines are learned. A singer can't approach the microphone or the audience until the throat is warmed up and the exercises done. A writer can't sit down to compose a major work without building up facility through reading, composing letters, or working on short pieces. And the leader of an Organizational Re-Invention can't begin without a period of practice in Executive Re-Invention.

When you begin anything after this transformation, the obvious first step will be to practice. Gifted practicers, such as performers and athletes, already live that way.

You might assume that successful performers and athletes, by nature, have special gifts that "normal" people can never aspire to. To a large extent, that's not true. Successful performers and athletes are not so much *gifted* as *practiced*.

The key to extraordinary performance is the practice. Practice is the threshold of capacity. The Olympic athlete learns very early that to achieve an impossible goal, a particular relationship to practice must be developed. Athletes such as Michael Jordan, Martina Navratilova, and Joe Montana know that the single factor separating them from other outstanding athletes is their long-term relationship to practice. The professional singer learns this lesson as well. If you look closely at the lives of, say, Luciano Pavarotti, Plácido Domingo and Leontyne Price, you'll see that each of these consummate artists has "paid the price" by establishing the practices of their profession as a priority in the daily discipline of their lives. The mastery of this relationship is the determining factor of whether or not what seems impossible becomes a living reality.

Having begun to develop their relationship with practice, the sense of "perpetual beginning" continues. It does not even end after you cross the threshold of mastery of the craft. In a sense, practice only starts then; it kicks into a more concentrated, more masterful phase. For example, you may develop proficiency in "declaring what's possible," instead of predicting it, when there is an opportunity. But once you have that practice down, you will move into a second phase: developing facility and skill at the choice of declarations you make, out of all the possible declarations you could make. Once you master that, there will be a third phase: gaining power and sophistication at wording that declaration, so that your language, when it is spoken, captures the power of the possibility that you are creating.

Great artists, whether singers, actors, or musicians, will tell you without hesitation that their rehearsal time is often the most difficult, fun, exciting, and challenging. They integrate the value of practice and rehearsal not just into their daily routine, but into their psyches. The athlete practices every day, no matter how many times he or she has won medals or games. The singer does not count a day complete without "exercising" his or her voice. Given their amount of rehearsal, their level of performance—even extraordinary performance—is often habitual. And as a result of this commitment to practice, they can count on themselves to be consistent even under the most stressful conditions or adverse circumstances.

Startlingly enough, practice is often heard as a dirty word in business circles, when in fact it refers to the opportunity to create remarkable speed within any area. Practice gives an individual absolute ownership of the field.

Consider the state of life in business *without* practice. Executives and leaders are used to doing whatever is necessary to get the job done. In the old competitive game of continuous improvement, paying the price has meant long hours, physical stress, relocation, absences from home, long hours in airplanes, absences from children's school activities, and many other sacrifices. And yet, that price alone is insufficient; in the new competitive game, enormous effort and sacrifice are not enough to guarantee the necessary results.

The price for being extraordinary calls for a relationship with practice that is equivalent to the commitment that artists and athletes have to the practices of their professions. In the process, there may be other rewards: With a sufficient commitment to practice, your effort may allay some of the need for long hours and physical stress—simply by reframing all of your work in a more effective manner.

Consider how a singer might spend years learning music and practicing scales, exercises, songs, languages, stagecraft, and performance techniques. But all of that is not enough to produce extraordinary results. Extraordinary results come when a singer is willing to re-invent himself or herself, to create a musical identity that the public has not already heard. *Being* extraordinary, in any field, requires a form of practice in which there is constant reexamination of all that's come before; in which the practicer lets go of everything that has worked before and creates a new future whenever it is needed.

The athlete and the artist recognize that each level of "mastery" is only a plateau on the way to another plateau. They also know that all they have at the moment of "performance" is habit—the habit developed in practice. The time to learn to sink a basketball is not in the game, it's during practice.

The same holds true for executive leadership and the skills required to play the competitive game of making the impossible happen. These skills are not manifested in the moment as though by a miracle. They are the result of a lifelong commitment to practice and the way of *being* that practice generates.

Sometimes business leaders "wing it," making intuitive decisions in unfamiliar situations, for which they are not prepared because they have not practiced. They hope not to get caught out of their depth. In many organizations, nearly *all* the executives are winging it, because they have never had any training in leading a Re-Invention, they are not aware of the practices that are needed, and they have had no opportunity to build their transformational "muscles" through practice. They are not noticed at first, because the visible manifestations of winging it fit the prevailing view of how managers are supposed to operate. But it's only a matter of time before the "frauds" get caught. That's not a great day. It's an unnecessary day, because practice is the determining distinction between the novice and the master.

In Chapter 5, I explained how a chemical plant transformed itself from being an extremely hazardous place to work to a factory that prided itself on safety standards implemented and maintained by the workers themselves. Everyone in the plant, not just the leaders, came to work with a totally new attitude, but it took some time for new systems to be implemented and for a new context of well-being to take hold. The leaders in this plant wisely saw the need to practice: not just talking about new types of action, but modeling that action from the platform of their own Re-Invention. When the workers saw they were serious—there would be room to act in ways unrelated to past practices, and time to learn and implement new practices—the plant transformed. Results followed only after that. The whole process took months, but it could not have been rushed.

THE WHOLE IS GREATER THAN THE SUM OF ITS PARTS

Inherent in each of the first six transformations that make up Executive Re-Invention is a specific form of practice. I have gathered them here, however, instead of putting them separately in each chapter, because they are holographic: These practices are components of a single transformation in themselves. They cannot be begun, let alone mastered, until you have completed the other six transformations. In working these practices on a day-to-day basis, you will deepen each of the previous transformations individually, and you will provide yourself with the power of the entire Executive Re-Invention process—the power to make the impossible happen.

In this respect, too, your practice is like that of an athlete. Master athletes are familiar with a wide range of practices, which may include jogging, gymnastics, stretching, and weight lifting, some of which seem like they have nothing at all to do with the athlete's main sport. The athletes also make use of nonathletic practices, involving meditation, mental exercise, dealing with fatigue and endurance, handling crowds, and even spiritual or ontological practice. (A pep talk can be seen as a practice session in declaring "what's possible" for the team.)

Any one of these practices is valuable in itself, but the athlete's power comes from the way they mix and reinforce each other, to produce a power, as a whole, that is greater than the sum of its individual components.

The same is true of the practices in this chapter. Each gives you access to a particular type of power, but only when they are put together do they add up to provide access to power to make the impossible happen.

Once you have experience with all those practices, your power increases in unforeseen, unpredictable ways. You can deal with making the impossible happen in situations that might have floored you before—when you're tired, injured, in the midst of a marital breakup, under emotional difficulties, being attacked, or navigating a crisis. Practice, in a variety of complementary arenas, gives you the mastery to make the impossible happen with grace under pressure.

Remember, to transform something is to alter how it *occurs* (how it exists, and how you are *being* in relation to it): from occurring in a way that constrains or limits you to occurring in a way that frees your actions. In each of the seven transformations, you are creating a new "clearing," in which the key elements of leadership (winning and succeeding, the past, taking risks, what's possible and not possible, the future, action, and being extraordinary) can exist as a component of your power to make the impossible happen.

Practice #1: Six impossible declarations before breakfast

The transformation in Chapter 2, "Uncovering Your Winning Strategy," involves your relationship with success and winning.

You are shifting from . . .

. . . *success and winning occurring as the desired outcome* . . .

. . . to . . .

. . . *success (in the form of your winning strategy) occurring as a compensation for what's not possible.*

Now, to deepen this transformation, you develop this practice:

Recognize your winning strategy in action, moment by moment, and—instead of acting out or giving in to that strategy—stop to ask, "What 'impossibility' am I compensating for here?"

To implement this practice, you must learn to stop and catch yourself. Stop doing what you normally do, for a moment, and ask yourself: "What is driving me?" You might catch yourself by hearing some component of your Winning Strategy, or by seeing it in action. You might see any element of it: the "listening for" component, the "so as to act by" component, or the "in order to" component.

Anytime any one of these elements is engaged, your whole Winning Strategy is engaged, whether you realize it or not.

Then ask yourself:

"In this situation, at this moment, what's *not possible* for me?"

What, in other words, are you dismissing from your mind because you *know* it's not possible? What impossibility are you compensating for by seeking the "success" that comes from your Winning Strategy instead?

For example, suppose you have a long-standing associate whom you like as a person—and you involve yourself in acknowledging, empowering, and encouraging your associate, in a perpetual effort to motivate that person to do better. Most of the time, you have no idea yourself that you have invoked your Winning Strategy, listening for "What can I connect to here?" so as to act by "empowering, motivating, or acknowledging other people" in order to "avoid danger and be secure."

You act to praise your associate despite his or her ineffectuality. You remind this person of something he or she is already good at. You hope that "connecting" with your associate will keep the relationship secure, avoiding the danger of upsetting or invalidating him or her, but somehow motivating the person to do better work. Maybe, without bringing up the dangerous direct comments, you can lead the associate to being better on the job.

Thus, you avoid the conversation that would allow either of you to deal with what you really want. You avoid the conversation your associate needs to hear: "These are the shortcomings I see. What's missing? Are you interested in providing what's missing?"

Most of the time, you don't even notice that you're avoiding the conversation you need. You get hooked by the hope that your associate, with enough praise, will naturally improve. You get seduced by the hope of improvement because nothing else is possible.

Every once in a while, you daydream about what you "know" is impossible: having an associate who is a full partner, who is two steps ahead of you, takes full initiative, and encourages *you* sometimes, instead of leaving you to be the responsible manager.

Can you catch yourself at the moment when, flush with resignation, you move to empower, motivate, and acknowledge your associate?

If you can, then ask: "What is the impossibility that I am compensating for right now with my Winning Strategy?"

The resolution may be to develop your associate to become a full partner. Or it may be more complex. You may just want to start your own small enterprise, where everyone working with you is a full partner—and you know, in your current Winning Strategy, *that's* impossible.

Having noticed this "impossibility," are you now willing to make a declaration? Are you now willing to declare the possibility of (for example) having an administrative associate who operates as a full partner? This might mean your current associate would step into that role. Or if that route requires more resources than you are willing to commit, or your associate is not interested, then it might mean finding another person to fill the role, and finding a different post for your current associate.

The "in order to" of another person's Winning Strategy—be respected—might prevent the risk-taking needed to be a truly creative marketing campaign leader. That person would not engage in any action where he or she could appear foolish.

You have your own individual Winning Strategy, with its own corollary impossibilities. What stops you from pursuing *your* impossibility? You'll find the answer somewhere in your Winning Strategy—probably in the "in order to" component. In this case, with your recalcitrant associate, your "in order to" component of avoiding pain would lead you to reject any action that might cause you to hurt people or be rejected.

Your Winning Strategy will pop up in a variety of circumstances, preventing you from attempting a wide range of "impossibilities." The practice of listening for your Winning Strategy requires a sort of continual vigilance.

That's why it's not enough to simply be aware of Winning Strategies as a concept, or even to be aware of your own Winning Strategy profile. "Okay, I know my characteristics—now let's move on." You must practice seeing it in action; hear it coming out of your mouth. Get to the place where you see your Winning Strategy as literally shaping every action you take. Become alert enough to step in and make a choice: In this instance, will you continue to compensate? Or will you declare the possibility of the "impossible" future and then move it to a reality?

When you intervene and ask the question "What's not possible for me right now?" you start to dislodge the effect of the Compensating Power Principle: As your Winning Strategy gets stronger and stronger and you expand what is possible—what you can be—at the same time, what expands along with it is what's not possible—what can't ever be. Your Winning Strategy compensates for the fact that you can't make the impossible happen. ("I cannot have what I most want, because that is impossible," you say to yourself, "but at least I can have the gains that my Winning Strategy produces.")

When you follow your Winning Strategy, you accept, more and more, the impossibility of what you really want in life. When you *stop* being led by your Winning Strategy, this acceptance begins to break up and dissolve. The more you stop following your Winning Strategy, the more it breaks up. Gradually, you disengage and emerge from under its power.

You begin to become aware of a whole *world* of impossibilities that could be possibilities—ones that you would accomplish if you could, but your Winning Strategy has shut you away from them and given you no access to them.

This practice is best managed on a day-to-day basis, rather than simply on "big" occasions for "serious" declarations. Most of the time, when people think about "declaring what's possible," they think in terms of a large future. But when you get into the habit of contradicting your Winning Strategy, declaring that "impossibilities" are possible becomes a way of life. You become like the White Queen in Lewis Carroll's *Through the Looking Glass*. When Alice said that there was no use trying, because "One can't believe impossible things," the White Queen retorted, "I daresay you haven't had much practice. When I was your age, I always did it for a half-an-hour a day. Why, sometimes I've believed as many as six impossible things before breakfast."

In this practice, you don't just "believe" impossible things; you *declare* them, incessantly and enthusiastically. You don't need to find a "designated" impossible *project* to declare as possible; new possibilities emerge constantly:

"Something must be sent in the last mail today and it's impossible to get it done in time. I declare it possible and promise that it will be done."

Or "It's impossible to be in two places at once, and we have been asked to attend two far-flung, simultaneous meetings. I declare that it is possible to participate fully in both. I request the dedicated help of the staff here in accomplishing this." (This declaration might lead, subsequently, to a request to establish an audio- or video-conferencing link, or some other heretofore unseen action.)

Or "No one here seems to believe that Joe Smith could be a powerful project leader. I declare that it *is* possible. I promise to relate to him from that stand. I promise to offer him my partnership as a coach for anything that is missing."

And then you design and play the game of making it possible. Sometimes you lose; sometimes you win, and achieve the impossible results.

Each of these results is small, in itself. But remember that each "impossibility" is a product of the way of *being* of the organization where you operate. Make enough declarations, and you alter that way of *being*.

Don't be stingy with your declarations. Certainly, use your judgment and discretion—you might not want to make every "Joe Smith" in your organization a great project leader—but don't hold yourself back. When you're enmeshed in a simple phone call, ask yourself: "In this phone call, what impossibilities have I given voice to—either in my listening, in my talking to myself, or in my actual speech? What have I implicitly declared to be impossible? Then, during that same conversation, declare that "impossibility" possible and make requests and promises to make it happen.

If you apply this practice constantly, in a variety of situations, you get so good at it that it becomes a way of life. Later, when a desperately important "designated possibility" comes along, you and your organization are ready.

Try this practice—for a month, a quarter, or six months—and watch your capability grow.

Practice #2: Tuning into the world of interpretations

The transformation that took place in Chapter 3, "The Universal Human Paradigm, involves your relationship with the past.

You are shifting from . . .

. . . *the past occurring as a series of events that "really happened" and are "the" truth* . . .

. . . to . . .

. . . *the past occurring as a series of interpretations you've made about events that happened, all of which are valid and none of which represent "the" truth.*

Now, to deepen this transformation, you develop this practice:

Become aware, day by day, of the extent to which you (and other people) automatically and immediately interpret everything that hap-

pens. Be able to hear that nearly every conversation is a reflection of the universal interpretation: "There is a way that things should be and there's something wrong with 'me, them, or it' when they are not that way."

The practice, simply enough, is to consciously pick up as much as you can the Universal Human Paradigm when it whispers to you and to other people. "Things shouldn't be this way." "I shouldn't have done that." "Things are turning out well for once." "I've been betrayed again." "They don't respect me." "They like me." "We've had some bad luck." "So-and-so has let me down." Expressions like these, and many others, all represent the Universal Human Paradigm's influence.

Can you hear its echo in conversations? Can you hear its echo in the silences between words, in the things that people stop themselves from saying, or in the things it doesn't occur to people to say, or in the things that don't need to be said (because the Universal Human Paradigm is so loud in the unsaid)?

Your own conversations change as you engage in this practice. Keep listening for the Universal Human Paradigm, and before long, naturally and without effort, you will stop engaging in arguments and discussions about what "really" happened, or what went wrong, or why things shouldn't be this way. You will stop complaining. You will ask, instead, "What's missing? What's the next action?"

When this practice becomes a part of who you are, a way of *being*, you'll also discover that you have the power and clarity to point out to others that they are expending their energies and resources examining what went "wrong" in the past. Instead, you'll be able to redirect the discussion from the future.

You'll become a better coach.

Every leader, like it or not, is a coach already. If you are a leader now, you are perpetually called upon by people to coach them about threats they face, in the form of problems they are having with people or projects. Inevitably, those problems involve manifestations of the Universal Human Paradigm—the fundamental, hardwired belief that "things should be" a certain way, and when they aren't, there is something wrong.

Coaching is not just a matter of setting an example; it involves finding ways to lead others to a new opening for action, so that they can become involved in the transformations that the organization has begun.

In this kind of coaching, you come to the other person from your knowledge and experience of the source of the "problem" he or she faces, in terms that help the person move forward.

Suppose someone named Terry comes to you with a request: "Help me understand my problem with my immediate boss." You ask for the details, and Terry relates the "story":

It seems that the boss has it in for Terry. The boss had promised, once upon a time, to be Terry's mentor, and made implicit promises about grooming Terry for advancement. But those promises haven't been fulfilled. Instead, Terry has been relegated to low-status positions. Terry has been singled out as "inferior" by the boss, or at least not recognized publicly as much as some of Terry's peers (who don't do nearly as much work or have nearly as much experience). It's now "obvious" that the boss has had it in for Terry ever since they began working together. All Terry can do is spin wheels and protest; and every time Terry protests, the boss gets angrier and cuts off more privileges. At this point, the two of them are drawn into a continually escalating cycle of anger and recrimination, from which it looks like there is no escape, and within which they are forced to keep working together.

You know Terry's boss and you immediately recognize that Terry is reacting to interpretations. You can hear the echo of "things shouldn't be this way" in Terry's comment. And you know, for instance, that the boss has not been getting up every day and thinking, "How can I ruin Terry's life *today*?" You can guess that the boss has been reacting to interpretations of Terry's actions that are every bit as overwhelming as Terry's own interpretations of the boss.

Your first task, as a coach, is to stay out of the cycle of Terry's interpretation. It doesn't matter whether you agree with Terry's view of the boss or not. As in martial arts, provide no place for a blow to land—no place for any interpretation of "how it went wrong" or "how it ought to be" to hook you and provoke your response.

In other words, don't get drawn into attacking the boss, defending the boss, agreeing with Terry, disagreeing with Terry, or analyzing Terry. If you're not pulled into Terry's state of being upset, you can be of some assistance. Don't get enmeshed in a conversation of assertions, about which interpretation of events is the "truth."

You may be tempted to think something like: "The real tragedy here is that Terry and the boss could work so well together if they gave each other half a chance. I'd better talk to Terry's boss and remonstrate." But that, too, is an interpretation of how the organization "should" be. It locks you into trying to "improve" Terry's relationship with the boss, based on what that relationship has been in the past, instead of helping lead Terry to a re-invented future.

In the place of interpretation, you can create an opening for action to land, coming from outside of the Universal Human Paradigm. To find that starting place, you need to find the future that is "impossible" for Terry in this situation. One approach to that starting place might be to ask, "Terry, what bothers you the most about everything that's happened?"

What bothers Terry the *most* might be any of a variety of things. It might be a feeling of being stuck, with no way out from under this boss. It might be the disappointment of seeing career opportunities lost, or the knowledge of how terrific a career Terry *could* have ("if only my boss gave me the right sort of mentoring"). It might be the drive to really show what Terry can do, a drive that seems continually blocked under this boss. It might be the stress of a personality conflict, or the desire to be vindicated, or the feeling that other people in the office have it easier.

Ultimately, the answer will undoubtedly come down to something with personal meaning for Terry. In this case, intentionally or not, Terry's answer might be: "I was struggling for credibility and vindication at my work; my boss knew how important it was to me; and my boss damaged it anyway."

Your next question would be designed to create an arena of possibility. "Then let me ask you something, Terry. In terms of the whole situation, if you could miraculously have your relationship with your boss altered, what would you have it be?"

Once again, you would want to bring this to as fundamental a level as possible. What Terry might want most could be a position of responsibility. It could be a mentoring relationship. It could be the chance to work on a beloved project. Or it could be "getting out."

Whatever Terry says, the next question you ask might be: "And do you think this is possible?"

Without ever mentioning the idea of "declaration," you are using this question to see if a declaration of possibility emerges naturally from the conversation. Terry will probably feel that, as things stand now, the most desired goal is *not* possible. But perhaps it *could* be possible. And now you have moved the conversation to a position where talk of action is possible.

What action would be effective in this case, *no matter what the truth about Terry's boss may be?*

Ultimately, in fact, Terry's two choices come down to operating from the Universal Human Paradigm and operating from the Re-Invention Master Paradigm. The first choice means focusing on the current situation, letting events escalate, and worrying primarily about who is "right." Terry won't get anything out of this choice except a kind of glee at being vindicated: "See, the boss was exactly as vicious as I feared."

The second choice means turning back to concentrate on the possibility that Terry wanted in the first place, the possibility that originally brought Terry to this situation. What Terry wants, after all, is bigger than merely a victory over the boss.

As a coach, therefore, your role is to create an opening for action that allows people to get untangled from their structure of interpretation, and focus on the future to which they are committed.

To help Terry answer these questions, you can do the most good as a coach by taking a stand on Terry. For example, I say ("I say" technically means, "I declare who I am (*being*) in the matter of") "Terry is more committed to a powerful relationship with the boss than to being right about the boss's motives." Relate to the commitment of Terry's future, rather than the commitment of the Universal Human Paradigm.

What is the most powerful action Terry can take—not to deal with what's "wrong," but to move forward to his deepest commitment?

The answer to that question is impossible to give, unless you know the details of the case. It may be that Terry is in a good position to call the boss and say, "I need an hour of your time—to make a request." The request would be an opportunity to be taken seriously, or a request to reframe their working relationship. "And if you're not interested in that sort of relationship, then can you help me find someone else to work with, or suggest any places to start looking?" It may be more appropriate for Terry to make a bold promise: "If you give me the level of support I want, I will promise to have such-and-such available to you by such-and-such a date."

You don't know what will come out of that conversation between Terry and the boss. No doubt, the boss will decline some of Terry's requests. (Terry may come back to you, needing to be reminded that the decline doesn't mean anything about Terry or the boss; it is simply a decline.) The boss may have counteroffers or counterrequests. It may be that several rounds of requests or promises will be necessary, until the right one is struck that allows Terry and the boss to move forward. And it may be that Terry discovers that the most fundamental goal *can't* be achieved working with this boss anymore; and Terry has to leave. Whatever the outcome, there is nothing to lose by having the meeting; the choice is between having the meeting and leaving things as they are.

This type of coaching requires finesse. Do not say flatly to someone who is inexperienced with Executive Re-Invention: "The injustice that has you upset is just your *interpretation* of events. You're bound by your opinion of what *'should'* happen, instead of by what actually happened." After all, the person you are coaching was *there;* that person "knows" what happened. If that person is typical, you can't easily dispute his or her knowledge.

Nor, as a coach, would you repeat to that person the explanation of the nature of the Universal Human Paradigm. A long exposition like that would hardly fall within the realm of accepted social discourse. More important, it wouldn't make any sense or any difference as a concept. All you need to do is leave him or her with an opening for action, without explaining why you said the particular things you said.

As with all practice, your ability as a coach will improve as you keep practicing. Indeed, as you work with the Universal Human Paradigm, it will increasingly come up as a coaching experience. As you become more capable, you become a "clearing" for action. People will be attracted to talk with you about their threats and problems. They may not quite be sure what happened in their conversation with you; it's not like you gave them an answer. But having talked with you, they are no longer stuck, or stopped in action. They are back in touch with their commitment, ready to move forward and out of the snares of interpretation.

You can be this sort of clearing because awareness of the Universal Human Paradigm creates a new set of distinctions in your mind. Thus, when someone talks to you about his or her problems, you can respond to those comments, coming from the context of the Re-Invention Master Paradigm: There's no such thing as "should" or "shouldn't," "right" or "wrong." To some extent you already have these distinctions; to some extent they probably seem mysterious. They will continue to seem mysterious until you have built up enough of the distinctions in your own mind between operating under the Universal Human Paradigm and operating under the Re-Invention Master Paradigm. These distinctions emerge through practice.

The CEO of an organization undergoing Re-Invention will find this particularly important. It is part of the job of this CEO to be a clearing in which a transformation of other people in the organization can take place. The CEO is the clearing for the organization's future. If the CEO never moves out of the frame of mind of the Universal Human Paradigm, that "something's wrong and it shouldn't be this way," the organization never will.

It's useful, in this context, to compare the two master paradigms in their entirety. Appendix 1, at the end of this book, lays out the elements of each.

Practice #3: Giving up the meaningfulness of your past

The transformation in Chapter 4 " 'Dying' before Going into Battle," involves your relationship with taking risks.

You are shifting from . . .

. . . *"taking risks" occurring as a serious threat, where the consequences might result in losing everything (if things don't turn out the way they "should") . . .*

. . . to . . .

. . . *"taking risks" occurring as "moving the action forward," with nothing to lose (since life does not turn out the way it "should"; it turns out the way it does).*

Now, to deepen this transformation, you develop this practice:

Taking the stand: The stories you tell about what happened in your life, your career, and your organization are not "true"—the events as you interpreted them never happened. Indeed, life itself is meaningless, and is all an interpretation that you made up. Finally, it doesn't mean anything that life is meaningless.

For many people, this is the most difficult transformation and the most difficult practice. It is hard enough to appreicate the need to "die before you go into battle," and to recognize, once, the freedom that comes from the meaninglessness of life.

In this practice, you create on a day-to-day basis the experience that accompanies a close call with death, or the shock of someone close to you unexpectedly dying. You take the freedom to engage in life for its own sake, as a gift, rather than for a purpose or outcome. You live without any "in order to" component in life. You live without a goal. To achieve this freedom, you need to take a stand for the meaninglessness of life, every day that you are alive.

Moreover, you take that stand about the aspect of life that rests for most people at the core of their identity—the stories they have told themselves that make up who they are.

When people tell a story about their life, it always sounds as if the events they describe really happened. "I grew up," someone will say, "in a poor family." Or "When I was young, my parents took me all over the world." Or "I really came into my own when I went to college." Whatever the story may be, the events sound verifiable, and they may indeed reflect actual events. But there is always an interpretation involved, always a reflection of the Universal Human Paradigm: "I grew up in a poor family, so I was always deprived and had to make my own way." Or "My parents took me all over the world, which was as it should have been, but that made me uniquely unrooted when I became an adult." Or "I should have come into my own before college, but that was the best I could do."

Look back at the stories you tell about your own life. Some stories are recent: "My boss (colleague, secretary, competitor) undermined (insulted, ignored, praised, rewarded) me (or my project)." Other stories took place long ago: "My mother (father, sister, brother) abandoned (rejected, criticized, took care of, depended on) me." You talk about those interpretations as if they *happened* rather than as the ways in which "what happened" occurred for you.

Throughout this book, I've been asking you to consider the ramifications of the fact that every story you hear from people, and every comment, is an interpretation. Now take this a step further. Consider the possibility that your entire life is an interpretation: a story you made up. If someone asked your mother, your father, your boss, your colleague, or any other character to describe the events, he or she would most likely tell a different story. Which of those stories really happened? Up to this point, it was enough to recognize that there is no "really happened." There is no "the truth." Now, in this component of the practice of Executive Re-Invention, it is important to up the ante.

I am now asking you to confront this concept: What you call "your life" is actually an interpretation. There is no "life" in your life story, only story. "Who you are" is the story in which you are engaged, and which wells up inside you. That is why it produces strong feelings, which emerge when you talk about it. But all of those feelings—whether they include pride, sadness, grief, happiness, anticipation, trust, mistrust, or any other feelings—are produced by the interpretations you have held (and hold now). History is an interpretation. The things you are upset about, that you have been upset about all your life, may or may not exist. When you say, "I feel this way," or "I think this way," or "I like this thing," or "I belong to this group," all of those emotions and thoughts are based on interpretations, not the "truth."

It is perfectly fine to have feelings, thoughts, likes, dislikes, and allegiances. Just recognize that they are not rooted in "truth." They are rooted in interpretations you have had all your life.

Why is this difficult to accept? Because (as anyone who has spent time working with human beings will find out), people are driven to be "right." If everything you feel, think, like, dislike, and belong to is rooted in interpretation, then none of that is "right." It is damn hard to be right when there is no "the truth." And if you can't be right, you can't survive.

If this game is what life is about—the game of surviving by "being right," by building up significance and meaning—then it is time to see the significance of this aspect of life. This cycle of interpretation, rooted in the Universal Human Paradigm, is using *you* for its survival. It is not a malevolent entity, brainwashing the entire human race; but it might as well be. Your life, to date, has been spent serving a by-product of the human condition, rather than any "significant" purpose you may have *felt* (or thought, or believed, or hoped) that you were serving. All your attempts to build something of significance have in one way or another been expressions of the futile quest for "meaningful" outcomes to your life.

This practice of Executive Re-Invention offers the freedom that is only available when you embrace the meaninglessness of life.

Hold your arm up over your head and wave it. What is the meaning of the action of your arm? It is void of meaning. You can make up a story about why you are waving your arm. You can wrap an interpretation around it, but it will still have no meaning. It's just what happened.

Similarly, it doesn't mean anything that your father lost his company when you were nine years old. It doesn't mean anything that you have no time to spend with your children because of the demands of your profession. It doesn't mean anything that your mother missed your big dance recital or football game. It doesn't mean anything that you got fired. It doesn't mean anything that the top position you worked for, for fifteen years, went to some-one else. Nor does it mean anything that the top position went to you; or that you got hired; or that your mother showed up, in the front row, of every public appearance you made in high school. All of the meanings you've assigned to what has hap-pened are all made up, like in a television soap opera.

You carry your life with you like a soap opera. You feel good or bad about it, like you do about a soap opera, but your life has no more meaning than a soap opera.

Suppose life doesn't mean anything, and it doesn't mean any-thing that life is meaningless. It is not sad that life is meaningless. Nor should it inspire happiness. It is meaningless that life is meaningless.

I ask you to accept this meaninglessness as a gift. It is a ticket to freedom. On a day-to-day level, while in one sense it changes nothing, in another sense it transforms all of reality.

What stops you from accepting it as a gift? It may be the fear that, if you see life as having no meaning, you will lose your drive and ambition. You will not consider anything worth striving *for*. You will be tempted to abandon your responsibilities, as nihilists have always done.

But consider for a minute what has happened when you ex-press this fear. Imagine that I say, "Life has no meaning." And you say, "If life has no meaning, why strive for anything?"

You have just enveloped the point of "life having no mean-ing" in a new set of interpretations. You have made "meaning-lessness" meaningful. If you abandon your responsibilities, you will have made meaninglessness the focus of a new Winning Strategy, as stifling as your old ones. Nihilism is, after all, just another way to try to "win."

All "meanings" you give to your life are your creations.

All meanings you give to any story you tell yourself are your creations.

All meanings you give to what happens to you, now or in the past, are your creations.

They may provide you with a whole range of emotions—happiness, joy, anger—but they are pure interpretation.

All you have left, after you give up meaning and interpretations, are actions.

You take actions.

Those actions have consequences.

Those consequences may lead you to take more actions.

If something goes "right," that's just an interpretation you've placed on it. If something goes "wrong," that's just an interpretation you've placed on it. The events that occur will occur, regardless of how they occur "for" you.

Can you begin to live, day by day, without assigning interpretations to what happens? Can you begin to live without thinking that your life, just because you happen to be living it, is special or meaningful in any way?

If you can, you can then take risks without "violating" this carefully tended structure of meaning. You can put all of your life at stake, in the service of whatever "designated impossibility" is important to you, because you know all of your life, to date, is meaningless. When you can do that, then you have met the challenge of this practice and completed the transformation of learning to "die before going into battle."

Practice #4: Having the "world" fit your "word"

The transformation in Chapter 5, "Creating the Re-Invention Paradigm," involves your relationship with "what's possible" and "what's not possible."

You are shifting from . . .

. . . *"what's possible" occurring as "what's predictable," bound by the limits of past experience* . . .

. . . to . . .

. . . "what's possible" occurring as what you say is possible and what you commit to make happen, based on nothing.

Now, to deepen this transformation, you develop this practice:

Replace "predicting the future" (by analyzing what's possible, benchmarking, setting objectives or goals, or making feasible promises) with "declaring the future" and making bold promises to fulfill it.

If you are serious about making the impossible happen, I ask you now to give up some of the most cherished programs in business today: benchmarking; "best practice" evaluations; stretch goals; forms of budgeting, appraisals, or measurements that are aimed at replicating someone else's results. Give up any endeavor where you think, "If other companies have accomplished such-and-such, we can do it too." Reserve these programs for commitments that call for improving what's already possible rather than commitments that require making the impossible happen.

Indeed, in this practice you give up every endeavor that you take on *primarily* because you know in advance that you can accomplish it successfully, or because you can predict the results. With this practice, you start listening for yourself saying things like, "If we start from our current position, and stretch ourselves a certain amount, then we'll produce such-and-such results." Or "Our analysis shows us that we can achieve good results in the future."

When you hear this language, ask yourself: "Am I proposing this action because I know in advance what will happen? Am I suggesting a direction because its results are predictable?" If the answer is "yes," then this practice suggests that you drop that course of action and replace it with one whose results are unpredictable.

Promises with predictable results represent a "word-to-world" fit. You make decisions and plans based on what the world says is possible. *You give your word, and thus make a promise, to fit the way the conventional wisdom of what is currently possible in the world.* By looking to the world to see what's possible, you are basing your promise on such factors as the current agreement, what's being done in other organizations, what management writers have said, your past experience, the gospel of management schools, and the strictures of regulations. Your statement about what you will accomplish sounds like a promise, but it is anything but "bold"—it is an expression of what authorities say is possible and therefore "acceptable."

When you operate this way, your ability to make bold promises atrophies. You—and your organization—become accustomed to every promise having a rationale that "legitimizes" it or that shows it is "feasible." There is no surer way to slip out of the power of your declaration and back to operating under the constraints of your Winning Strategy.

This dynamic explains why the "continuous improvement" mode is so limiting. Any promises you make in the name of continuous improvement will be absolutely "word-to-world": You give your word to some action designed, by its nature, to fit what the world says is "possible."

Under the Re-Invention Paradigm, instead of your word fitting the world, you design your promise as a "world-to-word" fit. You have the world lined up, to fit the promise you have made.

To make this happen, a declaration is necessary, but not sufficient. It must be followed by a promise. Mahatma Gandhi is a classic example. He declared that the British would walk out of India—a declaration that seemed absurd to the "world" when he first made it. But he followed that declaration with promises. He said, for example, that there would be no violence, starting at that moment. Others made that promise as well. Sometimes they kept it, and sometimes they didn't. But even when they didn't keep the promise, it provided an opening to move things forward. Gandhi also threatened not to eat until the violence stopped—a promise (remember, threats are promises) with enormous moral power.

Fred Smith, the CEO of Federal Express, made a declaration that a new type of postal service was possible: "Absolutely, positively overnight." That declaration was made when the world did not agree. There was no evidence that absolute overnight service, anywhere in the continental United States, was possible. Having made the declaration, however, Smith followed it up with promises. He took action to have the world fit his word. Some promises, to customers, concerned courtesy, reliability, response time, and a commitment to moving packages by air. Other promises, to employees, concerned empowerment, profit sharing, high pay levels, a lack of unnecessary paperwork, and the all-important promise that employees would be rewarded, not punished, for taking initiative to help customers.[1] The world has now lined up with his word. Not only is it possible for Federal Express to guarantee overnight delivery, but every courier, including the U.S. Postal Service, is now held to the same standard.

In previous chapters, I described Mike, the chief operating officer who declared that it was possible to meet his boss's four "impossible" objectives. That declaration was followed up with a series of bold promises that fed power to the original declaration. One of those promises was to reach the four objectives within three years. But that was just the beginning. Mike also promised that he would stop trying to convince the CEO (or anyone else) to cut down the number of objectives. And both he and the CEO promised the people working for them that there would be no reprisals for anyone who made bold promises on their own, and he invited his direct reports to point out when he was coming from the past.

How, then, do you fulfill this part of the practice of Re-Invention? By making declarations of possibility—lots of declarations, as practice #1 suggests—and following them with bold promises. Your promises are specifically designed without regard for what the old system is "capable" of handling, for any predictable outcome, or for what other organizations have achieved. You design a bold promise only with regard for the "designated possibility" that you have just declared.

The more you practice, the more you can make declarations on the spot, followed by bold promises, in times of stress. Suppose you walk into the office and there's a message from your key right-hand person that there's been a death in his family and he'll be gone for the week. He was managing a big presentation, due tomorrow. Your first reaction, inevitably influenced by the Universal Human Paradigm, would be something like: "Oh, shucks." Then you ask yourself: "Okay, now what am I going to do about it?" Already, you are compensating in some respect for the right-hand person's absence. From there, you might scurry frantically to make up the work, all the while blaming circumstance for what has happened, falling ever more deeply back into your Winning Strategy.

But with this practice in mind, you would switch instead to the Re-Invention Paradigm. As soon as you noticed your Winning Strategy or the Universal Human Paradigm at work, you would return to your original commitment. What was the commitment that led your organization to schedule that presentation in the first place? Then you ask, "What do I declare is possible, regarding that commitment?" You might declare that what's possible is for every part of the presentation to go off as scheduled. Or you might declare that it is possible to postpone the presentation without ill effects.

Following that declaration, you would make whatever bold promises are suggested to you by the imperative of your declaration. For instance, you might promise that you will make up the work on the presentation personally; or that you will use personal phone calls today to substitute for the presentation tomorrow.

Keep up that kind of practice, making and following up declarations of "impossible" possibility, and at some point you will hit a threshold where a significant enough part of the world will concur that "when you declare that something is possible, it happens." Making the impossible happen will no longer be a possibility you invented; it will be an expertise you *have*, as a function of who you are *being*.

Practice #5: Recognizing the cost of the tantrums you throw

The transformation in Chapter 6, "Inventing an Impossible Future," involves your relationship with the future.

You are shifting from . . .

. . . the future occurring as "someplace to get to" (from the present), where "what's wrong with you, them, or it" will be fixed or improved, and things will be the way they "should" . . .

. . . to . . .

. . . the future occurring as an invented "impossible" game, where there's no such thing as "should" or "shouldn't," as "right" or "wrong."

Now, to deepen this transformation, you develop this practice:

*Shift your focus of attention from what you are **doing** to the way you are **being**. Specifically: Are you being the "invented future and context" that you created, or are you being "right," dominating and avoiding domination, and justifying the way you are?*

Face it: Interpretation is addictive. You've been doing it all your life, and you're accustomed to the rewards and payoffs of interpretation. Even when you are engaged in playing the game of your invented future, what stops you from staying in action is your Winning Strategy.

We have discussed at length the pull of "what has worked in the past," the pull that begins the moment you react or interpret what happens. To stay engaged in your invented future, you must be able to recognize not only your Winning Strategy in action but the *dark* side of your Winning Strategy—the tantrums you throw when your Winning Strategy doesn't get you what you want.

Throwing a tantrum is a con game—a racket that you run.

When I think of a racket, I think of a storefront with penny candies in the window and a little old lady selling candy at the counter. But in the back room there's a gambling den, with a perpetual numbers game going on. The candy store is not what it appears to be, and even the innocent activities at the front are tinged with the malevolent flavor of the back room. Criminals, carrying illegal betting money, continually make their way past the children at the counter.

In any racket, there is a flavor of deceit. An unseen payoff is always going on, under the table. People only run rackets in the first place because there is a payoff—usually a big one. The size of the payoff justifies the ongoing deceit.

Because you are a human being, there is a part of you that is a con artist, and as accomplished as any racketeer. Clues to the nature of your own tantrums can be found in the unwanted conditions that persist in your life. The racket is elusive, perhaps, because it is not a "thing" you have; it is a condition, or a mode, that you adopt, on a recurring basis, when your Winning Strategy fails you.

Think about a persistent, unwanted condition that recurs in your life today. It may be that no one takes you seriously. Or you always end up being the "responsible person," both at work and in your family. Or you can't get your ideas across. If it changed, you know that would make a real difference in your leadership and your life. Whatever this condition is, no doubt you have been struggling with it for a long time. You've made many attempts to resolve it, but nothing has succeeded. So it keeps recurring. Every time it does, if you are not aware of it, it pulls you out of your invented future and throws you back into the game of surviving.

Many of the executives I have worked with have said, "I'm an intelligent, powerful, successful person. Why can't I solve this problem?" It doesn't make sense—to them or anyone around them—that such a successful person, with such an unparalleled track record, would be stymied by some unwanted, chronic condition. And yet the condition persists.

Rackets are dramatized in movies all the time. The hero, say, robs banks. He may not want to rob banks, but he keeps doing it. He tries to quit, but the payoff is too great. Without it, he'd have to take sme sort of drudgery job (or so he thinks) to take care of his children.

If someone said to you, "You're getting a payoff from that condition, and that payoff is worth more to you than getting rid of the condition would be," you might think that person was crazy. But that statement is absolutely right. You would appreciate being rid of the condition, but you have not been willing to give up the payoff.

To a great extent, that is because you are unaware of the payoff and the cost of keeping the unwanted condition.

Like the audience watching the bank robber, the rest of us can often see the nature of your payoffs, and what they cost you, even if you can't. The payoffs for maintaining your unwanted condition can be put in three categories. While all three apply, one of them will be the senior payoff—the most influential—for the particular unwanted condition that is persisting.

1. You get to be right. For human beings, being right is a very big payoff, particularly when you are right about the way things "should" be. This validates your tacit ties to the Universal Human Paradigm. You also get to make somebody else wrong.

The unwanted condition of never finding a relationship that works is an example of a racket. If this was your unwanted condition, you would probably swear up and down that you *really want* a working relationship. But you would never pick an appropriate partner—there's too much payoff in being right about how relationships can't work. Each failure would provide you more evidence that something is wrong with you, with your partner of the moment, and with marriage, relationships, and love in general. You would go from one relationship to another—frequently, from one marriage to another—involving yourself with the wrong person, over and over, to prove how hard you are trying to "make it work," but in reality, you would be thoroughly invested in being right about how relationships can't work. In short, you would be conning yourself, running a racket on anyone you were in a relationship with.

In business, the middle manager who doesn't say what he is thinking, because his ideas are never taken seriously, is running a racket. His payoff: He gets to be right about how difficult it is to advance in the company.

2. You get to dominate or avoid being dominated. This kind of domination is rarely spoken of directly, but it's the payoff for some of the biggest rackets humans have perpetuated. For centuries it has been the source of war-making. To many people, domination is almost a greater thrill than life itself.

The victim who always gets his or her feelings hurt is running a classic racket. Victims dominate everyone around them, because no one wants to hurt their feelings. Without having to be loud, forceful, or in charge, the victim can manipulate things to revolve around him or her. Similarly, when a teenager is nervous and cranky, everyone around him says, "Leave him alone. Let him do what he wants, or we'll have to hear about it all afternoon." No one wants to be bothered by his crankiness, and he knows that.

I know a writer and political consultant I'll call Gordon, someone with a national reputation, whose unwanted condition was to be constantly pulled into projects he didn't want to take on. When he looked at this from the point of view of it being a tantrum he was throwing, or a con game he was playing, he saw the payoff: that he could dominate the situation by insisting that he could leave any political campaign at any time, because he was not totally committed. "Then I could set the terms," he later said, "and others went along with those terms because they didn't want to lose me." It looked to him as if he would lose his power if he didn't dominate. From inside the Universal Human Paradigm, not dominating looks threatening.

For another example of the payoff of dominating, think of the people you know who dominate by having to express their opinion about everything. In a meeting, nothing can move forward until such people get to say everything that they want to say. This is true even if their points have already been made by other people. They will dominate the meeting until they can express it the way they want to express it.

3. Finally, you get to explain the way you are, and justify staying that way. This payoff, the strongest of the three, is directly connected to the "in order to" column of your Winning Strategy. Indeed, a racket can be thought of as the "dark side" of your Winning Strategy, the side that you would rather dismiss from sight, because you don't want to acknowledge its hold on you.

The film producer who never works up to her potential is running a racket. She can always say to herself, "I could have done more to make that work"—which becomes a handy justification for things staying the way they are.

An executive named Jack identified his racket accurately when he said, "I keep telling my people what I want them to do, but in the deep recesses of my mind, I wonder, with a good deal of concern, what would happen if they really did all the things I requested. In my gut, I can't help but feel I would no longer be necessary. Of course, that's very human of me and not something that readily comes into my mind, but whether I am aware of it or not, it lives very viscerally for me. Do I really *want* to be dispensable? I tell myself and everyone else, I want to be dispensable—I harp on it all the time—and yet I have the ugly confrontation with the truth inside my thoughts. The recurring fear is: If I become dispensable, I'll have to find something else to do."

Jack's Winning Strategy was listening for "What is the largest possibility?" so as to act by "challenging and arguing," in order to "be the best and avoid being ordinary." When he looked at the unwanted condition of being indispensable, saw it as a racket, and asked, "What is the payoff?" he replied, "The payoff is to justify staying the way I am—that is, being indispensable. If I were dispensable, I would be like anyone else—ordinary. And in my Winning Strategy, being ordinary is something that I'm constitutionally unwilling to tolerate."

Ultimately, in the movie about the bank robber, the hero becomes aware of a cost involved in robbing banks that's greater than the payoff. The cost might be his freedom, or the respect of his family, or his self-respect. When the robber can see the scenario in which the cost becomes greater than the payoff, an opportunity to relinquish the racket arises for the first time.

As with the payoff, you are unaware of the cost of running a racket, because your Winning Strategy has stopped you from experiencing the full impact of the cost. These costs can be categorized in four areas: (1) health and vitality, (2) happiness and the enjoyment of living, (3) being able to receive and express love, and affinity for others, and (4) full self-expression.

If you think about it, those four categories represent your whole life. A racket can diminish the joy of living to the point where you are merely surviving.

Consider the payoff that his racket extracted from Gordon, the nationally known writer and political consultant, in exchange for his ability to dominate. Today, looking back, he identifies the first sacrifice as his health and vitality. It took a lot of energy to maintain the resistance that kept him being pulled into campaigns—but not pulled *too* far. His racket never allowed Gordon to experience the vitality that came from full commitment to a project. He could never truly enjoy the great things he did. He got to the point where, in every new project, he calculated his fees based on how much it would drain his vitality. Instead of being in power and being energized by the work, he was drained by it.

The cost to his vitality was so great after one campaign—the management of which he handled well—that he retired from the political arena and retreated to his home to concentrate on his writing. He was worried that if he had kept up political work, it would have done him in. He was right; it would have. But it wasn't running the project that threatened to do him in; it was the unwanted, persistent condition—the racket—of not being able to say no, or fully commit to yes.

Similarly, Jack the executive understood all too well what his racket was costing him. "I'm having to deal with sadness right now," he said. "Such waste. I think the real weight of it just became obvious to me. I have not been able to express the love I feel for people—not just at work, but in my family, where I am also indispensable and must run everything. It has cost me the relationship I want with my oldest son, who can never replace me, and who (I can now see) doesn't want to, given the cost." That was a great cost for Jack, who had so much love to give that the results he had achieved with his Winning Strategy looked tiny by comparison. Identifying that cost allowed him to experience how being indispensable was costing him his life, and how the cost was not worth the payoff.

In this realm of practice, you bring yourself in touch with the enormous cost of your racket. You probably already know what your persistent, unwanted conditions are. (A clue is: They are the things that you complain the most about.) Like Jack, you need to allow yourself to experience that the cost is greater than the payoff. Only then will you stop conning yourself and running a racket.

The practice of viewing those unwanted conditions as a racket will allow you to recognize them for what they are. In recognizing them, you no longer have to act them out.

Once you have identified a racket, each time it occurs and you don't act it out, it will begin to dissolve itself. Again, like

Jack, you will ask yourself, "Am I more committed to running this racket, of being indispensable (or whatever), or am I more committed to leading this organization to an extraordinary future and having a loving relationship with my son?"

You will begin to ask yourself, "Which am I more committed to: running this racket or leading my organization to an extraordinary future?"

Another way to approach thinking about your rackets is to ask yourself, "Where in my life am I chronically concerned with being right? Where am I chronically concerned with dominating? Where am I chronically concerned with remaining the way I am?"

Do you see any links between those chronic concerns and the imperative of your Winning Strategy?

Exposing the racket that could prevent you from implementing your invented future opens the opportunity to make a choice between life and survival—or, as Jack described it, "If you run the Winning Strategy as well as I run it, then you're dead. You're not really alive. You only seem that way to those who want what you have or want to achieve what you've achieved."

Once you have exposed the persistent, unwanted condition as a racket, you are now free to make a choice between giving up the payoff and the unwanted condition, and keeping the payoff and continuing to pay the cost.

I have seen that awareness—once you have allowed yourself to experience the cost—move mountains and bring statues to tears.

Exposing the racket and giving it up allows for a whole new way of *being,* where vitality, happiness, love, full self-expression, and the freedom to make a choice become available to you.

To recognize your rackets is to understand what it means to say, "Your Winning Strategy is designed for survival." Rackets bring all of your concerns to a survival level, where just getting through the day is cause for celebration. Love, health, happiness, and full self-expression as a way of *being* are not what survival is about. They are the result of the freedom to *be,* and they come alive for you when your way of *being* is not dominated by the concern that "something's wrong."

Death is not the most profound loss or tragedy in life. That which dies inside of us as we live is a far greater loss. The loss of possibility, a loss that comes from running our personal rackets, has ravaged the lives of too many individuals who could have otherwise transformed the world.

Practice #6: Learning to see the "hook" coming before you swallow the "bait"

The transformation in Chapter 7, "Building the Bridge between 'Possibility' and 'Reality,' " involves your relationship with action.

You are shifting from . . .

. . . *action occurring as "a series of activities"* . . .

. . . to . . .

. . . *action occurring as a series of conversations.*

Now, to deepen this transformation, you develop this practice:

Replace reacting from the past with acting from the future.

This practice involves learning to *listen to* actions as elements of conversation: speech acts, such as requests and promises. Even when you recognize events as requests and promises, it is still easy to be swept away by your interpretations of what these events "mean." You become hooked by those interpretations.

One way to recognize a hook is to examine yourself regularly, to try to anticipate moments when you are getting worn out, upset, annoyed, or frustrated. When you do experience those feelings, they are probably not a direct result of the event that *actually happened*—the request or promise that was actually made. Chances are, your strong feeling stems directly from an interpretation or conclusion you've assigned or drawn.

For instance, if your boss, or a significant colleague, looks at a piece of your work and offers no positive comments, you may immediately feel bad. You may interpret this silence to mean that your work is poor, or even that your relationship with this person is in jeopardy.

Then your feeling may be reinforced, and made stronger and more debilitating, by the accompanying actions you take as a result of your interpretations. You may say something in reaction to your assumption, along the lines of: "I know this isn't my best work." You may then, hearing the self-deprecating tone of your own voice, and perhaps seeing the arch of your boss's eyebrow, feel even worse. You have then swallowed *two* hooks and are on your way to swallowing more.

But under the Re-Invention Paradigm, all that has happened is the following: You made an offer of your work, and your boss responded. That's all. You still have your feelings and thoughts, but they do not become the basis for action. There is no collapse between an event that happens and the meaning that you apply to the event. What happens is always and only what happens.

As you develop your expertise through this practice, you learn to avoid being hooked. Even in the heat of the moment, you learn to distinguish your reaction from the interpretation, and distinguish your interpretation from the event itself.

Timing is everything. You have to be able to see the hook coming before you swallow the bait. You have to see your interpretations arising, without being swept away into actions based on those interpretations.

If you're typical, you only get hooked by interpretations of events that touch you personally. If someone passes you on the street and says, "I think your work is terrible," you can probably remain clear-minded. But if someone whose opinion you value, or who has power over your position, says the same thing, then it becomes more personal. Now it is much easier to slip into interpreting that remark to mean there is something wrong with you—or that there is something wrong with the other person.

Listening for requests and promises, and making deliberate requests and promises of your own, gives you practice removing the meaning from events.

Suppose that you are in the retail business and your profits go down. Rather than making an assessment about the cause of the decline, and seeking to discover why things "have gone wrong," look at what happened: Profits decreased. In the language of the Re-Invention Paradigm, you offered your merchandise to your customers, and many of them (who had accepted offers you had made in the past) declined *this* offer.

If a customer doesn't pay your bill, it doesn't mean that customer is bad. It means that the customer broke a promise to you. In the Re-Invention Paradigm, breaking a promise and keeping a promise are events that happened—nothing more. They are not "good," "bad," "right," or "wrong"—just "what happened." And it's *all* that happened. Rather than looking backward to figure out the "cause" of the "effect" (why something happened), you stand in your invented future (the future that you created by declaration) and ask what request or promise you can make that will move that future forward.

In other words, the Re-Invention Master Paradigm is not anchored in "cause" and "effect." The Universal Human Paradigm enmeshes you in a continual effort to find the "cause" of everything that went "wrong" (or "right"), but the Re-Invention Master Paradigm is anchored only in "effect." There is only "what happened." There is only one event, then another, then another—with no discernible cause-effect relationship between them. The nature of their "causes" (the influence of one event on another, or the way in which one "effect" may have led to another "effect") is a matter of your interpretation. All "cause" is interpretation, and irrelevant to moving the action forward.

This doesn't mean that you do not take action. There is always action to take. Indeed, all that ever happens in the Re-Invention Master Paradigm are actions: requests, promises, and the responses (acceptances, declinations, and counteroffers).

Most people in everyday life do not speak in the terms of requests and promises. They speak primarily in the terms of "assessments"—they state opinions and evaluations—and in terms of "assertions"—they state facts, for which evidence (from the past) can be provided.

Thus, a key ingredient in transforming your relationship with action, and in mastering this practice, is your ability to transform what you "listen *for*." Train yourself to "listen for" requests and promises, rather than for assessments and assertions. "Listen for" requests and pomises, not for your Winning Strategy's version (or someone else's version) of what "should" or "shouldn't" be, what's "wrong," or what could go "wrong."

Often, as you listen closely, you will discover that people are only giving you their opinion, not making a request. They may tell you that your approach to a certain problem "isn't appropriate." Don't get hooked on an interpretation. They are not telling you your approach is wrong; nor are they requesting you to revise your approach. If you get hooked, then you quickly retreat back into protecting yourself from "life not working out." You can easily get caught in other people's evaluations, opinions, and judgments. The next thing you know, your Winning Strategy is back, in full operation, pushing you to spend fruitless hours to meet its needs for "succeeding" at that approach.

The following dialogue demonstrates the work that must be done sometimes to clarify other people's requests. Charlie, an executive at a large manufacturing firm, was well versed in corporate politics. But he became stymied when he received a request from the vice-president of his division. He even had a hard time describing, in retrospect, what had happened. "I think I made a counteroffer," he said.

"If you're not sure, the vice-president probably isn't either," I said. "From his point of view did you accept the request? Or do you think he heard your counteroffer instead?" I asked.

"Well, I don't think he heard my counteroffer. So I guess he probably thought I accepted."

The story had taken place during the week between Christmas and New Year's, when most people were not available at the plant. The vice-president had asked for full knowledge of the costs, day by day, on Charlie's project. Charlie couldn't provide those numbers, but said he could offer "a daily snapshot of our results." When the week was over, it was clear that Charlie's group had missed its cost projections—and that the vice-president held them responsible. Yet Charlie insisted that the necessary information was there, in the figures he had given the V.P., to show whether the project was on track or not.

"He didn't use what we gave him, to be honest," Charlie said. "We delivered a message that said things were off track. But since nobody received the information, the mark got missed. The vice-president didn't get the report personally."

"Hold on a second," I said. "When you say, 'The mark got

missed,' what did that have to do with you? That wasn't the request—or was it?"

"Perhaps it was," he said. "Maybe that's where the whole breakdown occurred. We didn't communicate the way we should."

When a request is vague, you can ask a set of questions in response. Here Charlie could have responded, "Are you asking me to be responsible for cost reduction? Are you asking me to monitor daily events? Or are you asking me to be personally responsible for providing you with information?"

But those questions would never occur as long as Charlie was "listening for" his own Winning Strategy. It never occurred to him to ask about accountability, because his Winning Strategy was geared to avoiding being weak. He didn't dare appear to be ignorant, because showing ignorance would surely kill him. He wouldn't survive, in the sense that his Winning Strategy had defined "survival" for him. So instead of putting his "survival" at risk, he did not clarify the question or make sure he understood what the vice-president intended.

When you have learned to listen well, you will be able to pick out the opinions from the requests, and when you hear an opinion, you can listen politely and say, "Thank you for your thoughts," without getting reeled into nonproductive conversations which lead nowhere. Or if you're uncertain whether an opinion is being offered or a request is being made, you'll ask, "Is there a request you have of me?" Or "Is there a specific action you're asking me to take?" They'll tell you. They may be vague at first: "Yes, fix it." Or "Just take care of it." Or "Get it handled." But with a few more direct questions from you, their request will become clear.

Sometimes people will tell you, "I just want to complain, and I want you to hear my complaint. And that's it, for now." Other times the complaint is actually a covert request, or a request they don't know they're making.

As you learn to listen, you will discover what people are committed to and you will begin to relate to them from their place of commitment. If you stop "listening for" assessments and "listen for" requests and promises, even when people speak in assessments (judgments, evaluations, and opinions) and assertions (facts for which there is evidence), you'll start to relate to people's commitments, rather than to their personalities or styles.

LEADING AN ORGANIZATIONAL RE-INVENTION

The six practices discussed above complete the last transformation of Executive Re-Invention. And the end of this book. But if you care primarily about Organizational Re-Invention, then what has come so far represents only a preliminary stage. With the transformations of Executive Re-Invention incorporated into your life, you are ready to move on to Organizational Re-Invention, which involves a series of specific transformations within your organization, each of which requires putting at stake the organization's success for the possibility it can be.

Organizational Re-Invention is even riskier than Executive Re-Invention, because it means going beyond all the ways that the organization has produced results in the past, including the basis of its reputation with shareholders. Nonetheless, unless the organization can be re-invented, it—like its leaders—will always be bound by its past habits and ways of being.

The practices of Organizational Re-Invention are still being invented. There is much to be written, and much to be learned, about it. It can't be delivered in recipe form; there are too many variations, from organization to organization. To do justice to all of its practices and ramifications would require a separate book.

Nonetheless, if you are about to lead an Organizational Re-Invention effort, then you should be aware of some basic principles. You should have a sense of what you are getting into and an awareness of the value, for your entire organization, of going down this path.

In that spirit, then, I offer you a set of guidelines from my experience in designing, consulting, and coaching Organizational Re-Invention. Together, these guidelines should give you a picture of what's involved in leading an Organizational Re-Invention.

1. Have all leaders who will play a key role in the Re-Invention of the organization complete the Executive Re-Invention process *before* taking any action.

The first step is to re-invent yourself. The next step is for *all* the key leaders (or, at least, a critical mass of key leaders) to re-invent themselves. This is crucial, because each organization's Re-Invention takes off from its own leaders' Executive Re-Inventions, and from the declarations and promises that they make.

In other words, every leader of an organization must become a "clearing" for Re-Invention, drawing anybody involved in the organization, automatically, to operate from the future.

This requires a concerted, orchestrated training effort. The recommended approach is to start with the people at the top of the organization—the chairman or CEO and their direct reports, across the organization—who will be playing a key role in the Re-Invention of the organization. Then leadership teams (usually made up of the direct reports of the first group) go through the Executive Re-Invention process, generally along with a few other key players from different parts of the organization.

2. Many of the steps of Organizational Re-Invention echo the steps of Executive Re-Invention, but this time from an organizational perspective.

One key process, early in the game, involves uncovering the organization's Winning Strategy. In Chapter 2, I described how every organization has a Winning Strategy. Often, these are produced by the Winning Strategies of the organization's leaders and founders, rippling through the network of people who are hired because they "fit" the leaders' Winning Strategies and who meld themselves to match those Strategies.

In Organizational Re-Invention, the leaders of the organization (and others who are involved in the effort) work together to bring that Winning Strategy to the surface and unveil its ramifications. Senior executives in the utilities industry, for example, have always listened closely for loyalty in their subordinates. Loyalty means fidelity and allegiance to your boss and the company above all else, as expressed through the rule book. This has been not just appropriate but endemic to companies with monopoly protection. It has been seen as essential in building a workforce primed for success.

An Organizational Re-Invention effort for a particular utility company might begin to ask what, in promoting this form of loyalty, the organization's members were "listening for." They would similarly work to recognize the "so as to act by" and "in order to" components: When an employee brusquely, bureaucratically denies a customer's request because of loyalty to the rule book, what has the employee been acting "in order to" accomplish?

Organizational Re-Invention will also typically include an effort to disclose the organization's "rackets." Each organizational Winning Strategy has one or more hidden con games, sometimes enshrined as standard practices, that members play because they desire the payoff. The costs of that racket are probably not evident. Indeed, in many organizations, the costs of the racket may occur in an entirely different part of the organization than the place that depends on the "payoff."

For instance, there may be a costly, difficult, and obnoxious work-flow tracking system, which everyone hates but everyone must follow. The racket persists because it allows one group to dominate and everyone else to be "right" about the pressure they feel from that group.

Organizational Re-Invention has analogues to the transformation of inventing an impossible future. Leaders of the Re-Invention declare possibilities and create games that move the entire organization forward. They make bold promises consistent with the invented futures. They assert "what is missing"; what is essential, and must be somehow produced, for the conditions of the promise to be fulfilled.

For example, the leaders of the Re-Invention effort might declare that an organization can develop a worldwide presence without taxing its resources. A series of promises would follow, from various people in various roles. The senior leaders would most likely promise to institute policies that reward effective communication between countries. They might also promise to heed requests for support, relevant to this game. There would be promises to develop new endeavors, promises to instill (and accept) new forms of training, promises to continue seeking out whatever is "missing" that this re-invented worldwide organization needs.

3. Much of the work of Organizational Re-Invention focuses around mobilizing people to identify the major "missing and essential" components of the overall Re-Invention and to make themselves accountable for leading and accomplishing the necessary transformations.

Perhaps you remember the story in Chapter 5 of the "Fisher Chemical Company," whose leader, Claude, had declared the possibility that their dye brand could become a household word. To implement this possibility, Claude drew his top management together, and for an entire day the group worked on articulating and designating the next steps for the business unit. About eighty people were involved, and they rapidly broke into subgroups. Through the work of the subgroups, and then when they returned to the plenary, they identified a variety of major transformations that were required:

They needed the leaders of the entire organization to be committed. They needed technical support, which presently did not exist and needed to be developed. They needed expertise to identify available technology. They needed a benefits package to reduce turnover, and work methods that were not in place. They needed training skills to teach analytical skills. And they needed a talented partner base.

Some of your "missing and essential" components can be accomplished through continuous improvement. Others will require transformations. All of them will have to be organized and coordinated.

One thing will be common to all of these components: Each will have a person, someone who has completed Executive Re-Invention, step forward and request overall accountability for leading it. It is important that this role not be assigned, but treated as an opportunity to be requested. The person who requests accountability need not be an expert in the technical, or "content," area of the component. For instance, if a particular component involves developing a new computerized information system, the person accountable need not be a computer expert. A "technical expert" can be assigned to handle technical concerns; the accountable executive is concerned with creating a context for the transformations that are necessary, the bold promises to deliver the component of Re-Invention on time, the conditions for fulfilling each of the bold promises, and whatever else is "missing and essential."

4. Organizational Re-Invention involves the entire organization in communicating from the future.

Even people who never go through any training will find themselves in a new milieu—an environment of committed speaking and listening. People must become aware that their actions are speech acts; they must know how to distinguish between declarations and assertions. They must know the value of requests and promises, in part because hundreds of explicit requests and promises will come their way as they take part in the organization's affairs.

This requires context-setting and coaching. You and other leaders will have to build support for your requests, as described in Chapter 7—paying attention to the audience's needs, to whether the audience is accountable, and to the offers and promises you need to make along with your requests. You will need to be explicit about which requests are demands, requirements, or prohibitions, versus which requests are supplications, invitations, or authorizations.

Somewhere along the line, some of the key people—a few from each area of the organization—are typically invited to be trained as coaches. This group can be composed of people from a variety of functions and backgrounds, or the coaching can all come from senior human resource leaders. Train the entire organization in the basic practices of transformation and how they differ from the basic practices of continuous improvement; train the entire organization to communicate with committed speaking and listening: to communicate with explicit attention to requests, promises, declarations, assertions, and assessments.

Gradually, committed speaking and listening becomes the communications system for the organization, and "making the impossible happen" becomes the organizational context, the water in which everyone is swimming. People may still individually gripe about "the way things should be around here," or voice other manifestations of the Universal Human Paradigm, but the environment of the organization no longer answers them back in kind. Instead, they are answered by manifestations of the Re-Invented Paradigm, and particularly by the future that this organization has invented for itself.

THE LAST WORD ON POWER

> Our worst fear is not that we are inadequate. Our deepest fear is that we are powerful beyond measure. It is our light, not our darkness, that most frightens us.
>
> We ask ourselves, "Who am I to be brilliant, gorgeous, talented, and fabulous?" Actually, who are you *not* to be? You are a child of God; your playing small doesn't serve the world. There is nothing enlightened about shrinking so that other people won't feel insecure around you.
>
> We were born to make manifest the glory of God within us. It is not just in some of us, it is in *everyone* and as we let our own light shine, we unconsciously give other people permission to do the same.
>
> As we are liberated from our own fear, our presence automatically liberates others.
>
> —Nelson Mandela, inaugural address, 1995

For centuries, philosophers have debated whether people create their destiny, or whether it is predetermined. I assert that you create your destiny *and* it is predetermined, through the interpretations you have made and the language you have spoken since childhood.

The Executive Re-Invention process is a systematic way to transcend the limits of your interpretations. It is a novel path; the sort of path that mystics and wise elders have traveled in the past. In our time, paths like this are open to more people than ever before. That availability is a tribute to declarations that various philosophers have made during this century: that the esoteric and the worldly can be merged in day-to-day practice, in every variety of organization.

By design, the whole of Executive Re-Invention is greater than the sum of its parts. The transformations of Executive Re-Invention are holographic, in the sense that each one provides, from its own angle, access to the same power—the "power to make the impossible happen." Through practice, you enter a state of freedom—freedom from the limitations of being human. You become free to operate at risk in the world, without the agreement or consensus of other people, and without fear of the consequences to yourself or your organization.

I declare the possibility: The time for a revolution in leadership has come. It is time to live in a world where a vast number of people are actively engaged in making the impossible happen.

I assert that nothing less than a revolution in leadership will allow the successful Re-Invention of our organizations, industries, and countries worldwide.

I thank you for the opportunity to share this conversation.

I take the stand that anyone who has read this book has the opportunity to re-invent himself or herself into an extraordinary leader, who makes the impossible happen.

I invite you to join me in taking the stand that you, personally, are such a leader.

I urge you to commit yourself and your organization's leaders to take on Executive Re-Invention.

I strongly recommend that you declare (for yourself) who you are, as a leader, before you close this book.

I assure you that if you seriously engage in the practices of Executive Re-Invention, you will realize each of the transformations.

I promise that when you accomplish all seven of the transformations, you will give yourself the gift of ultimate power—the power to get the world to match your words—the power to dance with the past, the present, and the future with complete and total *freedom!*

THE TWO MASTER PARADIGMS

	UNIVERSAL HUMAN PARADIGM	RE-INVENTION MASTER PARADIGM
Source:	Inherited as a human being	Acquired as an act of creation
Power:	Authority or control that is given and taken away based on position, accountability, results produced, or ability to influence	The speed with which you declare something impossible "possible" and transform it from a "possibility" to a "reality"
Designed to:	Improve what's possible	Make the impossible happen
Scope of results:	Anything inside of your reality that is currently possible	Anything outside of your reality that is currently impossible
Structure of reality:	Psychological system of cause and effect	Ontological system of committed speaking and listening
Mode of operation:	Change: Focus on what you are *doing* by altering the *process*	Transformation: Focus on how you are *being* by altering the *context*
Leadership skills:	Predicting the future based on past evidence Creating a vision Producing consensus Reaching goals Making feasible promises you can be counted on to keep Reacting from the past	Declaring the future based on no evidence Creating context Taking a stand Fulfilling realms of possibility Making bold promises you don't know how to keep Acting from the future

Context:	There is a way things should be, and when they're not, there's something wrong with me, them, or it	There's no such *thing* as should/shouldn't, right/wrong. They are always and only an interpretation
Action:	A series of activities to accomplish to produce a result	A series of conversations to engage in to transform a possibility into a reality
Relationship to problems:	Something that isn't the way it should be that requires fixing or improving	There are no problems; there is only what happened, what's missing, what's the next action
Life game:	Surviving: using your Winning Strategy in order to win and control so that life turns out the way it should, and doesn't turn out the way it shouldn't	Making the impossible happen: freely engaging in taking risks in a game that is worth playing while life turns out the way it does

TERMS OF EXECUTIVE RE-INVENTION

Being   As it pertains to transformation, the realm of possibility in which something exists, rather than an emotional or behavioral state. The way you are being at any given time determines what's possible.

Change vs. Transformation

Change   An alteration in the arena of *process*. You alter what you are *doing* to *improve* results you already have. Change provides an improvement in the existing way of doing business while the organization and its leaders essentially remain the same.

Transformation   An alteration in the arena of *context*. You alter the way you are *being* to *create* results that are not currently possible. Transformation provides the creation of that which does not yet exist in the organization and its leaders—a new realm of possibility leading to a new realm of results.

Clearing   A Heideggerian term that in German (*Lichtung*) means a clearing in the forest, a light, an opening. The clearing you are determines what is possible in the "opening" you are for others as a leader. The transformations of Executive Re-Invention are designed to produce a shift in your clearing as a leader: from being a clearing for fixing and improving what's wrong and shouldn't be as a compensation for what's not possible, to a clearing for making the impossible happen.

Committed Speaking and Listening   A series of speech acts that move what's not possible or impossible to a possibility, and a possibility to a reality.

Declaration An act of speaking that brings forth a future the moment it is spoken.

Declaration of Possibility A specific declaration that brings forth a new realm of possibility the moment it is spoken. A declaration of possibility creates a future that does not yet exist.

Promise Like a request, an act of speaking that is an action in itself. When you say "I promise," you are bringing forth a particular future as a commitment. Whether it is kept, not kept, or revoked, a promise moves a specific possibility forward to a reality.

Request An act of speaking that is an action in itself, not a representation of an action. A request brings forth a particular future as a possible commitment. Whether it is accepted, declined, or counteroffered, a request moves a specific possibility forward to a reality.

Compensating Power Principle Your Winning Strategy—your individual formula for winning (surviving) in life—is designed to compensate for what's not possible—for what you can't ever be. The Compensating Power Principle is: *As your Winning Strategy gets stronger and stronger and you expand what is possible—what you can be—at the same time, what expands along with it is what's not possible—what can't ever be.*

Context The human environment that determines the limitations of any process, and the scope of the results it can produce.

Extraordinary Leaders Ordinary human beings with the power to redefine reality by (1) taking a stand for what is currently impossible and (2) acting to make it happen regardless of past experience or current circumstances.

Impossible Anything that is outside of *your* reality—anything that occurs as something that is not possible for you to accomplish, or not possible for you to accomplish at this time and/or under these circumstances.

Invented Future A future that is not an extension of the past. An "impossible" leadership *game* that cannot be played from inside the limits of the Universal Human Paradigm and your Winning Strategy, that alters your identity and is the vehicle for making the impossible happen in life instead of improving/surviving.

Master Paradigm   The origin or source of all other paradigms. The Universal Human Paradigm is the master paradigm inherited by all human beings. The Re-Invention Master Paradigm is a new master paradigm designed to displace the inherited Universal Human Paradigm and is available only through re-inventing yourself.

Power   The speed with which you declare the impossible "possible" and turn that "possibility" into reality. Power is the *freedom* to act from the future without being constrained by the past.

Re-Invention   A deliberate series of transformations, putting at stake the success you've become for the possibility you can be.

  Executive Re-Invention   A series of seven radical transformations in which you put at stake the success you've become for the power of making the impossible happen. You completely re-invent yourself as a leader by redefining your reality of the past, present, and future and your relationship to taking risks, winning, action, and being extraordinary. Executive Re-Invention provides you, and allows you to provide others, with the capacity for making the impossible happen regardless of past experience or current circumstances.

  Organizational Re-Invention   A series of specific transformations necessary to re-invent an organization—either the entire organization or a division or business unit within an organization. Organizational Re-Invention always begins with Executive Re-Invention of the key leaders accountable for implementing the Organizational Re-Invention. This is a large-scale effort and involves not only identifying the transformations, specific to each organization, that must be accomplished to free the organization from its past and generate an "impossible future," but requires a transformation of the entire workforce to own and successfully implement the new future.

Survival   A condition that exists whenever you fear that you could lose something, the loss of which is threatening to your life. It could be a threat to your physical life, but commonly it's a threat to your professional life, or even more likely, a threat to any important aspect (family, finances, children) of your life. When we say survival, most of us think about the low end of survival, which is a last gasp for breath. *The high end of survival is success.* Some leaders succeed by never taking risks, while others succeed by taking risks all the time. Depending on what is popular in the leadership arena, or what the concerns of a particular organization or industry happen to be, either risk-takers or those who won't take risks will be in demand. In either case, risk-taking or risk-avoiding, the drive is to survive—code name: "succeed."

Taking a Stand   A declaration of commitment to act consistent with a specific "declared possibility" to move that possibility to a reality.

Universal Human Paradigm   The master paradigm shared by the largest community of people in the world—all human beings. It is designed for survival—being right, dominating and avoiding domination. The context of the Universal Human Paradigm— the water in which all human beings swim—is that there is a way things should be, and when they are that way, things are right, and when they are not that way, there's something wrong with me, them (other people), or it (anything in the world or the whole world in general). Each person's individual Winning Strategy is some version of this context.

Winning Strategy   A lifelong, unconscious formula for achieving success, which, unknown to you, has designed you as a human being and as a leader. It is the source of your success and at the same time the source of your limitations. It defines your reality, your way of being, and your way of thinking. It focuses your attention and shapes your action. It determines what's possible and not possible for you as a leader. Your individual Winning Strategy is a conversation that consists of three elements: *"listening for"*—the filter through which you interpret; *"so as to act by"*—your modus operandi; and *"in order to"*—your measure for knowing that life worked out.

FOR LEADERS ALREADY ENGAGED IN ORGANIZATIONAL RE-INVENTION OR REENGINEERING

WHY ORGANIZATIONAL RE-INVENTIONS FAIL

Too few people really care about leadership in organizations. Even those who pay lip service to it don't seem to care much. They don't seem to believe it's an important factor, for example, to ensure the success of their multimillion-dollar reengineering initiatives.

If they did believe, they would invest a few of those millions in learning how to create leaders. Every organization would have research-and-development initiatives in hot pursuit of knowledge about how to create effective transformational leadership. Senior management would make implementing that knowledge a priority. As a result, organizations would be full of visibly heroic people; they would be environments in which impossibly wonderful things happened constantly, with day-in, day-out regularity.

Instead, not one organization spends any significant money on research and development for creating breakthroughs in leadership and the management of transformation.

Thus, we have organizations in which extraordinary leadership is rare. The silver screen is full of people accomplishing extraordinary heroics. Yet there are no heroes where we need them most: in organizations. Worse still, there are no young heroes coming up through the ranks—no nascent Gandhis, Clark Kents, or even Indiana Joneses.

And yet, in today's post–Cold War business and political environment, the senior management of organizations is increasingly called upon to accomplish the impossible. Kodak, IBM, American Express, and General Motors have all sacked their CEOs during the last few years. Each of the incumbent CEOs had promised an organizational "transformation" (as they called it) that never actually came. All were able men with records of sustained success. They spearheaded vigorous programs of downsizing, delayering, and reengineering core business processes. Most of these endeavors showed promise . . . for a while. But beneath the sound and fury, competitive vitality continued to ebb away. Ultimately, the leaders were faulted for "inadequate leadership" and "lack of a strategic vision." And they all showed, in one way or another, that they were bewildered by the unraveling state of affairs that had led to their demise.[1]

These CEOs are hardly unique. People throughout business are attempting to stay on the cutting edge of management by directing a large-scale re-invention of their institutions. From roller skates to lip color to ice cream, from manufacturing techniques to joint-venture agreements to software design, from reporting responsibilities to human relations to accounting practices, all aspects of modern corporate life seem to be up for alteration.

Foreign competition threatens, so labor practices and technology purchases must be re-created from scratch. Employees are hidebound, so they must be manipulated somehow into becoming risk-taking innovators. Significant, sweeping overhauls are attempted in virtually every sector of the economy—as well as in education, public service, health care, parenting, religion, and the military.

This sort of sweeping re-invention has always been enviable, but it was never *needed* in the past. Organizations could survive very well without it.

Until now. As business competition grows sharper, and the global marketplace expands, the stakes for business capability are growing higher and higher. Continuous improvement, which was the mark of a distinctively "excellent" company in the 1980s, is now commonplace. Simply being a large corporation is no longer, in itself, sufficient for maintaining market leadership or leadership in society. Organizations (including companies, nonprofits, and government bodies) that could have gotten away with continuous improvement a decade ago are now in peril unless they can become radically different.

In the old game of "keeping pace," managers had to know how to predict, with reasonable accuracy, what results could be achieved. They had to be able to bring a group to consensus or alignment, so people felt "on board." They had to make promises that were feasible, and to deliver on them. They had to articulate visions and set goals, and to develop internal "change agents" who could spur others to increase performance.

The new game, setting the pace, is altogether different. It has different rules, requirements, and abilities. Hence the stress and difficulty involved in this shift. It's as if you were a championship baseball player suddenly forced to play football. Your basic athletic abilities carry with you, but all your specialized skills in fielding, pitching, and batting are no longer relevant. No matter how much you improve them, they will no longer help you score points. Instead, you need to cultivate new, unfamiliar skills—the equivalents of tackling, passing, and kicking. You become an expert at declaring the future, rather than predicting it. You excel at taking a stand rather than at generating consensus. You make bold promises that you don't know how to keep, instead of making feasible promises that you always deliver on. You learn to recruit and develop catalysts for transformation rather than change agents.

Jack Welch, the chief executive who "re-invented" General Electric during the 1980s and 1990s, recently described the imperative this way:

Managers confronting the need to revolutionize their organizations commonly fear chaos, or unforeseen outcomes at the least. Even in the best executives, such fear can breed timidity—the bane of corporate transformations . . . You've got to be on the cutting edge of change. You can't simply maintain the status quo, because somebody's always coming from another country with another product, or consumer tastes change, or the cost structure does, or there's a technology breakthrough . . . My biggest mistake was agonizing too long over difficult decisions. But we're all human . . . In hindsight, I was generally erring on the side of being afraid of breaking [GE]. GE would be better off if I had acted faster.[2]

Leaders are expected to rise to the occasion of managing these new "organizational revolutions." Re-invent your company, your institution, your industry, or your country? No problem. Everyone assumes that, even though they have taken on the task of completely re-inventing the organization, the leaders themselves will not need re-invention as individuals. Or, if they do, the process of taking on the job will naturally put them through the necessary transformations, without any special training or preparation. Magically, just by facing the challenges of a corporate overhaul, the CEO is supposed to become the person who is capable of whatever those challenges demand.

This expectation is a prescription for failure. It leads directly to the failure of the vast majority of efforts to reshape corporations.

THE MISSING PIECE OF REENGINEERING

As the most prominent organizational "change" strategy of the past few years, reengineering is a prime example. James Champy, one of the inventors of reengineering, acknowledges that many efforts fail because they do not recognize the need to transform people:

Everyone must change. The change will go deeper than technique. It touches not merely what managers do, but who they are. Not just their sense of the task, but their sense of themselves. Not just what they know, but how they think. Not just their way of seeing the world, but their way of living in the world.[3]

Most executives leading reengineering efforts are seriously committed to them. Yet so few reengineering efforts produce the expected gains that, by now, short-term failure is accepted as routine and inevitable, almost a necessary prerequisite. According to *Information Week*, two thirds of the reengineering efforts in place have never led to any significant productivity gains or valuable organizational changes at all. An estimated $52 billion will be spent on reengineering projects in 1997; if the two-thirds rule of thumb holds true, then a staggering $34 billion will be wasted.[4]

There is also a waste of human capital. The leader of a reengineering effort hopes that the opportunities in the effort will bring out the magnificence of the people in the company. But people only display their best qualities when they are unafraid. Most reengineering efforts, instead, paralyze people with fear of what might happen to them—undermining one of the primary original reasons for the reengineering move.

A third loss, still more intangible, may be even more devastating in the long run. "The real downside of a reengineering failure is not the hard costs," reports *Information Week,* "but the loss in credibility." After enough time has passed, strategies like reengineering will no longer provoke, excite, or incite executives to take on re-invention. The strategies will be discarded as "just one more management fad that failed to deliver on its promise." This attitude will not only unravel the commitment of the organizations that took them on, but will also set up the next "revolutionary" idea that comes down the pike as a failure waiting to happen.

The same dynamic seems to occur in every one of these cases. In theory, a reengineering effort should be a complete redesign:

"Starting over with a clean sheet of paper" (as authors Michael Hammer and James Champy put it), to re-create the company's processes and systems from scratch. But increasing failures indicate that, given human nature, reality will never live up to the theory.

One of the perennial problems with reengineering efforts, for instance, is the difficulty of getting rid of legacy accounting and information systems—the thirty- or forty-year-old procedures, channels, networks, and computer systems that reach into every corner of a company's procedures. Those legacy systems provided the company with its success in the past. While people will give lip service to the idea of replacing them, and will complain about the nuisance of their antediluvian ways, most people will never believe it's possible to give up the legacy systems. When push comes to shove, even the reformers will cling frantically to the old ways.

It's as if you asked them, "Would you give up your right arm if the fulfillment of your life genuinely depended on it?" People can intellectually imagine circumstances in which it would be worth agreeing to give up an arm. They might even agree in principle to give up an arm, if it meant their life would really work thereafter. But show up at their side with a surgical saw, and you'll see how quickly they renege. They'd like to believe they could give up their arm if they needed to, but when push comes to shove: "I need that arm." Similarly, they're happy to redesign the company from scratch in the abstract, but when push comes to shove: "We need that system."

Even if you could somehow magically remove those legacy systems, and start over from scratch, you'd just re-create the same problematic structure next time. After all, the same types of people who implemented the old processes are still responsible for making the new ones work. They're still thinking in the same types of ways, following the same strategies for success, and existing in the same organizational and personal context.

Before anyone makes a mark on that blank page, it's *already* filled—with the individual's past, the company's past, the things people think are appropriate for the business, and the qualities people think a company should and shouldn't have. To really start over with a clean sheet of paper, people would have to not only redesign the organization, but the identity of every key person, from the CEO on down.

NOTES

CHAPTER 1

1. Robert Heller, *The Leadership Imperative: What Innovative Business Leaders Are Doing Today to Create Successful Companies Tomorrow* (New York: New American Library, Dutton, 1995).

2. Martin Heidegger, "The Turning," in *The Question Concerning Technology and Other Essays,* trans. William Lovitt (New York: Harper & Row, 1977), p. 43.

3. Sherman Stratford, "A Master Class in Radical Change," *Fortune* 128, no. 15 (13 Dec. 1993), p. 82.

CHAPTER 3

1. Daniel Quinn, *Ishmael* (New York: Bantam, 1992), pp. 35–36.

CHAPTER 4

1. Thornton Wilder, *The Skin of Our Teeth* (New York: Harper & Row, 1957).

2. R. Buckminster Fuller, *Ideas and Integrities* (New York: Macmillan, 1963; reprint, New York: Collier Books, 1969), p. 45.

CHAPTER 5

1. Steven Levy, *Insanely Great* (New York: Viking-Penguin, 1994), pp. 60–61.

APPENDIX III

1. Tracy Goss, Richard Pascale, and Anthony Athos, "The Reinvention Roller Coaster," *Harvard Business Review* 71, no. 6 (November–December 1993).

2. John F. Welch, CEO, General Electric, as quoted in "A Master Class in Radical Change," *Fortune* 128, no. 15 (13 Dec. 1993), pp. 82–83.

3. James Champy, *Reengineering Management* (New York: Harper-Business, 1995), p. 10.

4. Bruce Caldwell, "Missteps, Miscues," in *Information Week* no. 480 (20 June 1994), pp. 50–60.

ABOUT THE AUTHOR

TRACY GOSS is one of the foremost experts in the field of transformational leadership. A consultant, lecturer, and author, she specializes in working with CEOs and their management teams to invent and implement an "impossible future," and to "re-invent" themselves and their executive cadre to lead a series of transformations into that new future. Over the past fifteen years, she has introduced the principles and practices of Executive Re-Invention and Organizational Re-Invention to major U.S. and international companies such as Paramount Pictures, IBM, Chase Manhattan Bank, Monsanto, Reebok, Europcar, Swiss Bank, Houston Lighting and Power, Owens-Corning, and Ciba-Geigy. Ms. Goss is cofounder of the Center for Executive Re-Invention and the President of Goss-Reid Associates, Inc., both based in Austin, Texas.

For further information on Tracy Goss's writing and speaking, Executive Re-Invention Programs, or Organizational Re-Invention Consulting, please contact the Center for Executive Re-Invention, 225 Corinthian, Austin, Texas 78734. Call (800) 491-1106, or fax (512) 261-3889.